Hard Lessons

of

Life and

Self-healing

Volume II

Raphael Ikechukwu Ogbuagu

(Aka Ik Poly, Odira Chukwu Mma)

For information about reprints rights, translation, or bulk purchases, please contact: **Raphael Ikechukwu Ogbuagu** at ik_ralph@yahoo.com

Title: Hard Lessons of Life and Self-healing Volume II
Author: Raphael Ikechukwu Ogbuagu
Cover designed by: BTP Marketing Group
ISBN: 978-0692569863
Published by: BTP International Group

Dedication

I dedicate this book to God, my creator, for giving me insight, knowledge, understanding, wisdom, and sustenance, and for preserving my destiny.

It is also dedicated to all motivational writers and speakers all over the world. I dedicated to my father, Chief (Engr.) Clement Ogbuagu (Nwachinemere, Ozo Ebube Nze Abagana). Finally in Shedding tears from my heart for those who are no longer with us. Although you are gone, you are always in my heart and will never been forgotten, my grandmother Gloria Ego Ogbuagu, my maternal grandmother Elizibeth Nwanyieke Akpua, my uncle, Samuel Olisa Akpua (Ejee Abba), my cousin Engr. Ferdinand Emeka Akpua (Ferdinando), Uncle Mr. Lazarus Ogbuagu (King Laz), Mrs. Florence Amah, Mr. Simon Obidigbo (Ossai), Mrs. Grace Ijeoma Onah, Chief Mrs. Sisi Dadiare, Mrs. Chinenye Emelife, Ms. Ekene Chukwu Achebe, Mr.Ugo Chukwu Ozor (Obataobie Abba), Mr.Lawrence Amobi, Mrs. Emily Amobi, Mr. Nnamdi Ogbuagu (AkuChukwu Abagana), Engr Simon Oraka, Mrs.Getruth Ogbuagu, Mr. Emeka Okoli (Mapito), The icon Nelson Mandela (Madiba), the late Mr. Senzo Mayiwe, the late Master Tintswalo Baloyi, Mr. Taiye Mensah (Rambo T), Ms. Leswana Mmebanyana Pholo, His Royal Highness Igwe Austin Ezenwa (Udene-gba-ona, Agbalanze Abagana), Chief Basil Ojinna Etusi (Ozoeome Eziowelle), Chief Stephen Osita Osadebe (Arusi Atani), Chief Akunwata Ozoemena Nsugbe (Ayaka Nsugbe), Icon Michael Jackson, High Priest Fela Anikulapo Kuti, Dr. Maya Angelou, Dr. Myles and Ruth Munroe, Chief Joseph. C. Onwubuya (Ichie Okutalukwu Abagana), and Chief /Sir Gabriel Onuorah (Ichie Akubueziokwu, Dike Udum Abagana) all of blessed memory. If tears could build a stairway I would walk right up to the heaven and bring you all home again. You all lived and you touched me in your various ways.

Table of Contents

ACKNOWLEDGMENT

The greatest strength in my life has been my family and I will not fail to acknowledge their tremendous contribution in all spheres of my life. My mother Mrs. Christina Adaeze Ogbuagu (Achala Ugo). My wonderful and God given siblings, Roseline, Obianuju, Anthony and Chinedu. The Ogbuagu, Akpua, and Ezulu Family for their support. My Cousins Prince Chukwuike , Chukwunonso, Paul, Tochukwu and Ifeanyi Ogbuagu, Ugochukwu, Chika, Dubem, Ikenna and Adaobi Akpua. Mrs. Loretta Obinabo, Tochukwu, Chidozie and Chidiebere Nnonye, My Aunties Mrs. Augustine Anyaji, Mrs. Florence Nnonye and Mrs. Josephine Akpua Thompson. Uncles Justin, Emmanuel, Cliford, John, Francis, Martin, Michael, Peter and Col. Innocent Ogbuagu.

Readers will realize that a book such as this could not have been written without the cooperation of many people. Being new in the field of writing, I want to thank all the people who have made my task easier and more rewarding. These are people who dedicated their precious time to edit and give me guidance without their help this work would not have been possible. These include: Dr. Don Mattera whom I fondly call "Daddy" Dr. Olive Ezeani, Mr. Celestine F. O. George, Ms. Nomhle Makabane, Rev. Chidozie Ejimadu (Ngwuru-Aja).

The works of John Maxwell have been a comforting rock in the time of need. His book "Leadership Gold" has exposed me to great leadership credentials. Besides, Maxwell's "Daily Planner" is a well-articulated piece of literary work filled with lots of inspiration. It stimulated my creative instinct, helped shaped my thoughts and inspired me to compile this book.

My special appreciation the Consul General of Nigerian in South Africa Ambassdor Mrs. Uche Ajulu Okeke (Anyanwu Njikoka, Ada Ezumezu) who have turned around the fortunes of Nigerians since her arrival in South Africa and giving us hope that all is well.

My friends who have supported me throughout life I will like to acknowledge their contribution and who have made the journey of writing this book a success, Henry and Vincent Molokwu, Emeka and Anthony Onuorah (Gabbson), Victor Ofoto, Prince Azubike Etusi, Chioma Enderline Agu, Ikechi and Kachi Uwaezuoke, Dominic and Anita Okwuh, Franklin and Siphokazi Omoluwa (Belushi), Clement and Esther Akhidenor, Ngozi and Rita Aminu, Nnamdi and Onochie Oraka, Barrister Robinson Akpua (Ozomma Abba), Ejikeme Akpua (Doctor), Barrister Chukwudi Hazes (Baba Hayes), Barrister Okechukwu Ifeji, Chukwuma Onyike, Olisa Akabike, Chukwunwike Amobi (007), Dr. Obinna Akabike, Aggrey Molokwu (Awilo), Sampson and Nkomzwayo Okorie, Samuel Kalu, Charles Nzeribe (Chaco), Daddy Anya, Ibe Nnaji (Action), Uchenna Bishop and Martha Amah (Igwe Elo Aka Awgbu/Ogbuefi Agu Bu Uzo Westrand), Albert and Gulda Oke, Donatus Oguama (Alhaji), Odinaka Agumadu, Nwabueze Nwaobele (Ngigi, Onowu Westrand), Okwuchukwu and Dudu Eze (Man CJ), Chidi and Thuli Madubugwu (Babe), Hrh Chidi Okoroji (Igweobi Merenma Westrand), Chukwudi Ogbodo (MC), Kennedy and Nonbuso Nwurah, Michael and Fatimah Emetuche, Abraham Oganbor, Emeka Otalor, Ikenna Adindeh (Daddy IK), Patrick Egbobe (Nwakaibeya, Skippo), Vincent Nwodili (Biggato), Godwin Ukoh, Chinedu Anyaele (Ezeiafiakaego), Julian Chijoke Omanukwue (Eribeagwuagwu N' Ifite Dunu, Ogbuefi Genesis), Ifeanyi Udemgba (Ego Ifite Dunu), Obiora Nnabugwu (Obi Nwelugo), Uche Udoji (Ebekudike Great Cali), Uchenna Ekeka (Ebubedike, Eto), Ikem Donzion Nwankwo (Awelle Ugo), Stanley Okpara, Michael Eze (Conipo), Emeka Egbo, (Udubunch N'South Africa), Vincent Obi, Prince Ikpe Ekong, Prince Joseph Kingsley (Sharp Joe), Melvin Udo Richmond (Ezennaya), Emeka Ezinteje (Embargo), Valentine Odidison, Anthony Uba (Ala Chiga–Achiga, Nwa Guy), Tijani Ushman (General), Nnabuike Onuzuluike (Ofuonye Nakwa Tipa), Ngozi Ogbuji (Aliye), Matthew Okafor (Matto), Marshal Momah (Pounds Euro), Nonso Osonwa (Shenshe), Hon Emmanuel Okoye, Ikechukwu Nkechi (Biggi), Ogechi Akatampho (Digidi Dunhill), Smart Njoku (Smartaman), Sunday John (Gabasheen, Supercat), Emeka Njeta

(Rowdy Roddy Piper), Ikechukwu Nwosu (Seal), Emeka Okonkwo (Dan Blocker), John Akwunobi (Sentence), Onyeka Ewezie, Cajetan Ugwuegbu (CJ), Kingsley Nzebe, Moses Ejapkovi (Ejoor), Leonard Iwuajoku (Leos Pee), Chidi Izuobi (Baby Face), Adolphus Ezennaya (Sege, Able Chair), Henry Izuogu Molocho, Raphael Shadrack (Above), Nathan Onwuliri, Vincent Obisie, (Udubunch), Einstein Nwachukwu (Papa), Iyke Otogbolu, Ms. Egwuagu Ify Miriam, Ms. Linda Okoroji, Victor Fevinn (Mc Hammer), Chidozie Kingsley Ndudim (KC), Hon Chukwura Osita (Ebekudike Abagana), Hon Ekos Jude Akpokabeyen, Hon Charles Amagba (Agbeego Ntkiti N' Orlu, Akudinanwa N'Imo State), Chief Chidozie Osita (Monty, Odogwu Ejimatu N' Nimo), Chief Stephen Chinedu (Nwabunnaya Ogidi), Kennedy Okeke, Uchenna Kuma (Vijay), Ms. Ntsako Mbhokota, Tochukwu Okonkwo (Tobosco), Andy Orakwe, Joseph Oduah (Black Mamba), Mrs. Thelma Ugwoke, Mrs. Ijeoma Olomina, Mrs. Beatrice Abache, Mrs. Ngozi Egbosionu, Mrs. Edith Okoroji Aknisola.

To my mentors, guardians and those that have been my inspirations all this while HRH Igwe M.U.N Okonkwo Etusi (Owelle of Eziowelle), Chief Engr Authur Eze (Ozorigbondu), HRM Eze Akuenwebe MJU Emechebe (Eze Ndigbo South Africa), His Highness Frank Times Ifeanyichukwu (Onyendu Ndigbo South Africa), HRH Anayo Igwilo (Igwe Mba N' Abo Na South Africa), Chief/Dr. Dennis Amobi (Chikiluba Abagana), Chief Emmanuel Nwude (Owelle Abagana), Chief/Dr. Innocent Onwubuya (Okosisi Abagana), Dr. Peter Obi (Okwute Ndi Igbo), Chief/Dr. Ifeanyi Patrick Ubah (Ebubechukwu Uzo/Capital Oil), Chief Sir Peter and Teresa Akpua (Owelle Owulu Odu Abba), Chief Okey Ezeibe (Oranyelueze Awgbu), Prince/Barrister Ephraim Ilonzeh (Enyi Abagana), Dr. Nwachuwku Anakanze (Okaa Omee Abagana/Ike Ndigbo), Chief Anayo Amobi (Chineyelugo Abagana), Chief Anthony Anaekwe (Ononenyi Abagana), Chief Innocent Amobi (Ochilozua Abagana), The family Chief Joseph and Elizabeth Anigbogu (Ichie Nzekwesi), Engr Innocent Nwobi, Chief Aloy Okonkwo (Ide Ifite Dunu, Aloy Standard), Chief Onyeka Oguegbo (Onwanatilora Obosi, Nwanne

Di Na Mba), Chief Ephraim Okafor (Ide Abagana,Awutolo), Chief Dennis Okafor (Ejimkayaeme Abagana), Chief Eugene Anene (Alupueaku Abagana, Eugenco), Chief Mrs. Eunice Onwubuya (Ochiora Abagana), Chief/Dame. Carol Nwazojie (Mmaluluno, Bicu and Sons Limited), Chief Mrs. Florence Nwazojie (Ochilozua, Flora Truworths Enterprises Ltd), Chief Mrs. Gloria Aniegboka (Adadiora mma Obosi/Nneoma Osilu ora N South), Chief Mrs. Justina Onuorah, Mrs. Uche Elochukwu, Mrs. Obioma Onwura, Chief Debe Odumegwu-Ojukwu (Akpunwa Nnewi), Pastor/ Dr. Richie Achukwu, The family of Mr. Leonard and Azuka Ogbonna (Litraco), The family of Koval Chibuko and Chika Ezeajughi, Mr. Ifeanyi Uzor, Prince Osita Ezenwa, Prince Pius Amobi , Mrs. Ebele Ozoh Liy, Mrs. Uzoamaka Ubabikem, Engr Mr./Mrs. Chukwu, Chief/Chief Mrs. Nwaeze, Chief Onyeka Chukwu Onyeka (Ebubedike I of Ozubulu), Chief Augustine Obele (Ana Egwu Ahara), Chief Jonas Udeji, (Onowu/Akajiofor N' SA), Chief Ikenna Obele (Okwu Nze N' Aguata, Agunwa Ezinifeti), Chief Sir E.K Anichebe (Ide Ukwu N' South Africa,Okosisi N' Oba), Chief Ogbuefi N.F. Ezeokenwa (Omenma Nkatego N'Oba), Chief Kycee Okafor (Chimuluezego N' Enugwu Agidi), Chief Emeka Anaekwe (Ezeudo N' Achina, Ezeugonna N' South Africa), Prince Ernest Afamfuna Agu (Mayor Dymanic Club,TEEJ), Chief Uchenna E.Eneanaya (Ezebunachi Oba), Chief Mark Muodum (Ichie Ezeani Ugonanabo 1of Akwaeze), Chief Tony Unigwe (Onwa Ozubulu), Chief Aloysius Ikegwuonu (Ebubechukwu Uzo N' Ozubulu, Bishop) Chief Uche Ejiofor, (Chinwatakueaku, Ojoto, Okaranmmadu Okara Mmuo), Chief Daniel Chigbo (Ije Ego Na Uga), Nze Chinedu Nwogwugwu (ISi Nze, Akubue Oba), Chief Christian Oruche (Eze Chukwu Na Emeh Ozubulu), Dr. Tochukwu Unigwe, Chief Vitus Okigbo Dunu (Otitodili Jesu), Chief Quintus Onyebinamma (Ogbuefi Dala Nwajiugonna Ozubulu,Obsanjo), Chief Uzo Dnc Ikedife (Ajibo), Chief Lawrence Odum (Akaonyewetalu, Zero), Chief Amadi.O.Amdi (Udozurumba N' Amsiri), Chief Michael Urama Nnaji (Omere-Igbo-Mma), Chief Obinna Muonaeke (Nwarupoaku Na Aro Ndi Izuogu), Chief Vincent Udobi, (Onwa Ifite-Dunu, Obeleagu), Chief Izuchukwu Nwankwo (Onowu Udene De Villers), Chief Uchenna Okoye (Idejiogwugwu N'

Awkuzu), Chief Chukwudi Nwobodo (Overall), Prince Rob Azonandu (Italian Mafia), Friday Nwankwo Kujah (Soccer Ambassador), Hon Emmanuel Nwogbo (Mgbedike), Hon Louis Ogugua Ndukwu, Hon Anthony Mekwunye (Zulu), Hon Ikechukwu Anyene (Nwachinemere), Hon Frank Anyaeche (Nwawerugo N'Agulu), Hon Benjamin Uchenna Onwurolu (Nzenaguora N' Oba), Hon IfeanyiChukwu Onwuanizu, Hon Johnson Umeh, Hon Jason Osuafor (Onyeogadrimma), Rabbai Chukwuemeka Ogbonna (Akajiaku Ishiagu), Hon Bemigho Eyeiyibo (Bermuda), Dr. Mayor Onyebueke, Hon Tony Muonagor (Oneweek), Hon Kupa Felix Edore, Hon Athanasius Ogbome, Hon Pascal Ogbome, Hon Pascal Adigwe, Hon Ifeanyi Osuoza (Agenda), Hon Valentine Kogolo, Hon Chima Onyeagba Umealo (Agbawo Dike Izu Na Mgbelu), Hon Jimmy Elozie, Nnamdi Okeke, Pastor Webster Nester Odili, Pastor Ethel Onyanta, Apostle Sam Gordon, Apostle Obinna Ezenwanne, Apostle Ken Morka, Pastor Edward Ikeomu, Pastor Joseph Nwadubasim, Pastor Enoch Phiri, Princess/Dr. Royal Mma Agwuna (Ada-Ife. Akwudoluagabala N'Igboland), Princess Dineo Meko, Mrs. Bose Ogbebor, Mrs. Pamela Nkenke Blessing, Mr. John Perry, Mr. Edward Lewis, Ms. Phindi Mahwayi, Ms. Mmatshilo Motsei, Ms. Elsie Janie, Ms. Emmarentia Moeketsi, Ms. Oprah Winfrey (Angel Network), Hon Graca Machel (Foundation for Community Development).

Finally, noteworthy is the level of cooperation I received from academics across ideological spectrums. I received inspiration and support from organizations such as Westrand Brothers Association and all its arms of government the football team, Igwe in council, Abagana Welfare Union, Neo Black Movement of Africa Worldwide, Apapa Development Association (ADAS), Ohaneze Ndigbo South Africa, Eze in Council SA,Nze Na Ozo SA, Anambra State Association South Africa, Nigerian Union South Africa, Ozubulu Development Union, Millennium Friends, Oba Brothers, Balogun Market Association, The Patriots Club of Nigeria International South Africa, Genesis Football Club, etc. Inadequacy of space precludes me from listing their members individually. It is also difficult to reflect on their individual views in this book. Collectively, however, their contributions were indispensable in shaping the impression that structured my research. I am thankful for I have gained tremendous knowledge and wisdom by associating myself with these organizations and their membership.

SPECIAL APOLOGY TO UNKNOWN AUTHORS

I wish to use this medium to give credit to authors of known and unknown quotes I have used in this book. I believe your marvellous and motivational words will have a very big impact on my readers and target audience. I state, categorically, here that without such an input, my desired message to my readers would not be fully accomplished.

In times of stress, troubles, betrayals, and disappointments your words became a cornerstone. I would not have made it this far without such inspirational words of yours. I once more salute you.

MY THEME AND PRAYERS

I have fed mouths that have been ungrateful and talked behind my back. I've wiped tears off the face of people that have caused mine. I have picked up people that have tried to knock me down. I've done favors for people that can do nothing for me. I have been there for people that have not been there for me. Crazy maybe. But I will not lose myself in the hatred of others, I continue to be me because, I am who I am and it is my nature. Life isn't easy but even through all of the challenges, I will still be here being me and by the Grace of the God I will remain who He created me to be in Jesus Name Amen.

Comrade Raphael Ikechukwu Ogbuagu "Ik Poly"
(Odiraa Chukwu Mma, Abagana)

FOREWORD

Comrade Raphael Ikechukwu Ogbuagu writes with enviable clarity devoid of dogma and renders even the most complex ideas accessible. The beginning of the book provides one of the most intriguing and simple explanations of how to know your calling, your assignment with God and how to fulfil your destiny. In this book he takes the reader on a well organized journey by drawing on the insights and quotations of several philosophers, elder statesmen, clergies, and how we can apply their experiences and observations in order to empower and liberate ourselves. It will be erroneous to claim that this book offers solution to all problems in life. However, it does, give much clarity on some of the dilemmas and constraints that confront us as we try to find answers to the puzzles of life.

Thus, the author avoided the temptation of indulging in complex analysis. He used his personal experiences and tragedies to reveal the dilemma associated with career choice and how you can make the right choice. It is no exaggeration that some people will make a conscious decision to change their career after reading this book. The book is full of quotations and voices of reason that will help lift your soul and make you prosper. This is a life changing book. I am confident your life will be greatly enriched and renewed as you assimilate the truth this book brings to light.

As different voices clamour to assert their views of a world free of violence and crime, the message of love has become a reoccurring sermon being preached and interpreted in various ways. Raphael Ikechukwu Ogbuagu, through this book, has documented his views for global peace and love for one another with emphasis on man returning to the true nature of love as originally planned by God. His work has added invaluable contribution to our understanding of a troubled society in search for peace, which can only be attained through love.

Suffice it to say that love is one of the few terminologies in social and religious theories that have been used so lavishly. Yet, despite its inflated presence and usage, the term is still obscured, undertheorised, and has failed to defuse the resort to violence and crime by people. The author rises to the challenge of conceptualising love through a philosophical examination of its usage and its interpretation in contemporary times. This book is well researched and impressive. Important and difficult terms are well explained and easy to understand. Reading this book is like having a one and one interaction with the writer as he speaks from his mind. The book is recommended for people from all walks of life. Be blessed as you pick up a copy for yourself and another for someone you love.

Celestine F. O. George

Deputy Personnel Manager

Hitech Construction Company Limited Okrika (Base) Rivers State Nigeria

INTRODUCTION

"Many of us have shame, guilt, pain and anger attached to things we have done or experienced. We go to great lengths to hide what we have done or what has been done to us. You are as sick as your secrets. Until you reveal, examine, and unpack the negative emotions attached to the secrets, thoughts, feelings, and experiences, you are held captive by them." **(Iyanla Vanzant)**

When you have been hurt and betrayed, it tends to carry a lot of anger within you. Medical research has shown that harbouring anger and resentment for a long period causes physical and psychological stress that weakens your immune system and breaks down your vital organs. When you hold on to old hurts, you only give power and control to those who have hurt you, but when you forgive them, you cut the ties to them. They can no longer yank on your chain. Don't get hung up on thinking that by not forgiving them you are doing them a favour; if nothing else, do it for yourself . Forgive all those who have hurt you by doing this you release yourself of anger and resentment. Just enjoy what forgiving them does to you. Once you have adopted an attitude of forgiveness, you will lighten your load so that you can chase dreams without being weight down by baggages from the past. Self-forgiveness is just as important as forgiving others, I have made mistakes. So have you.

The bibles says that "we reap what we sow." If you are bitter, angry, self-pitying, and unforgiving, what do you think those attitude will get you? What joy is there in a life like that? So reject those dark and pessimistic moods, load up on optimism, and charge up an attitude of gratitude, an attitude of action, an attitude of empathy and an attitude of forgiveness. Our thoughts has the power to affect and influence how we feel, and how we feel has the power to influence our behaviour. Acceptance of what has happened is the first step to overcoming the consequence of any misfortune.

Do not hold on to any loss if you still want to live free! Healing does not mean the damage never existed, it just means the damage no longer controls our lives. And with this we free our minds from factors that stand in the way of our happiness, joy, love, peace and advancement in life. We can get a clear vision of moving forward to help us create a life filled with peace and harmory.

"The mind is a powerful force. It can enslave us or empower us. It can plunge us into the depths of misery or take us to the heights of ecstasy. Learn to use the power wisely." **(David Cuschieri)**

"No matter what you have gone through and what others have put you through, you are still you. To embrace happiness, to find your passion and to love yourself, remember these things were never taken away from you. Nothing can stop you from rediscovering yourself. The greatest journey always begins within YOU." **(Dodinsky)**

"We are what our thoughts have made us; so take care about what you think. Words are secondary. Thoughts live, they travel far." **(Swami Vieekananda)**

"A mind preoccupied with thoughts of resentment and bitterness cannot change the past nor does it wound anyone but the soul that beholds them." **(Dodinsky)**

"Anger, fear, resentment are all by-products of compulsiveness. What you need to overcome is your compulsiveness." **(Sadhguru)**

Seeking professional help is advisable but one should have the inner desire to heal. Self-healing is very important to any individual who has passed through losses, tribulations, pains etc. The most important aspect of healing comes through acceptance of what has happened. Nobody can heal on your behalf; people seek healing in various ways; some resort to drinking, isolation, smoking, sports, painting, or writing and even to drugs. Loving and accepting yourself is the only cure for self pity and overcoming the victimhood mentality. The use of drugs, alcohol, and sex offer temporary reliefs, and eventually they bring only more pain. When you come to see yourself as a child of God and a part of His plan, your life will change forever. You may not be a believer in Christ, but you are valuable in the eyes of God.

Self healing in a positive way could be taking up a hobby to occupy one's mind, whichever way you may choose to heal is personal to you. If anger isn't brought up into conscious awareness, it has no place to go. It either turns into an attack on self or an inappropriate unconscious attack on others. We keep blaming someone in the present for something else did in the past. Our defences reflect our wounds. But no person can heal those wounds.

The fundamental change will occur with the change of mind. Life is too short and precious to be wasted on things beyond the power of our own will, because therapy can be such a waste of time, energy, and resources. I have a choice. You have a choice. We can choose to dwell on disappointments, short comings, hurts and pains. We can choose to be bitter, angry or sad. Or when faced with hard times and hurtful people or situation, we can choose to learn from the experience and move forward, taking responsibility for your own happiness is something nobody can do for you. Think about how you want to respond to challenges that come your way. Life may not be going well for you now, but as long as you are here press forward, anything is possible. Hold on to hope.

How to begin: Rebuilding life from within. Love yourself. Love can heal a wounded soul. We all have scars from our past. Scars on wrists and throats can be healed with time but there are some scars which are much deeper than those on the body. They are the scars on our hearts, minds and on our souls which take a long time to heal. Embrace people who love you because love has an amazing power to heal and bring radiance in our life. Nurture your inner strength. Stop apologizing for being you, surrounding yourself with positive people. Create for yourself an environment where love abides, where love rules and you will see other things will fall in place.

"After rain come sunshine; after darkness comes the glorious dawn. There is no sorrow without its alloy of joy; there is no joy without its admixture of sorrow. Behind the ugly terrible mask of misfortune lies the beautiful soothing countenance of prosperity. So, tear the mask." **(Chief Obafemi Awolowo)**

"People can be more forgiving than you can imagine. But you have to forgive yourself. Let go of what's bitter and move on." **(Bill Cosby)**

"Acceptance is simply recognition. When you recognize a thing, you see it for what it is. All of our experiences, no matter how awful they appear to be, are temporary. Acceptance of an experience as a temporary situation can make it a lot easier to handle." **(Iyanla Vanzant)**

"Even though you may want to move forward in your life, you may have one foot on the brakes. In order to be free, we must learn how to let go. Release the hurt. Release the fear. Refuse to entertain your old pain. The energy it takes to hang onto the past is holding you back from a new life. What is it you would let go of today?" **(Mary Manin Morrissey)**

"Everything happens for a reason. People change so you can learn to let go. Things go wrong so that you can appreciate them when they are right. You believe lies so that you will eventually learn to trust no one but yourself, and sometimes good things fall apart so that better things will fall together." **(Marily Monroe)**

"The purpose of life, after all, is to live it, to taste experience to the utmost, to reach out eagerly and without fear for newer and richer experience." **(Eleanor Roosevelt)**

"Someday we will forget the hurt. The reason we cried and what caused us the pain. We will finally realise that the secret of being free is not revenge, but letting things unfold in their own way and own time. After all what matter is not the first, but the last chapter of our life which shows how well we ran the race. So smile, laugh, forgive, believe and love all over again." **(Unknown)**

The compilation of this book dates back to 1992. It is a product of 18 years of research. It is recommended for social institutions and government agencies such as:

1.   Churches

2.   Schools

3.   Families

4.   Prisons

5.   Security

6.   Agencies/Outfits

7.   Governmental Institutions

8.   Non-governmental Organisations etc

This book will help you to discover your purpose and provide you with the courage to follow your own unique life path. Chapter one talks about knowing our callings in life. Unfortunately many people don't know what thier calling is. God created us with a purpose. When you find what that calling is it opens a lot of doors for you and makes your life more fulfilling. Chapter two is full of philosophical quotes from the best brains the world has ever produced. Chapter three reflects on the selection of a career path that will make you a more fulfilled person. Many of us for the sake of earning a living have gone into occupations that are not necessary what will elavate our general wellbeing. Chapter four will empower you to believe in yourself and that positivity is the key to survival. Chapter five focuses on the self healing power of love. Many of us have been betrayed, stabbed in the back and forsaken by our loved ones, however to overcome this we have to learn to love and forgive so that we don't hold ourselfs down in the moment of grief, regrets and self pity.

Chapter Six is a romantical adventure for lovers, the up and downs of life have taken our minds away for wooing and sustaining the flame of our various love life. You can revive and maintain a healthly loving relationship by sending out such message to your spouse. I have no doubt that this piece of work I have taken the time to research will bring out the best in YOU. Enjoy your reading.

CHAPTER 1
KNOWING YOUR CALLING, YOUR ASSIGNMENT WITH GOD AND YOUR DESTINY

Unless you know what you are looking for, you may not be able to identify it when you find it. It is one thing to know what you want; it is another thing to know what it looks like. God has put something inside and around you to productively occupy you until He comes. What you need to discover it is insight. However, the insight you require demands humility. If you despise the days of little things, you may not see great days. Everyone is unique in his or her own way and has a calling from God. Simply put, everyone has an assignment he or she came with into this world.

Service is the rent you pay for your time here on this earth. The higher the rent, the bigger the purpose. In every human being there is a sleeping lion, an untapped greatness. In every one of us there is a calling; a calling to be greater than we are today, a calling to achieve more and a calling to leave a legacy.

We all have it; the most difficult problem is discovering it. No matter how odd this calling might be, if you find it, stick to it. One of the greatest problems of our generation is trying to be like the other person which is not possible. There are no two of you in this world, you are the only one, no matter the resemblance. Even twins are different and unique in their own ways. This is evidenced by the fact that among the 7 billion people on this planet, no two individual are alike; their fingerprints, genetic code, and the chromosome combinations are all distinct and unique. The untold wealth within you is uniquely yours because God creates no two people for the same purpose, your personality, abilities and resources are God's gift, bestowed on you. He gave you the breath of life, and they contain the possibility for bringing meaning and fulfilment into your life.

God wants you to release all He gave you for the benefit of others and the blessing of your own life. You were designed to be distinctive, special, irreplaceable, and unique, so refuse to be "Normal"! Go beyond average! Do not strive to be accepted; rather strive to be yourself. The most difficult task we face is having the courage to trust ourselves, to be ourselves, when we become ourselves we stop being distorted of others. When God calls you to do something, you may not understand or be enthusiastic at first. Have you been able to ask yourself these questions? Where am I heading in life? How do I want my life to end? What would I like to be remembered for when I am gone? If you are able to give yourself an honest and genuine answer, it is likely going to help you fulfil your destiny and calling with God.

"If we had no purpose God would not have planted us unto our mother's womb and gave us life. We have a purpose in life, discover it and let His grace lead you to live it." **(Osadebe Ibegbu)**

"We must believe that we are gifted for something, and that this thing, at whatever cost, must be attained." **(Marie Curie)**

"I've come to believe that each of us has a personal calling that's as unique as a fingerprint - and that the best way to succeed is to discover what you love and then find a way to offer it to others in the form of service, working hard, and also allowing the energy of the universe to lead you." **(Oprah Winfrey)**

"I don't know what my calling is, but I want to be here for a bigger reason. I strive to be like the greatest people who have ever lived." **(Will Smith)**

"The tragedy in life doesn't lie in not reaching your goal. The tragedy lies in having no goal to reach." **(Benjamin Mays)**

"Your destiny is to fulfil those things upon which you focus most intently. So choose to keep your focus on that which is truly magnificent, beautiful, uplifting and joyful. Your life is always moving toward something." **(Ralph Marston)**

Everyone has the perfect gift to give the world and if each of us is freed up to give the gift that is uniquely ours to give, the world will be in a total harmony." **(Buckminister Fuller)**

Calling is a divine revelation that God's purpose for your live. God exercises His right to assign anyone via revelation to any assignment of His choice. It has nothing to do with your abilities but God's abilities at work in you. Every divine calling naturally enjoys divine backing.

Vision is the faculty or state of being able to see, the ability to think about or plan the future with imagination or wisdom, a mental image of what the future will or could be like.

Dreams are visual manifestation of the seed of destiny planted in the spirit and sour of each human by His creature. The dream God gives you guarantees, no matter what it looks like now, when it is all over, your dream will come to pass.

Gifting is when you discover the natural endowment inherent in you, the productive abilities that flow out of you naturally. There is no ungifted being on the earth. Everyone is divinely endowed for a profitable life. In case you have not heard a voice, and have not seen a vision, look inward and identify your gifting. There is enough inside you to occupy you till He comes.

Choice God made you a creature of choice and as long as your choice is not contradictory to His convent previsions for you, you have His backing. The power of your choice in locating God's Purpose for your life covers areas like academics, business, professional practices, so whatever you discovered either by calling, vision, gifting or choice, nurture it and do all you can to develop yourself in it because the brightest stars in the kingdom are those who know where they are going and give it all it takes to get there. Whenever we are presented with a situation to make choice in order to fulfil our dreams, we should be careful not to be lured into compromising ourselves and what the word of God teaches, for that is a recipe for disaster.

"You are defined by your choices, and you have thousands of them spread through a lifetime to continue re-inventing yourself." **(Dodinsky)**

"The two most important days in your life are the day you were born and the day you find out why." **(Mark Twain)**

"We have all been placed on this earth to discover our path, and we will never be happy if we live someone else's idea of life." **(Sibongile Mthembu)**

"Life is the most difficult exam. Many people fail because they try to copy others not realising that everyone has a different question paper" **(Unknown)**

"Know well what leads you forward and what holds you back, and choose the path that leads to wisdom." **(Buddha)**

"Understand that the right to choose your own path is a sacred privilege. Use it. Dwell in possibility." **(Oprah Winfrey)**

"On my journey, I have found that the path to self-discovery is the most liberating choice of all." **(Muhammad Ali)**

When you refuse to follow your calling, you deny yourself the opportunity to fulfil your potential and purpose and you forfeit the productivity that could have blessed you and others. Therefore you steal from the world. If you already understand your purpose, are you prepared to change your plans to match God's will? If you aren't, you can easily become bitter because things that used to work for you may no longer work. A lack of purpose and unfulfilled potentials is epidemic in our world, yet just as the gold status was hidden inside the clay there is " **Gold** " in each of us is waiting to be revealed.

No matter whom you are or which country you live in, you have a personal purpose and calling, for every human being is born with one. God created each person with a unique vision. He has tremendous plans for you that no one else can accomplish. When all that is in you fuses with the world around you, you become part of a greater purpose. Most of the reasons why men fail are our inabilities to discover our purpose. We came into this world to thrive, not to survive, the worst tragedy of life is not death but a life without a purpose, to be alive and not fulfilling your destiny is as if you had never lived.

"You lose nothing when fighting for a cause. In my mind the losers are those who don't have a cause they care about." **(Muhammad Ali)**

"God gives a pay package for only the function He has assigned you; other activities make you famous without eternal reward." **(Apostle Sam Gordon)**

"When God decides to bless you, He will baffle the spectators. He doesn't make normal moves. When God moves in your life, no one will be able to deny His presence." **(Tony Gaskins Jr)**

"When you're doing what you were put here to do, there may be opposition but there is no competition." **(Tony Gaskins Jr)**

"When the purpose of anything is not known, abuse is inevitable. What is the purpose of your marriage, the wealth God gave you, the beautiful gifts (Children), He gave to you that place working etc. You need to understand the purpose" **(Chika Nwankwo)**

"You were not created to live in fear; you are born to take action." **(Pastor Matthew Hagee)**

"Those who desire to reach, and keep their places at the top in any calling must be prepared to do so the hard way." **(Chief Obafemi Awolowo)**

The tragic thing is that many people live their whole lives without ever recognizing their vision and calling. How do you remove the clay and uncover the gold within you? Your dreams, talent, and desires can be refined in a process of discovering and fulfilling your life's vision so that the pure gold of your unique and personal gift to this world can shine forth. Bear in mind that the most powerful force in life is the force of vision which is tied to your destiny and calling; once there is no vision you will simply relive the past with its disappointment and failures. Therefore vision is the key to your future and destiny.

To fulfill your vision in life you will have to swim upstream against the tide of popular opinion. Compromised vision always kills potential because a vision that is attempted outside God's guidance cannot reveal His power; you will find yourself struggling when you are out of His Purpose for you. Take your dream, and be willing to die for it. Understanding your purpose is the key to operating in excellence. When you understand this specific plan that God has for your life, you are able to plan and prioritize accordingly. Many of us fail to operate in excellence because we tend to bite than we can chew. When you understand your purpose, you are able to accept the assignments that are aligned to your God given purpose.

You determine the measure of your own success, success that is established by the creator's assignment for your life. The purpose for every created thing pre-existed its creation. This means that the creator of a thing knows the attributes it must possess in order to fulfill the reason for its existence. Consequently, when it is created, they are incorporated in its design and manufacture producing a fully competent creation. There are a few ways to discover the purpose of a created thing; observe the service it provides while in operation (the need it is meeting), understand its attributes and their collective potential (what they could be used for) or simply ask its creator (and get the answer directly).

The created thing can never choose its purpose; it can only discover it. It operates at maximum efficiency, effectiveness and ease when it is fulfilling that which it was created to do. When purpose is not known, abuse is inevitable. The result is a creation easily damaged, broken or neglected. The challenge then is, what questions should you be asking to whom to discover your purpose? Your gift will make a way for you but you need to believe, be strong, positive and smart. All you need is someone that can help you find direction and to trust God. Think of anything that makes you happy, do it for that is your calling.

"Each of us has been put on earth with the ability to do something well. We cheat ourselves and the world if we don't use that ability as best we can." **(George Allen, Snr)**

"As you become clearer about who you really are, you'll be better able to decide what is best for you - the first time around." **(Oprah Winfrey)**

"Almighty God made us unique from the moment we were conceived; from our personality right down to our fingerprints. When we interact with other people it is important to recognize and celebrate our own uniqueness. In spirit, it is impossible to always agree with someone. There will always be some little difference." **(Unknown)**

"If you had the talents of another person, it wouldn't help you; it would hinder you. They have a different destiny. Quit trying to outperform others and be happy with whom you are." **(Joel Osteen)**

"You may find people who can share your dreams and goals with, but hoping that they will be identical to you is unrealistic" **(Unknown)**

"We all have different faces, characters and names. If God wanted us to be all same, He would have done it. Not to respect the differences, to accuse the others for our fault is not to respect God." **(Shams Tabrizi)**

"There are four kinds of people in the world. Those who build walls. Those who protect walls. Those who breach walls. And those who tear down walls. Much of life is discovering who you are. When you find out, you also realize there are places you can no longer go, things you can no longer do, words you can no longer say." **(P.S. Baber)**

It is interesting to note that when you get to discover "**your calling**" everything about your life will give you joy, laughter, confidence, faith, and satisfaction. This in turn helps to increase your lifespan. Events around you tend to make way on their own accord without you knowing how it came about. Purpose is not something you can easily explain, it is very sad that many people will never get to fulfill their calling before death takes them away from this world. The world is proficient at aborting potential and destiny, not only will it do nothing to help you reveal and use the hidden treasure in you discovering your calling, it will mostly discourage you by measuring your effort against its standard or following the trend of what people. Bear in mind that when you are doing what God has called you to do jealously and envy will arose and people will want to pull you down for no reason.

"Put your heart into what you're called to do, and let God determine the result." **(Hasheem Francis, CEO Built to Prosper)**

"When you understand PURPOSE and PROMISE you don't feel the need to race or compete, your goal is to complete!" **(Letwin Dadirai Mandishona)**

"Actualizing greatness will often cost you people, places and things. The price is so high that many opt out and embrace normalcy. But those who understand they were born for greatness and choose to weather the storm of transition and change will experience a limitless and unfathomable existence." **(Unknown)**

"When you accept God's high standards of integrity, the world will come to find you, and everything you ever wanted will come to you without you even trying." **(Dr. Richie Achukwu)**

"I know why I am here and my only real focused goal is to live each day to the fullest and to try and honour God and be an encouragement to others. What the future holds is firmly in God's hands, and I am very happy about that!" **(Ken Hensley)**

It is for this reason some have argued that the graveyard is the richest place on earth, as a result of so many potentials who are buried at the point of death without utilization. One of the greatest tragedies of life is to watch potential live unreleased. How sad to know that majority of people on this planet will never discover who they really are or their true calling in life while others settle for only a portion of their true self and calling. If you leave this world without fulfilling your purpose; you are a disgrace and a waste and owe your generation an apology. Without purpose we lose direction and this is dangerous for anyone —to be alive and not know why. Bear in mind that what you love is a clue to your assignment and purpose in life. You were created because there is something God wants done that demanded your presence on this planet. You were designed and dispatched for destiny.

Destiny and purpose is also the key to your ability. If by chance, you're among the few who get to find their calling, there is nothing like the experience of living out your purpose. Most of the time your purpose will be accompanied with a lot of unseen forces, tribulations, attacks, and challenges if your faith is shaky and you do not have the confidence in yourself, you may deviate from it. The key to moving forward, even in hard times, is to let your vision for your life be guided not by what you can see but by what you can imagine. You must have faith in God and His plans for your life and destiny. Most times in life we focus on our limitations instead of our possibilities which are all tied in our destiny and relationship with God.

There is great power in believing in your destiny. You can move mountains. God is able. Read *Isaiah 41:10*. I can tell you now that there is no greater feeling than discovering your purpose in life. It spars you on to want to do the unthinkable and confronts things that you never thought were possible. Such a feeling can only come from Almighty God and nowhere else. I was once told by Pastor Ethel Onyanta that "God operates like a car navigation system; irrespective of how lost you are in life, if you're diligent and seek Him with all your heart, God will always find a way to bring you back to fulfill your dream and purpose of creation."

Anything God asks of you is for your own good and that of others, for the healing of the world, on a small or large scale. Without purpose; life lacks substance. Without dream, we reach nothing. Without love we feel nothing. And without God, we are nothing. I want you to bear in mind that your purpose is greater than your pain so stick to it no matter what happens along the line.

"So many people out there are afraid to live their dreams. Just keep doing your best and the world will definitely notice. I always say, the toughest part about following your dreams is having the guts to go after them, once that is done, you are on the right track." **(Ntsako Mbhokota)**

"To survive is to remain alive or in existence, to thrive is to grow vigorously or realize a goal despite the circumstances of your life." **(Dr. Richie Achukwu)**

"When I tried to live my purpose, I failed miserably. But when I decided to follow God instead, heaven backed me up." **(Paballo Sefara)**

"Passion and purpose go hand in hand. When you discover your purpose; you will find something you are tremendously passionate about. Follow your heart but be quiet for a while. Ask questions then feel the answer. Learn to trust your heart. Absence diminishes little passion and increases great ones just as wind extinguishes candle yet fans a fire. Fuel your passion, igniting your potential in all aspects of life" **(Anna La Torre)**

"Everyone has talent, what is rare is the courage to follow the talent to the dark place where it leads. " **(Erica Jong)**

"Thought leads to purpose, purpose goes forth in action, action form habits, habits decide character, and character fixes our destiny." **(Anna La Torre)**

"My fighting had a purpose. I had to be successful in order to get people to listen to the things I had to say." **(Muhammad Ali)**

"My life has always been about service. I am focused on serving my creator, family and my country to the best of my ability and with your help I aim to be better at doing that." **(President Goodluck Jonathan)**

Over the years my life has been an epitome of someone gifted to serve people and to be a leader in any capacity. Thus, I have been able to unravel the potential in me to touch people's lives through my words, speeches, writings, empathy, and actions. Time and again, I have tried to shy away from this calling and responsibility. However, many are surprised that regardless of my quiet and humble disposition I have been able to lead and command respect even among the most brutal, rugged and ruthless environments one can imagine.

I have realized that with God's blessing and purpose upon my life, I can start by making a small yet steady difference in the world while working towards enlarging my life to extend God's kingdom. I do not have to change the world on my own, but the few people that I can touch with my life and the resources that God has given me, can have positive impact on those people's lives, the fact also is that when you serve others, your own heart heals. I encourage you to sow good seeds by serving others; you may find that the life you transformed is your own life. Our mission on this planet is that of service.

"Full time is time full and when you get to that place you can be used by God to turn Nations and empower them no forces on earth can hold you back." **(Pastor Ray McCauley)**

"You don't have to be superhuman to do what you believe in." **(Debbi Fields)**

"Truly great people in history never wanted to be great for themselves. All they wanted was the chance to do good for others and be close to God." **(Muhammad Ali)**

"Life is not easy for any of us. But what of that? We must have perseverance and above all confidence in ourselves. We must believe that we are gifted for something and that this thing must be attained." **(Marie Curie)**

"When I started my music career, I was a maid. I used to clean houses. My mother was a proud janitor. My stepfather, who raised me like his very own, worked at the post office and my father was a trash-man. They all wore uniforms and that is why I stand here today, in my black and white, and I wear my uniform to honour them. This is a reminder that I have work to do. I have people to uplift. I have people to inspire. And today, I wear my uniform proudly as a Cover Girl. I want to be clear, young girls, I did not have to change who I was to become a Cover Girl. I didn't have to become perfect because I've learned throughout my journey that perfection is the enemy of greatness. Embrace what makes you unique, even if it makes others uncomfortable." **(Janelle Monáe)**

"A good head and a good heart are always a formidable combination." **(Nelson Rolihlahla Mandela"Madiba)**

I have rendered service to humanity by serving in different capacities right from my high school days till date. There is hardly a gap in my life where I have not been entrusted with responsibilities or leadership positions to enable me make impact in the lives of those around me. Whatever the magic is, I do not know. All I know is that I deliver results. It is no gain saying that being placed in a position of trust and responsibility tends to bring out the best qualities in me - qualities I never knew I had. I have always refused to accept failure as an option and have often seen myself as someone destined to excel. Consequently, I have often seen problems and difficult situations as opportunities to make a difference in the lives of those around me. Hence, through courage, perseverance, hard work, and faith in God I have been able to overcome these challenges and touched the lives of many. In doing so, I had to deny myself some of the basic comforts of life and sacrifice a great deal of my time and resources for the benefit of others. The bigger your life purpose, the more your ego tries to distract you, and bring down your courage. Stay strong and focus on your spiritual path.

"I expect to pass through this world but only just once. Any good thing that I can do, or any kindness that I can show to my fellow mates; let me do it & let me not defer nor neglect it, for I shall not pass this road again." **(Raphael Ikechukwu Ogbuagu)**

"Unless someone like you cares a whole awful lot, nothing is going to get better. It's not." **(Theodore Seuss Geisel)**

"If I change one life by touching another with my story. I have done my duty." **(Zelda La Grange)**

"Doing good to others is not a duty; it is a joy for it increases your own health and happiness" **(Zoroaster)**

"Those of us placed in a position of leadership must be prepared to grasp the nettle if we unite in doing so, and if, in addition, we set a worthy example and a Marat on pace in probity, unselfishness, and self-sacrifice, the people will follow, all too readily, in our footsteps." **(Chief Obafemi Awolowo)**

It is awkward that people in trusted positions and leadership want to be worshipped, served, feared, dreaded, respected, adored, and praised. However, my idea of leadership is one that sees leadership as a sport that serves the need of the people and brings joy rather than an opportunity that paves way for self-enrichment. Simply put, leadership, in my view, is service that gives positive response to public desires and expectations. It is on this basis that I have always wanted to serve others, help them actualize their dreams and elevate their status, and give meaning to their existence. Suffice to say that most contemporary leaders are basically lured to preside over others as a result of what they stand to gain; the reverse is the case with me. It is with humility, therefore, that I wish to add that I have a penchant for embracing people in difficult situations and helping them seek ways and means of solving their problems; rather than identifying with them on the basis of what I stand to gain. As a leader, do you have plans to "grow" the people you are leading irrespective of their backgrounds? Or are you disconnected because everything has to revolve around you?

"I have always maintained that character and values, when cherished by leaders, are far more important than their contributions in other areas of public service." **(Hon Peter Obi)**

"When people respect you as a person, they admire you. When they respect you as a friend they love you. When they respect you as a partner, they cherish you. When they respect you as a leader, they follow you." **(John Maxwell)**

"Before you are a leader, success is all about growing yourself. When you become a leader, success is all about growing others." **(Jack Welch)**

"As a leader, if all you do is look for something wrong with people...you are sure going to find it. Be different, look for the positive." **(Matthew Okafor)**

"A leader is great, not because of his or her power, but because of his or her ability to empower others." **(John Maxwell)**

"No man will make a great leader who wants to do it all himself or get all the credit for doing it." **(Andrew Carnegie)**

"A lot of leaders want to be accorded respect and honour by virtue of their position, but what most of them fail to understand is that they have to earn such by deeds and actions." **(Raphael Ikechukwu Ogbuagu)**

"Most people don't reach their potential....because they distance themselves away from people who challenge them...good leaders welcome dissenting voices!" **(Matthew Okafor)**

"Leadership is solving problems. The day soldiers stop bringing you their problems is the day you have stopped leading them. They have either lost confidence that you can help or concluded you do not care. Either case is a failure of leadership." **(Collin Powell)**

"Leadership is the capacity to translate vision into reality." **(Warren Bennis)**

There are three great personalities that have greatly shaped & influenced my ideology and perception of leadership as a result of their actions. The first is my mother, Mrs. Christiana Adaeze Ogbuagu, who has demonstrated, through her devotion and selfless service to her family and community, that it is possible for us to positively impact and touch the lives of people around us. The two major attributes of her which make her a good leader are: her willingness to love people and her commitment to assisting others achieve their desired goals and aspirations.

The second figure was Chief J. C. Onwubuya (Ichie Okutalukwu Abagana), of blessed memory who was a selfless servant to the community of Abagana where he came from. He took up others' problems as if they were his own. He died doing just that. I wept so much at his death because I had never seen anybody as passionate in the upliftment of others as him. The third figure is my mentor and friend, the honourable Louis Ogugua Ndukwe, who taught me through his pitfalls as a leader what not to do. His words were, "Don't make, or allow money to be your driving force in leadership. Whatever agenda you intend to pursue or actualize don't let it be personal; it should be an agenda that benefits mankind in general." Today Louis Ndukwu is a local government chairperson I pray that his mandate as a leader will be executed to the highest level and that more life's are touched by his empathy. With these principles I have excelled in various positions I have been privileged to occupy in life. Sometimes, in leadership you may have to step on the toes of your closest allies in order to secure a fair result. Moreover, you may have enemies you don't deserve in your bid to do things right for your followers and others that look up to you. Hence, regardless of the persecution, accusation, gossip, and tribulation that may come your way don't give in or deviate from your principles. Always stay focused on the vision and victory will surely be yours by God's grace.

"Most leaders never experience what is best in them; because they live their lives trying to be what they feel is acceptable to the masses. That's not authentic leadership, that's conformity leadership." **(Hasheem Francis, CEO Built to Prosper)**

My first leadership motto is not to blend in the general trend. In other words, I do not jump on the bandwagon. My second leadership motto is to believe and do only those things that are in line with God's will and are pleasing in his sight. Thus, whatever I do, I do as a result of my commitment and passion to serve God and humanity; devoid of any personal benefit. I have also learned that the quickest way to failure as a leader is to try to please everybody.

"The closer you get to you get to your excellence in life, the more friends you will lose. People love you when you are average because it makes them comfortable. But when you pursue greatness it makes people uncomfortable. Be prepared to lose some people on your journey." **(Tony.A.Gaskins Jnr)**

"A man should never be appointed into a leadership position if his vision focuses on people's weaknesses rather than on their strengths." **(Hasheem Francis, CEO Built to Prosper)**

"Whenever you are going with the general trend, you are not doing your own thinking." **(John Maxwell)**

"I think whether you're having setbacks or not, the role of a leader is to always display a winning attitude." **(Colin Powell)**

"Problems only emerge when there solutions for them. The role of leadership is to guide people towards those solutions." **(Walter Sisulu)**

"Real leader must be ready to sacrifice all for the freedom of their people." **(Nelson Rolihlahla Mandela"Madiba)**

Though leadership may be hard to define the common characteristic among leaders is the ability to actualize a dream or vision. Leadership is that quality of mind that enables a person to assess a problem in larger context and see how solutions can be found to such problems. Leadership is an attribute of the mind and human experience which enables people to task themselves to engage problems, offer solutions and move society or a group of people forward including the leaders themselves in the process. One of African greatest son Mohamed ElBaradei once said that "you cannot intend to be a President when you don't really know what is the duty and responsibility of a President." Many want to occupy the position, have a name tag attached to their name yet they don't know the meaning or duty of a leader, in so doing they misuse authority, power and resources when they find themselves in position of influence. One has got to know what a job description entails before applying for such a job in the first place.

What is Leadership?

Leadership is the reciprocal process of mobilizing by persons with certain motives and values, various economic, political and other resources in context of competition and conflict, in order to realize goals independently or mutually held by both leaders and followers. Leadership is an influence relationship among leaders and followers who intend real changes that reflects their mutual purpose.

Put in another way leadership is a process by which members of a group are empowered to work together synergistically towards a common goal or vision that create change, transform institutions, and thus improve the quality of life.

Are you a Spiritual Leader?

This is a true saying, if a man desires the office of a bishop, he desires a good work. **(1 Timothy 3:1)**

Leadership is a subject everyone talks about. It's a pity however that only few understand it. Most people want to be leaders but only few achieve it. What is leadership? What is spiritual leadership? It can be deduced from today's Bible reading that spiritual leadership is not the same as inordinate ambition. Inordinate ambition denotes canvassing for promotion with the motive of being seen and approved of by men. Such a person desires to be popular, to stand tall among one's contemporaries and to exercise control over others. It is perilous to put an ambitious man in office. Ambitious men enjoy the powers that money or authority gives. They lobby for promotion and are carnally minded. This kind of attitude is strongly discouraged by the scriptures **(1 Peter 5:2-3)**. God and men are constantly searching for leaders who are willing to suffer for the sake of objectives great enough to demand their wholehearted obedience.

There is a rising need for leadership that is authoritative, spiritual and sacrificial. Spiritual leadership is not won by promotion but by many prayers and tears. It is attained by confession of sin, soul searching and a humble attitude before God. It is attained by self-surrender, a courageous elimination of every idol, a bold, undying, uncompromising and uncomplaining embrace of the cross, and also by an eternal, unfaltering focus on Jesus Christ. It is not gained by seeking great things for ourselves, but rather by counting all things as loss for Christ. Are you a spiritual leader? Follow the Master's master principles for effective leadership.

What are the Master's master principles for effective leadership? The first is the principle of dependence. Jesus voluntarily emptied Himself, surrendering His privileges and the independent exercise of His will to God. His dependence upon the Father was voluntary **(Philippians 2:7)**. Secondly, there is the principle of approval. Jesus was approved of God. To excel as a spiritual leader, you need the approval of the Almighty **(Acts 2:22)**. The third principle is the principle of modesty. Christ was modest. A spiritual leader should not be strident and flamboyant, but modest and unassuming. Fourthly, we have the principle of empathy.

Leadership involves being sympathetic and understanding with the weak and erring. The fifth principle is the principle of optimism. Jesus was full of faith. Leadership requires hope and optimism since a true servant of God battles with the powers of darkness. A pessimist cannot make an inspiring leader. The sixth principle is the principle of the anointing. Christ was anointed with the Holy Ghost and power. Leadership requires a touch of the supernatural **(Acts 10:38)**.

"If your action inspires others to dream more, learn more, do more and become more, you are a leader." **(John Quincy Adams)**

"Let our various positions be it in government, politic, organisations or family be driven by passion not ambition." **(Raphael Ikechukwu Ogbuagu)**

"Leadership is about falling in love with the people you serve." **(Nelson Rolihlahla Mandela"Madiba)**

"Visionary leaders are the people who are breaking the rules. They cannot be held by circumstances." **(Hasheem Francis, CEO Built to Prosper)**

"Leadership is not about titles, positions or flowcharts. It is about one life influencing another." **(John C. Maxwell)**

"Successful leaders have the courage to take action when others hesitate to do so." **(John Maxwell)**

"The first responsibility of a leader is to define reality." **(Max Dupree)**

"If you want to change the life of people you lead don't attack their value or idea, but give them better information than they have." **(Dr. Richie Achukwu)**

"Leading well is not about enriching yourself, it's about empowering others." **(John Maxwell)**

"A great leader's courage to fulfil his vision comes from passion, not position." **(Sibongile Mthembu)**

"If you are a leader, you will find that realistic thinking helps people to buy into you and your vision." **(John Maxwell)**

"A leader is not a person who can perform better than his people but someone who can inspire and support his people to perform better than himself." **(Hon Pascal Adigwe)**

"As we look ahead into the next century, leaders will be those who empower others." **(Bill Gates)**

"Leaders have two characteristics. First, they are going somewhere and second they are able to persuade other people to go with them." **(John Maxwell)**

"The challenge of leadership is to be strong, but not rude; be kind, but not weak; be bold, but not bully; be thoughtful, but not lazy; be humble, but not timid; be proud, but not arrogant; have humour, but without folly." **(Jim Rohn)**

"Management is doing things right; leadership is doing the right things." **(Peter Drucker)**

"Leaders should sketch a picture of where the team is going." **(John Maxwell)**

"Great leaders gain authority by giving it away." **(James B. Steckdale)**

"The number one enemy of empowerment is the fear of losing what we have." **(John Maxwell)**

"Leadership is getting someone to do what they don't want to do, to achieve what they want to achieve. " **(Tom Landry)**

"A true leader has no ego, understands consistency, and is always willing to serve others." **(Tony Gaskins)**

"Leaders not only see the big picture before others do, they also see more of it." **(John Maxwell)**

"Real leaders are ordinary people with extraordinary determination." **(Unknown)**

"A leader is one who sees more than others see who sees farther than others see, and who sees before others do." **(Leroy Eims)**

"A leader is like a shepherd. He stays behind the flock, letting the most nimble go out ahead, whereupon the others follow, not realizing that all along they are being directed from behind." **(Nelson Rolihlahla Mandela"Madiba)**

In the course of my career and personal life, I have taken up different responsibilities and served in various leadership positions such as:

1. Deputy Class Labour Prefect: Christ the Kings College Onitsha

2. Class Labour Prefect: Christ the kings College Onitsha

3. Okagbue House Captain: Christ the kings College Onitsha.

4. Store Keeper: Christ the Kings College Onitsha

5. Vice Chairperson: Apapa Development Association (ADAS) Lagos.

6. Chairperson: Apapa Development Association (ADAS) Lagos

7. Mr. Polytechnic: Federal Polytechnic Oko Anambra State, Nigeria.

8. Mr. Ultimate: Federal Polytechnic Oko Anambra State

9. Treasurer Excellencio Exclusive: Federal Polytechnic Oko Anambra State, Nigeria.

10. Director of Social: Business Administration and Management, Federal Polytechnic Oko Anambra State

11. Chairman: Neo Black Movement of Africa (KKT)

12. Coordinator: Neo Black Movement of Africa Youth service Abudu Edo State.

13. Coordinator: Neo Black Movement of Africa Germinston Forum

14. Public Relation Officer: Neo Black Movement of Africa South Africa Zone.

15. Chairperson: Westrand Brothers Association Gauteng South Africa.

16. Zonal Head: Neo Black Movement of Africa, South Africa Zone.

17. Chairperson: Nigerian Union, Roodepoort Ward

18. Financial Secretary: Abagana Welfare union South African branch

19. Public Relations Officer: Anambra State Association South Africa Chapter (ASA SA)

20. Life Member: Council of Elders Neo Black Movement of Africa, South Africa Zone

In the light of the above, I have also given myself a target to achieve goals and aspirations that some people thought were unattainable. I have laid down a standard that would be used as a reference point and, most importantly, something that would move my followers forward and give them other dimensions of thinking. I want to be able to stand before God, my creator, at any day and boast that I made use of the talent, resources, vigour, and energy that He gave me at the point of my entry into this world to empower people in my little way.

"Do not follow where the path may lead. Go instead where there is no path and leave a trail." **(George Bernard Shaw)**

"Innovation distinguishes between a leader and a follower." **(Steve Jobs)**

"Leadership is more than a title. It is an obligation to set the example for you to lead**." (Hasheem Francis, CEO Built to Prosper)**

"A true leader is one who puts the interest of his subjects before his no matter the consequence." **(Raphael Ikechukwu Ogbuagu)**

In all associations, I have been privileged to lead one such as Westrand Brothers Association, Neo Black Movement of Africa World Wide South African Zone. I have achieved goals only a few associations of the same manner have managed to achieve. I have always had faith in the possibility of all things by the grace and direction of God. I intend to continue: to promote the good image of Nigeria so that Nigeria will be heard and admired for good reasons, not for bad ones as it has often triggered a negative connotation in the world; and to help erase the impression that everything which comes out of our great nation is corrupt and evil; to assist the poverty-stricken and underprivileged people of this world, the orphans, HIV/AIDS victims, the oppressed, the needy, the lonely; to facilitate and promote quality education by providing books and other educational materials; to promote a crime free society and contribute to the safety and security of our society by constantly liaising with the law enforcement agencies, reporting suspicious characters and their actions, in order to make our society a better place for all. I want to continue to contribute to churches which over the years have continued to serve as a centre for spiritual revival.

"A leader owes it as a solemn duty to protect and provide for the needy and the vulnerable in our society." **(Dr. Oby Ezekwesili)**

"Any leader without compassion and empathy will hardly do well as a leader as those are special attributes of good leadership." **(Raphael Ikechukwu Ogbuagu)**

"Good leaders must first become good servants." **(Robert Greenleaf)**

"Let me pass, I have to follow them, I am their leader." **(Alexandre LeDru-Rollin)**

"The challenge of leadership is to be strong, but not rude; be kind, but not weak; be bold, but not bully; be thoughtful, but not lazy; be humble, but not timid; be proud, but not arrogant; have humour, but without folly." **(Jim Rohn)**

The knowledge and ideas I have shared in this book will help to motivate, guide, and inspire readers and people from all works of life. Finally, that this book will help to resurrect lives that were dead; give hope to the hopeless and help others to acquire wider knowledge and be successful in life.

"The greatest danger for most of us is not that our aim is high and we miss it, but that it is too low and we reach it." **(Michael Angelo)**

"The greatest pleasure in life is doing what people say you cannot do." **(Walter Bagehot)**

"The biggest enemy of great is good. While good people follow rules, great people rewrite the rules." **(Shilpa Prasad)**

I want to make history, rewrite events, and create the prospect and possibility of a better environment and a worthy name for my country and myself. I want to be a reference of worthy virtues. I want to be able to nurture this small vision that God has given me and turn it into a bigger dream that I will stand someday and be able to say that despite all odds and setbacks I made it, that we made it. To be a person of influence means that one is able either to touch other people's lives directly or indirectly to bring about positive change in their lives. John Maxwell says that if you desire to be successful or to make a positive impact on your world, you need to become a person of influence; I have been a person of influence with my vision, ethics, and zeal in any association I found myself.

"Men make history and not the other way around. In periods where there is no leadership, society stands still. Progress occurs when courageous, skillful leaders seize the opportunity to change things for the better." **(Harry S. Truman)**

"We are not makers of history. We are made by history." **(Dr. Martin Luther King Jr)**

"The respect that leadership must have requires that one's ethics be without question. A leader not only stays above the line between rights and wrong, he stays well clear of the gray areas." **(G. Alan Bernard)**

"Love and respect do not automatically accompany a position of leadership. They must be earned." **(Jason Chiwuzie Osuafor)**

"You can't lead the people if you don't love the people. You can't save the people if you don't serve the people." **(Cornel West)**

"From this day on, when I look back on the past, I will smile and say to myself, I never thought I could do it but I did. I overcome all the people who tried to bring me down." **(Broken Angel)**

"Honesty is the best policy when there is money in it." **(Mark Twain)**

"You have got to think about big things while you are doing small things, so that all the small things go in the right direction." **(Alvin Toffler)**

"To give real service you must add something which cannot be bought or measured with money & that is sincerity and integrity." **(Douglas Adam)**

"You will meet rejection in your path and you must not let it deceive you into believing it is THE path. Part ways and move on." **(Dodinsky)**

"Everyone has greatness within them. But it is buried deep within their souls and those who fight to obtain their greatness will use it to conquer and succeed." **(Hasheem Francis, CEO Built to Prosper)**

"I shall argue that strong men conversely know when to compromise and that all principles can be compromised to serve a greater purpose." **(Andrew Carnegie)**

"Leadership means discomfort. If you're going to be an effective leader, you must live outside your comfort zone." **(Dr. Oby Ezekwesili)**

"Move out of your comfort zone. You can grow if you are willing to feel awkward and uncomfortable when you try something new." **(Brain Tracy)**

"A good goal is like a strenuous exercise, it makes you stretch." **(Mary Kay Ash)**

Finally, I want people to know that in carrying out the assignment given to me by God, I am human and not a perfect being. In so doing, I am bound to make lots of mistakes, stumble and fall lots of times, have cold feet here and there, judge situations incorrectly; step on people's toes unintentionally; feel bigheaded once in a while and have my weakness. But, most importantly, I will have an open ear towards being advised, corrected; be in dialogues, deliberations, accept criticisms and to be properly guided by friends, associates, colleagues and mentors. In life the moment you accept your flaws no one can use it against you. I am prepared to learn and exchange ideas with people in order to make my calling as a leader a worthwhile and fulfilling experience to God and my followers. This is a task I have no doubt in my mind I will accomplish.

When you pray every morning, ask God to show you your assignment and calling and to lead you to the people who will help you to accomplish this calling as you cannot do it alone. Just as Pastors, Prophets, Evangelist, Apostles, Song ministers etc, are called to use their calling to liberate and free the captives and give hope to the hopeless, so are the doctors, engineers, nurses, leaders and other professions in alignment with the will of God upon our lives. When you connect to your purpose, you tap into the power of the divine. As a result of your walk in His plan for your life, nature will respect and honour you, all God's creation will hearken to your voice and the earth will obey your words.

"A good intention clothes itself with sudden power." **(Ralph Waldo Emerson)**

"At the end of our lives we will all ask, "Did I live? Did I Love? Did I matter?" **(Brendon Burchard)**

"Don't aspire to make a living, aspire to make a difference." **(Denzel Washington)**

Your purpose arrives dressed in strange clothes, it is an old friend dressed in shabby clothes. Drape it in silk and it will shine. The right path to follow is the hidden trail covered with brambles switch your focus to find the entry point, gain insight into your purpose, and learn how to follow your destiny.

Turn your passion into a profitable business. You were born to fulfill a great purpose, it begins today. There is no direct route, no high way to your destiny. Do not worry about your destination while you are travelling, your destiny will find you. Living your purpose fully is a choice that requires courage. The alternatives are bitterness, boredom, and emotional death. You do not achieve a purpose you live it: day-by-day, minutes by minutes, activity by activity. Focus your full attention on your dream, when you follow your calling with faith, and action, life conspires to smooth your way. You cannot see your world through another's eyes. You cannot hear your message through another person's voices. You cannot discover your destiny in someone else's space, your destiny and calling in life is only what you alone can discover for yourself with little assistance from your mentors. We are born to be creative, to do, to risk, to shine our own light.

During our life journey, we choose which lands we wish to visit; Excitement or boredom? Courage or helplessness? Adventure or excuses. Excuses drags you down. Courage lifts you up. Waiting is a slow death. Action changes the world. You owe it to yourself and others to become what makes you special and the uniqueness that God planted in you on your creation. What matters is not what you do for others but what you do for yourself the greatest sense of all is an insight into you calling from God in accordance with the reason for your creation on earth. If you are still searching for your path in life, know that is okay to feel a little frustration.

This is a marathon, not a sprint, your yearning for more meaning is a sign that you are growing, moving beyond limitations, and developing your talents. It is healthy to look at where you are from time to time and consider whether your actions and priorities are serving your highest purpose. When you are committed to bringing forth what God has placed in you, you will have to push against all the odds. God is willing to help us but not until we push. So do not fail to give birth to what God has put in you, it is time for you to bring it forth. Take control of your own destiny. Understand yourself in order to better understand others. Visualize it. Want it more than anything does. Accelerate your efforts. You are unique of all God's creations, nothing can replace YOU. Zero in on your target and go for it! On your journey to destiny; plans may change but purpose remains constant. Always have in mind that you are not an experiment but a creature of purpose.

"I am here for a purpose and that purpose is to grow into a mountain, not to shrink to a grain of sand. Henceforth I will apply ALL my efforts to become the highest mountain of all and I will strain my potential until it cries for mercy." **(OG Mandino)**

"God didn't make a mistake when He made you. You need to see yourself as God sees you." **(Joel Osteen)**

"Power is not really good or bad; it is neutral. Power itself is not negative or positive, although our feelings about it may be. Power is the potential to influence others for good or evil, to be a blessing or a scourge. Like nuclear energy, it can provide the electricity to light a city, or it can fuel the bomb that destroys it." **(Blaine Lee)**

"I always try to turn my personal struggles into something helpful for others." **(Henri Nouwen)**

"To be a leader, you have to make people want to follow you, and nobody wants to follow someone who doesn't know where he is going." **(Joe Namath)**

"Leaders are dealers in hope." **(Napoleon Hill)**

"Leadership is action, not position." **(Donald H. McGannon)**

"The most awful thing about power is not that it corrupts absolutely but that it makes people so utterly boring, so predictable." **(Professor Chinua Achebe)**

"You gain strength, courage, and confidence by every experience in which you really stop to look fear in the face. You must do the things you think you cannot do." **(Eleanor Roosevelt)**

"There is a difference between interest and commitment. When you are interested in something you do it only when it's convenient. When you are committed to something, you accept no excuses only results." **(Ken Blanchard)**

"I am of the opinion that my life belongs to the whole community and as I live, it is my privilege to do whatever I can with it." **(George Bernard Shaw)**

"A leader is one who climbs the tallest tree, surveys the entire situation, and yell, wrong jungle." **(Stephen Covey)**

"That was one thing that worried me to be raised to the position of a semi god because then you are no longer a human being. I wanted to be known as Mandela, a man with weaknesses, some of which are fundamental, and a man who is committed but nevertheless sometimes, fails to live up to expectation." **(Nelson Rolihlahla Mandela"Madiba)**

Leaders, whether in the family, in business, in government, or in education, must not allow themselves to make mistakes intentions for accomplishment. Managers help people to see themselves as they are. Leaders help people to see themselves better than they are. Leaders must not be naive. I used to say, Liars shouldn't lie," What a sad waste of words that is! I found out liars are supposed to lie. That is why we call them liars- they lie what else would you expect them to do? We must learn to help those who deserve it, not just those who need it. Life responds to deserve not need.

My mentor said," Let's go do it," not go do it, How powerful when someone says," Let's"! Leaders must understand that some people will inevitably sell-out to the evil side. Don't waste your time wondering why; spend your time discovering who. When dealing with people I generally take obvious approach when someone says, "This always happens to me and that always happens to me. Why do these things always happen to me? I simply say," Beats me". I don't know. All I know is that those kinds of things seem to happen to people like you." We could all use a little coaching. When you're playing the game, it's hard to think of everybody. A good objective of leadership is to help those who are doing poorly to do well and to help those who are doing well to do even better. "As a leader you should always start where people are before you try to take them to where you want them to go." **(Jim Rohn)**

In conclusion, as a leader you have to build a dream team of supporters who have your best interest at heart, you must first prove yourself trustworthy as a leader to them by standing for them. Your subordinates will treat you the way you treat them. If you invest in their success, support them, encourage them, and give them your honest feedback, you can expect them to do the same for you. If they don't you should move on and find other people willing to be on your team as that will make your task as a leader easier and more fulfilling. One of the biggest mistakes you can make is to try and win your followers only by telling them about yourself: your fears, frustrations, and pleasure. The truth is that you win followers and allies by learning about them and finding shared interest to build bonds that will provide mutual benefits. Building a relationship in leadership is like building a saving account; you can't expect to take anything out of it if you haven't put something into it.

We need Supportive relationship in all spheres of our lives, leadership is not an exception. We all must engage with kindred spirit. To do effectively, we must build trust as a leader and prove ourselves trustworthy. Leaders must understand that most people instinctively act out of self interest ,but if you show them that you are interested in them and can invest in their success, mostly they will do the same for you in seeing that your agendas as a leaders succeeds at all cost. There is this saying walk the talk, we have all heard of those who say talk the talk but don't walk the walk. You may be a great leader, good listener, highly empathetic, engaging, and a charming tactful leader, but if you don't step up and reach out to your followers when situation requires it, then all other skills are meaningless. Just saying "I feel for you" doesn't cover it.

Your action speaks louder than words. In work relationship this means not doing your job and striving to be successful but helping others to do their jobs and supporting them in their effort to succeed. What Makes a Bad Leader? One of the characteristics of a bad leader includes failure to communicate, either at all or effectively with subordinates. Bad leaders also do not like to listen to the input of others .What makes a Good Leader? A good leader knows how to communicate what their desires are and is good at rallying people and supporters together to succeed at a common goal. They possess good character and set .What makes An Effective Leader? An effective leader is a leader that works with their people, one who is able to reach his employees, or followers on a base level that creates a positive relationship.

What Makes a Great Leader? A great leader is someone who is able to make decisions quickly and efficiently, appoint tasks to others and is generally well respected by peers. Leadership is a service and so being appointed to a leadership position is like being given an opportunity to serve. A good leader should be able to work with all kinds of people - one cannot say they are a good leader simply because they work only with people who agree with them. The real test of our leadership comes when we have to work with those we do not like or those who do not always agree with us. A leader should focus on those they are leading rather than on the opposition. If we focus on improving our service to those whom we lead then the fact that there is an opposition will become irrelevant.

Leaders are not, as we are often led to think, people who go along with huge crowds following them. Leaders are people who go their own way without caring, or even looking to see, whether anyone is following them. "Leadership qualities" are not the qualities that enable people to attract followers, but those that enable them to do without them. They include, at the very least, courage, endurance, patience, humor, flexibility, resourcefulness, stubbornness, a keen sense of reality, and the ability to keep a cool and clear head, even when things are going badly. True leaders, in short, do not make people into followers, but into other leaders.

"A good objective of leadership is to help those who are doing poorly to do well and to help those who are doing well to do even better." **(Jim Rohn)**

"As a leader, you must be willing to accept the truth without attacking the messenger." **(Matthew Okafor)**

"A true leader has the confidence to stand alone, the courage to make tough decisions, and the compassion to listen to the needs of others. He does not set out to be a leader, but becomes one by the equality of his actions and the integrity of his intent." **(Douglas MacArthur)**

"The shepherd leader casts a shadow of protection over his flock." **(Glen A. McQuirk)**

"The stronger the relationship and connection between individuals, the more likely the followers will want to help the leader. " **(Unknown)**

"You must understand where the people stand to be able to represent or serve the people." **(Contributed by Matthew Okafor)**

"The proof of leadership is found in followers. The very essence of all power to influence lies in getting the other person to participate." **(Harry A. Overstreet)**

"Leadership and learning are indispensable to each other." **(John F. Kennedy)**

"The function of leadership is to produce more leaders, not more followers." **(Ralph Nader)**

"Leaders make decisions that create the future they desire." **(Mike Murdock)**

"A good Leader tackles the problem and not the person….in whom the problem lies with…no time to be petty!!" **(Matthew Okafor)**

"It may sound corny, but it's really true: People don't care how much you know until they know how much you care." **(Unknown)**

"Leaders don't create followers, they create more leaders." **(Tom Peters)**

"When the right leader and the right timing come together, incredible things happen." **(Unknown)**

"Only leaders of special calibre and integrity are able to see the basic problems that affect us all." **(Nelson Rolihlahla Mandela'Madiba)**

"You can't move people to action unless you first move them with emotions. The heart comes before the head." **(Unknown)**

"To build trust, a leader must exhibit competence, connection, and character." **(Unknown)**

"Character makes trust possible and trust makes leadership possible that is the law of solid ground." **(Unknown)**

Essential qualities of a leader

1. **Character:** Be Authentic.

2. **Charisma:** Show interest in others.

3. **Commitment:** Be consistent and persistent.

4. **Communication:** Be an effective communicator.

5. **Competence:** Lead by example.

6. **Courage:** Take risk and responsibility for the results

7. **Discernment:** Put an end to unsolved mysteries.

8. **Focus:** Don't get distracted by the critics.
9. **Generosity:** Spread the wealth. Share your wisdom.

10. **Initiative:** Step outside the box. Be creative

11. **Listening:** Learn to listen with your heart.

12. **Passion:** Fuel your purpose with passion.

13. **Positive Attitude:** If you believe you can. YOU CAN!

14. **Problem Solving:** Be know as solution oriented.

15. **Relationships:** Build them and cherish them.

16. **Responsibility:** Take ownership of the outcome.

17. **Security:** Be secure in the vision and mission.

18. **Self-Discipline:** You are the first person to lead.

19. **Servant hood:** Serve with an open hand.

20. **A Teachable Disposition:** Keep Growing.

21. **Vision:** You must see it, before others can see it.

Theories of leadership:

There are scores of leadership theories, models, and studies available for you to examine, if you choose developed primarily in the 20th century by scholars, leadership ideas have existed at least A.D 100. Thanks to these great men and women. In addition to the theories, there are countless leadership survey, tests, and aptitude indicators that are available to determine a leader's style and interest. What can you do when faced with complexity of leadership information? Most leaders do not study the many theories of leadership in detail. Some general knowledge is helpful, however, to know what the relevant major issues are so that you can use that knowledge in your specific situation. These issues will be explained.

There are five leadership Orientation

We will briefly examine five leadership orientations since every leader has a distinct style made up of combination of these orientation, it is impossible to account accurately predict your style without a thoroughly analysis. As with most leaders, you will tend to use different styles when faced with different situations. Each orientation presents two extreme between which leaders have determine the right balance for themselves based upon their personality and specific leadership challenges. For example , there are effective leaders who have high orientation score in relationship and task, others score high in relationship and low in task; by understanding these five leadership orientations, you will be better able to understand the framework within which most leaders operate.

1.   Democratic or autocratic

2.   Participation or direction

3.   Relationship or task

4.   Consideration or initiation

5.   Action or inaction.

Democracy or autocracy: The two orientations are the first classification because the encompass attributes of the other four orientations. It makes sense that leaders tend to lean naturally toward one or the other because followers will so wither one or two things.

They will do what they are asked to do. Thus requiring the supervision of a teaching and facilitating type of democratic leader, or they will do what they are made to do, which requires a more punishing and coercing autocrat. There is no conclusive proof as to what type of orientation is more effective at getting bottom-line results. One may be more effective in different organization or situation than the other may. A person's style of leadership, however does affect employee job satisfaction, although the effects vary among employees.

A higher degree of satisfaction in an organization will encourage loyalty, teamwork, and sharing of the leader's goal; each of these can lead to higher level of personal and organization productivity.

Democratic leaders focus on their followers because they feel the welfare of their team is great importance. They tend to be easily approachable, relationship-oriented, and considerate of others' feeling. These leaders prefer to lead their teammates by collaboration and empowerment. They are convinced that tasks will be better accomplished if they consider their subordinates' needs. These teammates tend to have high job satisfaction.

Autocratic primarily are concerned with tasked for which they are responsible. They believe the key is to focus less on subordinates and their needs and more on the work related issues. In doing so, they use their position to prescribe solutions and direct others to comply. This type of leader usually has more subordinates with low level of job satisfaction than des the democratic leader.

Participation or Direction Orientation: Leaders also can be analyzed in terms of how much contribution the leader obtains from subordinates before solving a problem or making a decision. As previously discussed, most leaders are situational and they use both styles on different occasion. A popular leadership trend since the 1980s has been to encourage employee participation in problem solving and decision-making. By obtaining and considering the suggestions of subordinates, a leader has access to more data, experience, and opinions. Participation can occur when the leader either delegates total responsibility for a task or allows subordinates to participate in problem-solving decision-making process.

A more restrictive form of participation is used when a leader discusses the task with subordinates but ultimately makes the decision as to what will be done. By using a participative style of leadership a leader does not relinquish the responsibility to get the job done, but gives subordinates the authority to help arrive at the right decision to get the job done correctly. Participation is particularly effective in less structured or rapidly changing work environments.

Leaders who have a **direction orientation** decide what needs to be done and communicate this to subordinates. They may or may not explain why they chose a course of action and they may use persuasion techniques to bolster their directive. These leaders autocratically assume that, since they know the right answer, seeking input from subordinates is unnecessary.

They may rationalize the use of a directive style by citing organizational problems, such as low employee educational level and competence, even though this may not be applicable. The degree to which a leader may be directive depends upon a number of factors. For example, leaders tend to be more directives when there is high uncertainty on the situation, little time available, short-term increase in productivity is needed, or they exercise a high degree of positional or organizational power. Directive leadership tends to be used more than participative leadership in slow-changing situation or where employee input is needed.

Relationship or task Orientation: The best leaders concern themselves both with people relationship and the tasks for which they are responsible, because tasks usually are accomplished more effectively when human factors are considered. The degree of integration of task and relationship varies considerably with each leader; the exact mix partly depends upon task urgently, subordinate 'work performance and the ability, organizational climate, and the leader's natural inclination toward one orientation or the other.

Leaders who set **relationship** as a priority recognize the synergistic effects of attending to human side of work. This does not mean they are less concerned with accomplishing tasks but that they know the best way to achieve high quality success is to make sure they consider subordinates' and team members needs. They do this by maintaining warm, close, and friendly relations with their followers and co-workers and by opening trusting and supporting them.

A complete **task orientation** means that a leader has foremost in mind the job that must be done. Without seeking inputs from subordinates, the leader structure the work, define the goals allocate resources, and focus on achieving production quotas or delivery of services. People are concern but only because they are necessary to get the work done. This leader uses an inflexible, no-nonsense approach with subordinates.

Consideration or Initiation Orientation: Considerate leaders do what any considerate person would do, but in context of leader. Since they concern themselves with subordinates' interest and well-being, they seek suggestion from subordinates and consider what effects these decisions will have on the team. By openly praising and privately correcting subordinates, they a working environment in which people trust, respect, and follow them.

Initiation refers to a leaders' ability to start activities and organize work. Strong initiators prefer not to let the group completely structure its work or make all of the on-the-job decisions. They prefer not only to determine what must be done but also who does it and how it is to be done. Consequently, they focus on task: most of their daily initiatives occur simply to facilitate achievement of work-related goals. Since there can be overlap in these two orientations, a leader could be both highly considerate and initiative and still be effective.

Action or Inaction Orientation: Action-oriented leader in themselves with fulfilling work responsibilities. They take charge of these responsibilities by using the leadership and management principles discussed in this angel as outlined by Randall Ponder and by realizing that subordinates perform better when their leaders are aware of work-related issues, interested in seeing goals achieved, and actively monitoring performance. Active leaders establish and communicate their subordinates' authority, responsibilities, and work parameters.

Having this knowledge of what is expected of them and the encouragement to perform well, employee will gain the autonomy that most of them crave. There are distinctions between action and in-action. By asking a subordinate to complete a task, for example, the leader is actively delegating an assignment, not avoiding taking action.

Leaders who are **in-active** are much less engaged in their work than active leaders. On a spectrum of reasons for such inactivity, you will find leaders who consciously shirk their responsibilities and those who do not realize that they are less active than they need to be. Inactive leaders tend to react to a daily challenge after someone tells them about it, whereas the active leader proactively seeks out impending obstacles. In addition to the risk that inactive leaders pose to their organization's ability to achieve goals, the leaders themselves risk being perceived irrelevant or ineffective by their subordinates.

Personality, Psychology, and Leadership

The previous discussion of leadership orientation shows you there is so much room for leaders who have various combinations of leadership styles. Most leaders take a situational approach and use different style under different conditions, depending upon the urgency and nature of the task, experience and expectation of subordinates, and the degree of trust and rapport in the work relationship. A central concept in leadership study is that to better understand the behaviours of leaders and subordinates, it is useful to understand the psychological nature of people involved. One popular and extensively used resource is the Myers-Briggs type indicator. After individual respond to questions based upon how they usually would feel or act in different situations, this survey classifies them into 16 types, based on four continual: extraversion-introversion, sensing-intuition, thinking feeling, and judging-perceiving. These types will provide insight into their work preference and decision-making patterns. A leader can use this as a tool to gain insight into his or her subordinates or team members; it can be a useful way to increase understanding.

Although these resources will give you a quick profile of your subordinates, it is important to be careful when using them and never completely rely on them. They should be used only in conjunction with skill development tools and other resources. There are several reasons for this. Firstly, though many companies use the tests, the experts disagree considerably as to their reliability. Unfortunately, there is no magic no magic formula for what test is best. It is up to you to examine those that are available and make the best choice for you and your organization. Second, these resources are sometimes misunderstood. People often make major style changes based upon the result of one survey, without realizing the extent of which those results were due to bad testing conditions or the person's mood at the time of the survey. Third, some people are skeptical of tests or resentful of been arbitrarily typecast. You can avoid this reaction if you take time to explain the process and rest to them.

"Leaders are rewarded or condemned publicly, for what they practice privately." **(Hasheem Francis, CEO Built to Prosper)**

The 10 major causes of failure in leadership

We come now to the major faults of leaders who fail, because it is just as essential to know what not to do as it is to know what to do.

1. **Inability to organize details**: Efficient leadership calls for ability to organize and to master details. No genuine leader is ever "too busy" to do anything which may be required of him in his capacity as leader. When a man, whether he is a leader or follower, admits that he is "too busy" to change his plan, or to give attention to any emergency, he admits his inefficiency. The successful leader must the master of all detail connected with his position. That means, of course, that he must acquire the habit of relegating details to capable lieutenants.

2.   **Unwillingness to render humble service**: Truly great leaders are willing, when occasion demands; to perform any sort of labour which they would ask another to perform. "The greatest among ye shall be the servant of all" is a truth which all able leaders observe and respect.

3.   **Expectation of pay for what they "know" instead of what they do with that which they know.** That world does not pay men for that which they "know" it pays them for what they do, or induce others to do.

4.   **Fear of competition from followers;** The leader who fears that one of his followers may take his position is practically sure to realize that fear sooner or later. The able leader trains understudies to whom he may delegate, at will, any of the details of his position. Only in the way may a leader multiply himself and prepare himself to be at many places, and give attention to many things at one time. It is an eternal truth that men receive more pay for their abilities to get others to perform, than they could possibly earn by their own efforts. An efficient leader may, through his knowledge of his job and magnetism of his personality, greatly increase the efficiency of others, and induce them render more service and better service then they could render without this aid.

5.   **Lack of Imagination:** without imagination, the leader is incapable of meeting emergencies, and of creating plans by which to guide his follower's efficiently.

6.   **Selfishness:** The leaders who claim all the honour for the work of his followers, is sure to be met by resentment. The really great leader claims none of the honours. He is contented to see honours, when there are any, go to his followers. Because he knows that men will work harder for commendation and recognition than they will for money alone.

7. **Intemperance:** Followers do not respect an intemperate leader. More so, intemperance in any of its various forms destroys the endurance and vitality of all who indulge in it.

8. **Disloyalty**: Perhaps this should have come at the head of the list. The leader who is not loyal to his trust, and to his associates, those above him, and those below him, cannot long maintain his leadership. Disloyalty marks one of being less than the dust of the earth, and brings down on one's head the contempt he deserves. Lack of loyalty is one of the major causes of failure in every walk of life.

9. **Emphasis of the "Authority" of leadership**: The efficient leader leads by encouraging and not by trying to install fear in the heart of his followers. The leader who tries to impress his followers with his "authority" comes within the category of leadership through force. If a leader is a real leader, he will have no need to advertise that fact except by his conduct-his sympathy, understanding, fairness, and a demonstration that he knows his job.

10. **Emphasis of Title**: The competent leader requires no "title" to give him the respect of his followers. The man who makes too much over his title generally has little else emphasize. The doors of the office of the real leader are open to all who which to enter, and his working quarters are free from formality or ostentation.

These are among the more common of the causes of failure in leadership. Any one of these faults is sufficient to induce failure. Study the list carefully if you aspire to leadership, and make sure that you are free of these faults

"To supervise people, you must either surpass them in their accomplishments or despise them." **(Benjamin Disraeli)**

"To succeed in business, you must not have the "do-it-all-yourself" mentality. Effective leaders are not afraid to hand the job to those who are more suited for the task at hand." **(Hasheem Francis, CEO Built to Prosper)**

"True power is not measured by how many people you control but how well you practice "self control." **(Matthew Okafor)**

Kegan's scientific research has shown leaders depending of their level of consciousness can be:

1. Self-sovereign
2. Socialized
3. Self-authored
4. Self-transforming

Imagine 4 leaders and a mountain

1. **The self-sovereign leader** is at the base of the mountain, he can't see the beautiful landscape. This leader looks only for his umbilical and just sees others as facilitators or obstacles to the realization of his own desires. Thus, for him corporate sustainability is just obeying the law (when obeying), just for the fear of being caught.

2. **A little bit higher up the mountain is the socialized leader,** he can see a small part of the landscape and he is very busy waving for the friends. He likes to show others that he applies corporate sustainability, in small practices and philanthropy to show off in the media.

3. **At the middle of the mountain we find the self-authored leader** that can see more landscape than the socialized leader. He can see more than his own group. Thus, for him corporate sustainability is being focused on stakeholders' management and triple bottom line.

4. At the top of the mountain, the leader who climbed the most, with the most developed mindset, **is the self-transforming**

leader. He can see the entire landscape, is a visionary, ahead of time. His corporate Sustainability is about creating value for stakeholders and the entire society. Not very surprising, there are not many people in this last category.

"Like the gardener, a leader must take responsibility for what he cultivates; he must mind his work, try to repel enemies, preserve what can be preserved, and eliminate what cannot succeed." **(Nelson Rolihlahla Mandela"Madiba)**

"There are times when a leader must move out ahead of the flock, go off in a new direction, confident that he is leading his people the right way." **(Nelson Rolihlahla Mandela"Madiba)**

CHAPTER 2
EMPOWERING AND LIBERATING YOU
VOLUME ONE

This Chapter will empower and liberate your wellbeing; it contains strong and powerful words of inspiration, motivation and encouragement. Within these pages you will find encouraging words from some of the world's greatest teachers, philosophers, and ordinary people. Please read in order to attain the knowledge, wisdom, and understanding, and in turn get to grow inwardly.

"Motivation is the fuel, necessary to keep the human engine running." **(Zig Zigler)**

12 Thoughts that will help you grow strongly if applied.

· Never interrupt when you are being flattered.

· Pray; there is immeasurable power in it.

· Don't trust someone who doesn't close their eyes when you kiss them.

· Once a year, go somewhere you have never been before.

· If you make a lot of money, put it to use by helping others while you are   still alive; that is wealth's greatest satisfaction.

· Remember that not getting what you want is sometimes a stroke of luck.

· Learn the rules; then break some.

· Remember that the best relationship is where love for each other is greater than your need for each other.

· Judge success by what you had to give up, in order to get it.

· Remember that your character is your destiny.

· Approach love and cooking with reckless abandon.

· Share your knowledge; it is a way to immortality.

This is Sampson's way of reminding you that life is short and precious; enjoy it while it last. With your life, exercise your kindness and turn your frustration into opportunity (Author Unknown)

Inspirational Quotes from Authors, writers and philosophers from the African Continent.

"The acquisition of knowledge is a personal responsibility which no one can do on your behalf; just as no one can be saved on your behalf and no one can prosper or succeed for you. Learning is a non-transferable responsibility." **(Bishop David Oyedepo)**

"To me, being an intellectual doesn't mean knowing about intellectual issues; it means taking pleasure in them." **(Professor Chinua Achebe)**

"Nigeria confuses kids by telling them to be patriotic irrespective of ethnicity only to use state of origin as admission criteria in schools." **(Ben Murray Bruce)**

"The greatest threat to freedom is the absence of criticism" **(Professor Wole Soyinka)**

"The beauty of wealth or its greatest satisfaction is how many people you have been able to help." **(Raphael Ikechukwu Ogbuagu)**

"The poor prey on one another because their lives offer no hope and communicate the tragic message to these human beings; that they have no possibility to attaining a decent standard of living." **(Thabo Mbeki)**

"The knowledge of truth is the power behind the enthronement of the saints, as nothing can stop the truth." **(Bishop David Oyedepo)**

"Your branding must be able to deliver something unique; it is who you are when people are not watching." **(Dr. Richie Achukwu)**

"As soon as you cannot keep anything from a woman/man; it means that you love that person." **(Raphael Ikechukwu Ogbuagu)**

"Let's start engaging in the girl child development now, in terms of capacity building, of which education takes a central Theme!" **(Dr. Carl Oshodi-Isibor)**

"There is a thinking stuff from which all things are made, and which, in its original state, permeates, penetrates, and fills the interspaces of the universe. A thought in this substance produces the thing that is imaged by the thought." **(Jason Chiwuzie Osuafor)**

"If the United States of America or Britain is having elections, they don't ask for observers from Africa or from Asia, but when we have an election they want observers." **(Nelson Rolihlahla Mandela"Madiba)**

"A man without integrity is equally a tragedy waiting to happen." **(Chima Onyeagba Umealo)**

"Its mental slavery to allow foreign media dictates what we think about Nigeria & her institutions. They can't love Nigeria more than Nigerians." **(Ben Murray Bruce)**

"If God did not will it, we will not be Nigerians." **(President Goodluck Jonathan)**

"Nothing in life is gained without sacrifice." **(Raphael Ikechukwu Ogbuagu)**

"Will not let the circumstances I see make me forget that I'm equipped with all I need to succeed." **(Letwin Dadirai Mandishona)**

"When you pray always, you create a celestial database for supernatural activity." **(Rev Omotoso)**

"How you speak about others is a reflection of who you are as a person because "If you damage the character of another, you damage your own." **(Yoruba proverb)**

"Almost 100% of Nigeria's elite became what they are through free education, yet after climbing up we removed the ladder that got us there!" **(Ben Murray Bruce)**

"We understood how the future was shaping and nobody ever saw us despair." **(Emperor Haile Salassie)**

"Any lady who goes about calling guys stingly must be a first class beggar' And really should make a sign that says' please no amount is too small." **(Kollenz Sospctacular Chukwuma)**

"There are two set of people in this world. Men of will and those who enjoy what the men of will have done." **(Raphael Ikechukwu Ogbuagu)**

"Fools does not lead a community else, the community would be or become a compound full of fools." **(Collins Thomas Mgbo)**

"Being a Nigerian is a blessing and a great responsibility, the first responsibility is to use the ballot." **(President Goodluck Jonathan)**

"History will continue to vindicate the just." **(Dr. Nnamdi Azikiwe)**

"It's not what one says but what one does that defines the kind of person they are." **(Theodorah Malapane)**

"When you find people fighting, don't take sides because when their dispute is resolved you won't know what to do." **(Paul Light)**

"Only buses will stop here, not your time, so keep walking towards your goal." **(Bruno Ezeani)**

"You don't choose your family. They are God's gift to you, as you are to them." **(Arch Bishop Desmond Tutu)**

"I'm a lawyer. I go for due process; I go for fairness and equity - these values mean a lot to me." **(Mohamed ElBaradei)**

"Nigeria is a nation of resilient people. We will never yield to forces of darkness. Nigeria will never, ever disintegrate." **(President Goodluck Jonathan)**

"A Man's reputation is the opinion people have of him; his character is what he really is." **(Chukwuma Onyike)**

"In life you always find what you look for, the only thing that matters is what you choose to see." **(Bruno Ezeani)**

"The first to apologize is the bravest. The first to forgive is the strongest. The first to forget is the happiest." **(Dave Ugochukwu Chima)**

"General Obsanjo is beginning to see himself as a second god in Nigeria and believes he has the remedy to make Nigeria right this should call for concern from well meaningful Nigerians as this same person was in power for 8 years without anything to show for it." **(Raphael Ikechukwu Ogbuagu)**

"In the war between falsehood and truth, falsehood wins the first battle, but truth wins the war." **(Rev Elias Ndeda)**

"The greatest mistake you can make in life is to continually be afraid you will make one." **(Melvin Udo Richmond)**

"One of the best feelings in the world is knowing that our presence and absence both means something to someone!"He who does not understand your silence will probably not understand your words.One thorn of experience is worth life time of good advice and warning!" **(Lilian Ngozi)**

"There is nothing wrong with being poor; but there is everything wrong with remaining poor after you have discovered your riches in Christ." **(Pastor Chris Oyakhilome)**

"Well, the first thing is that truth and power for me forms an antithesis, an antagonism, which will hardly ever be resolved. I can define in fact; can simplify the history of human society, the evolution of human society, as a contest between power and freedom." **(Professor Wole Soyinka)**

"Some people are born great, some made themselves great. Messi was born great, Ronaldo made himself great." **(Nwike Amobi)**

"In our world today people now fear what witches and wizards will do to them than what God can do for them." **(Raphael Ikechukwu Ogbuagu)**

"I am an ordinary woman who chooses everyday to make extra-ordinary decisions...I am driven by a dream and nothing will stop me, I made that choice long ago." **(Phophi Rhinah Muguru)**

"The lie that some people are white and others are black will come to pass because we are human first, of these denominations of power of status." **(Dr. Don Mattera)**

"I am the conqueror of the British empire, the black Hitler of Africa." **(Idi Amin)**

"A wise man never knows all, only a fool knows everything." **(African Proverb)**

"Love is like a chewing gum, it tastes only in the beginning. But friendship is like a chocolate, it tastes till its ends." **(Contributed by Elizabeth Lizzy)**

"If you see wrong-doing or evil and say nothing against it, you become its victim." **(Namibia Proverb)**

"Fela was real force in my life, the way I believe, the way I live. He made me a very proud African." **(Yeni Kutii)**

"Arrogance of illiteracy has no end in sight." **(Dr. Godson Ezejiofor)**

"Racism should not be allowed to undermine and demoralise our God's given talent neither should we allow ridicules of the envious people to bring us down." **(Chief Jonas Ndubueze Udeji)**

"To be at rest while active and active while at rest is an exclusive preserve of those who live in the realm of spiritual freedom." **(Rev Chidozie Ejimadu)**

"In our today's world people now worship the messanger instead of the sender of the message. People now look for miracles instead of looking for the creator of the universe. People now believe in signs and wonders instead in believing in the word of God." **(Raphael Ikechukwu Ogbuagu)**

"Managing a country is like managing a company in many ways. It maybe involves more complicated issues, but it's the same skills." **(Mohamed ElBaradei)**

"The beauty of being close to your siblings is getting to know the beautiful people they bring into the family. Understanding love is a powerful thing. Hating love is a foolish & weak thing. Love your siblings, their spouses & their children. Those are the people who are the love that surrounds you on this earth." **(Khosi Buhle Khumalo)**

"The tongue is one of the most powerful forces on earth. Learn how to use it." **(Rev Elias Ndeda)**

"Race doesn't really exist for you because it has never been a barrier. Black folks don't have that choice." **(Chimamanda Ngozi Adichie)**

"I prefer to see the silver lining in the dark cloud rather than the dark cloud in the silver lining" **(President Goodluck Jonathan)**

"Some people dream of success whiles other wake up and work hard for it, make it your business to chase your dream." **(Phophi Rhinah Muguru)**

"When a man unbuttons your bra with one finger, do not sleep with him, basically he has had a lot of practice with other women's bras." **(Digidi Dunhill)**

"In order for you to shine, never let your struggle define you, let it refine you instead." **(Ntsako Mbhokota)**

"When suffering knocks at your door and you say there is no seat for him, he tells you not to worry because he has brought his own stool." **(Professor Chinua Achebe)**

"Painful loss holds the seed of transformation."**(Bruno Ezeani)**

"The money you steal will do nothing good for you, it will boast your pride but your spirit will be killed within." **(Raphael Ikechukwu Ogbuagu)**

"Sometimes you will look back at the girls you spent your money on instead of your mother and you realise witchcraft is real." **(President Robert Mugabe)**

"So, there is no alternative for me, I must make my stand, and if Allah wishes, I shall die by following His path, the path that has made our country rich with farmland, with food and health, and even allowed us to help our African and Arab brothers and sisters." **(Col Muammar Gaddafi)**

"As I have said, the first thing is to be honest with yourself. You can never have an impact on society if you have not changed yourself... Great peacemakers are all people of integrity, of honesty, but humility." **(Nelson Rolihlahla Mandela" Madiba)**

"Fix yourself before you try to fix someone else. Don't tell people what they're doing wrong, when you're doing nothing right!" **(Letwin Dadirai Mandishona)**

"People are constantly applying double standards. Take the United States, for example. Washington wants the whole world to admire the country for its democracy. Then the government sends out its army, in the name of this democracy, and leaves behind the kind of chaos we see in Iraq." **(President Jacob Zuma)**

"We cannot trample upon the humanity of others without devaluing our own." **(Professor Chinua Achebe)**

"I do not wish to die, but if it comes to that, to save this land, my people, all the thousands who are all my children, then so be it. Let this testament be my voice to the world, that I stood up to crusader attacks of NATO, stood up to cruelty, stoop up to betrayal, stood up to the West and its colonialist ambitions, and that I stood with my African brothers, my true Arab and Muslim brothers, as a beacon of light ." **(Col Muammar Gaddafi)**

"Distinguished ladies and gentlemen, leadership is about staying focused to achieve goals despite challenges. I have been faced with many challenges since coming to office as President. With your support and encouragement, we have stayed the course." **(President Goodluck Jonathan)**

"I stand for simple justice, equal opportunity and human right. The indispensable element in a democratic society and well worth fight for." **(Helen Suzman)**

"Sometime you've got to play the role of a fool, to fool the fools who think they are fooling you." **(Ndidi Agbodike)**

"The state must be the first to be organized and totally committed to serving the interests of the people." **(Samora Machel)**

"The damage done in one year can sometimes take ten or twenty years to repair." **(Professor Chinua Achebe)**

"Politicians are like prostitutes. Every good paying client is a sweetheart. When they're in power government works but when in opposition government become underachievers." **(Chima Onyeagba Umealo)**

"Most times your position does not guarantee you respect, you gain your respect from your personality, and how you mould and coordinate your activities." **(Raphael Ikechukwu Ogbuagu)**

"Money won't create success, the freedom to make it will." **(Nelson Rolihlahla Mandela"Madiba)**

"Rich people tell their story and they get paid for it. Every great person has a story to tell." **(Dr. Richie Achukwu)**

"I want us to understand that if we have fallen from the grace of God, We can rise up again. If God has kept you up until this moment, HE has a plan for you and me. Do not forget." **(Rev Omotoso)**

"When you know who you are, a title doesn't matter." **(Matthew Okafor)**

"Wisdom is your capital! Your mind is your asset." **(Pastor Chris Oyakhilome)**

"Give so much time to the improvement of yourself that you have no time to criticize others." **(Sibongile Mthembu)**

"If you don't like someone's story, write your own." **(Professor Chinua Achebe)**

"Without gratitude & appreciation for what you already have you will never know true fulfillment." **(Phophi Rhinah Muguru)**

"Life has taught me no matter how sincerely and diligently you go about your duty, you will be misunderstood by some as having a wrong motive. Some will criticize you out of jealousy; others will falsely accuse you and attempt to destroy your reputation, because of your strong testimony. But in all these, pay them back in love, good deed, and prayer." **(Hrm Eze Akuenwebe Emechebe)**

"God does not quit on what He has started in our lives. Once you are focused, with zeal and believe you can do it through Christ Jesus." **(Raphael Ikechukwu Ogbuagu)**

"Democracy is a collective action, energized by individual responsibility. Your mandate at this time will inspire in me the strength to complete the good work we have started together." **(President Goodluck Jonathan)**

"Don't trust a female that pull her panties and jeans down at the same time." **(Pamela Mbatha)**

"For you to be taken seriously you do not have to have a lot of money or be a tall big man, you have to love your country and your people. The power of change does not lie in what you have but what you believe in." **(Pacifique Sukisa Makasi)**

"When I try to go back to certain people or certain circumstances, I think back on what caused me to leave them in the first place." **(Letwin Dadirai Mandishona)**

"A capitalist Nigger is endowed with the highest level of intelligence. It is within his power to change the course of Black economy slavery to that of Black independence." **(Dr. Chika Onyeani)**

"The biggest mistake a man will make in life my mum told me is to marry a woman that is not supposed to be your wife." **(Pastor Idah Peterside)**

"Let us not retire, if you do you will expire." **(Pastor Ethel Onyanta)**

"To create a balance life, you need to put limits to everything. Work must remain exactly there, at work, in order to have a harmonious life at home." **(Dudu Debe)**

"If your father is a poor man it is your fate but if your father in-law is a poor man, it is your own stupidity." **(Gauteng Love)**

"I Believe That a Strong Relationship Is Not Based Only on Sex Life but That a Strong Relationship Builds a Strong Love Life That Leads to a Strong and Great Sex Life and Can Only Happen With Open Communication." **(Mell Khumalo)**

"It is the meaning of what my life has been since a youth – to try to fight for the dignity and the freedom of my own people." **(Graca Machel)**

"I think back to the old people I knew when I was growing up, and they always seemed larger than life." **(Professor Chinua Achebe)**

"That is a very silly question because I have never claimed to be a Nigerian Army General and truth be told, I would rather be a Private in the Biafra Army than a General in the Nigerian Army for one simple reason. A Private in the Biafra Army had more combat experience than most Nigerian Army Generals. I know them very well because most of them were my friends or my students. There are many Generals in the Nigerian Army who cannot tell the difference between a battlefield and a cornfield." **(Dim Chukwuemeka Odumegwu Ojukwu, Ikemba Nnewi)**

"Now, I am under attack by the biggest force in military history, my little African son, Obama wants to kill me, to take away the freedom of our country, to take away our free housing, our free medicine, our free education, our free food, and replace it with American style thievery, called "capitalism", but all of us in the Third World know what that means, it means corporations run the countries, run the world, and the people suffer." **(Col Muammar Gaddafi)**

"South Africans will kick down a statue of dead white man but won't even attempt to slap a live one. Yet they can stone to death a black man simply because he's a foreigner." **(President Robert Mugabe)**

"Though it may seem to be ages but one thing is sure and certain. For your honesty and services to humanity the good Lord shall surely bless us in this present life." **(Chima Onyeagba Umealo)**

"Like cause always produce like effect. In kind, we always reap what we sow; but quantitatively, we always reap much more than we sow." **(Chief Obafemi Awolowo)**

"In the days of our fathers, even in my own days, before now, when a man takes a lady to meet his parents, it means that he is in for a serious business, but nowadays! If you like let him take you to his ancestors, it means nothing!!!" **(Chika Nwankwo)**

"I have found out that the older you become you need stability in finance and most importantly stability in your relationship. You become distress staying without a partner you can love, cherish, share, communicate, laugh, fight, quarrel, smile, hug and wake up beside each other in the morning." **(Raphael Ikechukwu Ogbuagu)**

"You know, I don't think of myself as anything like a 'global citizen' or anything of the sort. I am just a Nigerian who's comfortable in other places." **(Chimamanda Ngozi Adichie)**

"I am the product of the masses of my country and the product of my enemy." **(Winnie Madikizela-Mandela)**

"If you bet on individuals instead of the people, you are going to fail." **(Mohamed ElBaradei)**

"It may be that writers too have failed us. For seduced by their freedom, their freedom to entertain, they may have been ignoring the monsters growling deep in our sleep, monsters that may, one day, devour us...Writers are dangerous when they tell the truth...Writers are dangerous when they tell lies." **(Ben Okri)**

"Very honest people have few friends**." (Pastor Idah Peterside)**

"I have told my friends and myself to stop being a typical hypocrite; one sentence is enough for all of us, to find ourselves first before with locate others, as finding ourselves first is strength and Mastery!" **(Dr. Carl Oshodi-Isibor)**

"We can change the world and make it a better place. It is in your hand to make a difference." **(Nelson Rolihlahla Mandela "Madiba)**

"Just when the caterpillar thought the world was over it became a butterfly." **(Bruno Ezeani)**

"Nigeria is too poor for her leaders to act like multi - billionaires and Nigeria is too rich for her people to be so poor." **(Ben Murray Bruce)**

"The struggle you're in today is developing the strength you need for tomorrow. Don't give up." **(Melvin Udo Richmond)**

"Life gives us the things we need, the things that need us and the people who need us. But life does not make us perfect for the people and the things we need. Nor are we surrounded with perfect people in our short lives. But all the time we have, all the people we have, all that we are and we can be, and all the things we have are perfectly perfect. We can only respond in gratitude with grace and humility at the wonderful gifts of life and time." **(Professor Sam Maluleke)**

"Our small and peaceful country is threatened daily by covetous and bigoted big powers whose hunger for domination and control of other nations and their resources knows no bounds." **(President Robert Mugabe)**

"If they throw stones at you, don't throw back instead use them to build your own foundation." **(Letwin Dadirai Mandishona)**

"We Africans used to carry Europeans, but now Europeans are carrying us. We are now the masters .They came from Britain and wanted to show that they really have power in my country." **(Idi Amin)**

"Our value system have been side tracked from what you can offer, who you are, the potentials in you to how much do you have in our pocket, that has become the greatest nightmare that our beloveth country Nigeria has become." **(Raphael Ikechukwu Ogbuagu)**

"For this greater good to become the chariot of our purpose, there is need to do the needful, while bring serene joy and Peace to others and ourselves; to liberate the family from which we hail. To do justice to others and be truthful to yourself. The greater good of all must not outweighs our consciousness to remain positive, joy filled, believing and Kind in the tiniest measure to all in our ways. I've the hope that this greater good is in all of us, irrespective of our present situation. Even the most dastardly human being has an element of this greater good in them! This is just my one Dollar observation though!" **(Dr. Carl Oshodi-Isibor)**

"Just because the hands can wash the feet but the feet cannot wash the hands, it is no excuse for the hands not to wash the feet." **(African proverb)**

"Once it gets to a point where it becomes a matter of life and death to occupy a position of leadership or not, with an eye on future opportunities, therein lays the danger." **(Kgalema Motlanthe)**

"If you want to be great be ready to make yourself a fool." **(Dr. Richie Achikwu)**

"History has shown that the path of honour for any true leader is not to walk away from his people in moments of challenges. We must stand together in adversity and overcome all threats to our development. We must defend our future, for the sake of our children." **(President Goodluck Jonathan)**

"The problem is not the problem. The problem is your attitude about the problem." **(Johnny Muteba)**

"I am not from the East, but I admire the custom of our brothers from that part of the country to take community development as a core duty of any individual that has the means." **(Ben Murray Bruce)**

"I don't want to be remembered as a great man, but as one who paved the way for others to be great and to realise their destiny." **(President Robert Mugabe)**

"Things work out best for those who make the best of how things work out." **(Lawrence Katleho Khekhe)**

"Mediocrity will always try to drag excellence down to its level. Don't trade your superiority for inferiority." **(Chris Arukwe)**

"The most beautiful thing that a woman can wear is self confidence." **(Ntsako Mbhokota)**

"Good Sex can fix a bad argument - Not a bad relationship." **(Letwin Dadirai Mandishona)**

"Any acclaimed rich man that is liquidated by a woman was never rich in the first instance." **(Raphael Ikechukwu Ogbuagu)**

"I have always been curious about how much of our cultural baggage we bring to what and how we read. I suspect we bring a lot, although we like to think we don't." **(Chimamanda Ngozi Adichie)**

"Whether approached in the context of religion, human rights, societal norms and or politically, what is wrong when inflicted by the other party to the other can never be right when positions are swopped. Oppression can never be right now even if we swop positions." **(Mickey Meji)**

"People talk about smart sanctions and crippling sanctions. I've never seen smart sanctions, and crippling sanctions cripple everyone, including innocent civilians, and make the government more popular." **(Mohamed ElBaradei)**

"Originality is the essence of true scholarship. Creativity is the soul of the true scholar." **(Dr. Nnamdi Azikiwe)**

"It is said that no one truly knows a nation until one has been inside its jails. A nation should not be judged by how it treats its highest citizens, but its lowest ones." **(Nelson Rolihlahla Mandela"Madiba)**

"No matter how hard you try, there are things you can't change."The frown on the face of the goat will not stop it from being taken to the market." **(Igbo proverb)**

"Charisma might open a door, but it takes character to maintain it." **(Pastor David Adeoye)**

"Poverty is not the lack of wealth opportunity but an evidence of wasted wealth/opportunity." **(Jimmy Elozie)**

"Women are basically greedy; they want all things from one man, while men are so simple, they only want one thing from all women." **(Gauteng Love)**

"A chameleon cannot change its majestic step because there is a fire on the mountain." **(Nwike Amobi)**

"Until you prevail with God, you cannot prevail with men; your victory has to be spiritual first, before it is physical." **(Pastor Chris Oyakhilome)**

"Don't tell me what I'm doing "wrong", if your actions aren't showing me how to do it right." **(Letwin Dadirai Mandishona)**

"Those who succeed are those who have failed. Those who fail are those who do nothing." **(Rev Elias Ndeda)**

"They're all good men before something happens to them. Some of them still stay good. No matter how they were treated." **(Pamela Mbatha)**

"Do you know that a sexy and intelligent woman can make an average man do anything?" **(Raphael Ikechukwu Ogbuagu)**

"Sorry is not just a word, it's a deed. It is an act." **(Dr. Don Mattera)**

"The lion does not turn around when a small dog barks." **(Namibia Proverb)**

"A good businessman must have nose for business the same way a journalist has nose for news. Once your eyes, ears, nose, heart and brain are trained on business, you sniff business opportunities everywhere." **(Dr. Orji Uzor Kalu)**

"Throughout history, it has been the inaction of those who could have acted; the indifference of those who should have known better; the silence of the voice of justice when it mattered most; that has made it possible for evil to triumph." **(Emperor Haile Sellasie)**

"Together we have travelled a long road to be where we are today. This has been a road of struggle against colonial and apartheid oppression." **(Thabo Mbeki)**

"Today, however, God has repaid me in several folds. I can hardly keep pace with all my investments in different parts of the world, and I virtually live in the air now, crisscrossing continents." **(Dr. Orji Kalu)**

"Your intention is more important than your feeling in order to reach your dream. Don't you ever give up even when you feel you can't?" **(Johnny Muteba)**

"Having a female best friend is like having a chicken as a pet, you'll eat it one day." **(African Proverb)**

"People are attracted to you by what they see in you; they remain attracted to you by what you see in yourself." **(Melvin Udo Richmond)**

"A capitalist Nigger loves money. There is absolutely nothing wrong with the love of money. He loves money to live a better life. He loves money to change the poverty and economy slavery of the black race." **(Dr. Chika Onyeani)**

"Every time you celebrate the little win, it builds your confidence that leads you to a bigger win." **(Dr. Richie Achukwu)**

"There is no easy walk to freedom anywhere and many of us will have to pass through the valley of shadow of death again and again before we reach the mountain of our desire." **(Nelson Rolihlahla Mandela"Madiba)**

"The cleared path is not my route, and where it leads is not my destination. My route is the bush which I must clear for others to pass." **(Rev Chidozie Ejimadu)**

"The problem with looking in the mirror is that you never know how you will feel about what you see. Sometimes, when my hormones are out of sync, I have no interest in the mirror, and if I do look I think everything is all wrong. Other times, I am quite pleased with what I see." **(Chimamanda Ngozi Adichie)**

"Wife, when you get to know what your husband doesn't like, you will save yourself from a lot of unnecessary prayer and fasting. All you need is to apply wisdom and do away with the things he doesn't like." **(Dr. Uma Ukpai)**

"The quality of life you live here on earth depends on the knowledge of God that you have." **(Pastor Chris Oyakhilome)**

"We must agree as African leaders that acts of terror against one nation are an act of terror against all nations." **(President Goodluck Jonathan)**

"Anxiety and anxiousness is a form of doubt and it is the greatest enemy to break through." **(Pastor Ethel Onyanta)**

"We pass through this world but once and opportunities you miss will never be available to you again." **(Nelson Rolihlahla Mandela"Madiba)**

"The devil will not look for you unless you have something shinning in you he wants to destroy." **(Dr. Richie Achukwu)**

"Sincerity, truthfulness, straight forwardness and the grace of God is the number one key to succeed in every area of life." **(Raphael Ikechukwu Ogbuagu)**

"Time is money. If someone is wasting your time they are stealing from you." **(Letwin Dadirai Mandishona)**

"Many of our own people here in this country do not ask about computers, telephones and television sets. They ask when we will get a road to our village." **(Thabo Mbeki)**

"When I joined the ANC, I never thought I would be anything. In no way, did I say, 'One day I could be the president. I think I am good material for the presidency.' Not at all." **(President Jacob Zuma)**

"The white man is very clever. He came quietly and peaceably with his religion. We were amused at his foolishness and allowed him to stay. Now he has won our brothers, and our clan can no longer act like one. He has put a knife on the things that held us together and we have fallen apart." **(Professor Chinua Achebe)**

"What counts in life is not the mere fact we have lived. It is what difference we have made to the lives of others that will determine the significance of life we lead." **(Nelson Rolihlahla Mandela "Madiba)**

"If you want to solve a problem permanently, then you must deal with the cause for "You need to take care of the root in order to heal the tree" **(Gullah proverb)**

"A dream doesn't become reality through magic; it takes sweat, determination & hard work." **(Violet Namo)**

"When we hold onto our past pains and bitterness, we become slaves to our emotions." **(Raphael Ikechukwu Ogbuagu)**

"The passion of love makes people impervious to advise, for as they say, "You can't advise a man who is after a woman (love is blind)" **(Kenyan Proverb)**

"2000 years ago Rome knew how many people it had. Mary & Joseph were counted in Bethlehem. In 2015 does Nigeria know how many people she has?" **(Ben Murray Bruce)**

"Everybody wants to be a diamond but very few are will to be cut. To be the best, be prepared to handle the worst and get cut in the process." **(Ntsako Mbhokota)**

"What the Edo election has confirmed is that when the President and Commander-in-Chief puts the country first and foremost conducts himself as a statesman and not just a party leader, credible elections are possible." **(Hon Adams Oshiomhole)**

"What you absorb can completely alter your peace of mind, be mindful of what you're listening to, reading and allowing into your space!" **(Pamela Mbatha)**

"My horizon on humanity is enlarged by reading the writers of poems, seeing a painting, listening to some music, some opera, which has nothing at all to do with a volatile human condition or struggle or whatever. It enriches me as a human being." **(Professor Wole Soyinka)**

"A capitalist Nigger who wants something must move mountains to get it without begging for it. He is a man and he has to behave like a man." **(Dr. Chika Onyeani)**

"Mothers should always be loving and caring to everyone around them because "Mother is god number two" **(Chewa proverb)**

"Victory will last a time but excellence will last forever." **(Raphael Ikechukwu Ogbuagu)**

"Our country is full of needy people, overflowing with men and women who know they're missing out on something, bursting with hurting individuals who come to us with hands outstretched. Our hard-working, innovative, and imaginative youth have become hopeless, deflated, and disengaged." **(Dr. Oby Ezekwesili)**

"Nothing significant has ever been accomplished without controversy, with criticism." **(Rev. Elias Ndeda)**

"When our actions are based on good intentions our soul has no regrets" **(Simangele Mngomezulu)**

"Find someone who will change your life, not just your status." **(Johnny Muteba)**

"I'm in a space of gratitude, acceptance allowance. I am grateful to be alive. I am thankful for every drop of tears I shed in the past few years when no one was there for me. Being homeless helped me to find a permanent address in my heart. Having no food to eat taught me to feed my soul. Now I know for sure, I am loved and my purpose on earth is to be loved. I give thanks to who I am becoming every day of my life. I send you tons of blessings. May each day reveal to you why you were born. May you be blessed with all the resources you need to live your purpose Amen." **(Mmatshilo Motsei)**

"You children of nowadays only run to elders when you have finished making the damage." **(General Olusegun Obasanjo)**

"Behind every successful man there is a woman and behind every unsuccessful man there are two women." **(Gauteng Love)**

"As long as the mindset is limited you can never succeed." **(Raphael Ikechukwu Ogbuagu)**

"The forces that unite us are intrinsic and greater than the superimposed influences that keep us apart." **(Kwame Nkrumah)**

"Selfish people promise you things to extend their time in your life; while still keeping you as an option. However, a person with real intentions makes good on their promises and makes you a priority." **(Letwin Dadirai Mandishona)**

"It is only in South Africa that an illerate villager thinks a qualified medical doctor from another African country is the reason for his unemployment." **(President Robert Mugabe)**

"The greatest legacy you can give to yourself and your family is to build a good name that will always stand the test of time." **(Raphael Ikechukwu Ogbuagu)**

"Regret is a power drainer."I wish I would not have. I wish I would have." Well, if you did not you did not, and if you did you did. So this is today and lets us be now people because faith is now." **(Sophie la Belle)**

"Good men obey orders and follow the existing path. Great men disobey orders, reconstruct the existing path or create a new path." **(Rev Chidozie Ejimadu)**

"A realization that work is a place where money is made and a home is where love is created. You need to be able to separate the two in order for your life to stay balanced." **(Noxolo Ndlovu)**

"There is no triumph without travail; there is no delivery without labour." **(Bishop David Oyedepo)**

"Where you stay does not define what stays within you. We can live in mansions and still be homeless. What is small to you may be Monte Casino to the other person." **(Esmeralda Sharon)**

"Surround yourself with people who will offer uplifting advice because "When a king has good counsellors, his reign is peaceful." **(Ashanti proverb)**

"Relationships are easy to start; it cost a lot to develop them and it takes guts to break them." **(Rev Elias Ndeda)**

"Americans think African writers will write about the exotic, about wildlife, poverty, maybe AIDS. They come to Africa and African books with certain expectations." **(Chimamanda Ngozi Adichie)**

"For me, before public office, I was active in business, involved in corporate governance, both nationally and internationally. And when I left office, I returned to my original calling, which is business. That is the way it should be." **(Dr. Orji Kalu)**

"There is no cloud above my head - there is not even a mist." **(President Jacob Zuma)**

"So many of us are trying to find LIFE in the things that don't make us feel alive." **(Letwin Dadirai Mandishona)**

"For 25 years of my life I fought for freedom of Nigeria, Nigeria will obtain independent on October 1st 1960, it makes no difference who becomes the prime minister whether Balewa, Chief Awolowo or myself, so long as Nigeria is free I will be satisfied." **(Dr. Nnamdi Azikiwe)**

"The future is not some place we are going to but one we are creating. The paths to it are not found but made." **(Sibongile Mthembu)**

"A man is not finished when he is defeated, he is finished when he quits. In trying times too many people quit trying." **(Rev. Elias Ndeda)**

"When old people speak it is not because of the sweetness of words in our mouths; it is because we see something which you do not see." **(Professor Chinua Achebe)**

"Many people when they go to church they need the help of God, but they don't need the face of God." **(Raphael Ikechukwu Ogbuagu)**

"The enemies of a people are those who keep them in ignorance." **(Thomas Sankara)**

"Racial discrimination, South Africa's economic power, its oppression and exploitation of all the black peoples, are part and parcel of the same thing." **(Oliver Tambo)**

"Because the truth is, it doesn't really matter who I used to be. It's all about who I've become." **(Letwin Dadirai Mandishona)**

"Loneliness is not the lack of affection but the lack of direction." **(Jimmy Elozie)**

"When a person is ignorant of what kind of treasures are within them, they live their lives like trash." **(Pastor David Adeoye)**

"There is a difference between obedience and compulsion. Obedience allows for choice from within whereas compulsion is a form of bondage." **(Osadebe Ibegbu)**

"Success is a relative term. It brings so many relatives." **(Gauteng Love)**

"Overcome poverty is not a gesture of charity. It is an act of justice. It is the protection of a fundamental human right to dignity and a decent life while poverty persists, there is no true freedom." **(Nelson Rolihlahla Mandela"Madiba)**

"We paid the ultimate price for it and we are determined never to relinquish our sovereignty and remain master of our destiny." **(President Robert Mugabe)**

"The person who loves sorrow will always find something to moan about." **(Johnny Muteba)**

"Whatever happens to you doesn't fall in despair. Even if all the doors are closed, a secret path will be there for you that no one knows. You can't see it yet but so many paradises are at the end of this path. Be grateful! It is easy to thank after obtaining what you want, thank before having what you want." **(Dr. Carl Oshodi-Isibor)**

"Saying is different from acting. Saying gives hope while acting brings change." **(Raphael Ikechukwu Ogbuagu)**

"There is no winning without warfare; there is no opportunity without opposition; there is no victory without vigilance." **(Pamela Nkenke Blessing)**

"Never tell a man anything evil about a woman he loves, he will not hear you." **(Pastor Idah Peterside)**

"The ability to triumph begins with you. Never let the odds keep you from doing what you know in your heart you were meant to do." **(Obinna Nwizu)**

"Gratitude unlocks the fullness of life. It turns what we have into enough, and more. It turns denial into acceptance, chaos to order, confusion to clarity. It can turn a meal into a feast, a house into a home, a stranger into a friend." That is what an expression of appreciation can do. I hope your healths are good. Enjoy." **(Jason Chiwuzie Osuafor)**

"Don't blame the past or others for your downfalls or failures; choices that you make are the ones that carry you to where you set your mind to. Look from where you were to where you are; look how far you have come and faced. Admire your accomplishments, large or small, tremendous or tiny; they contribute to the well being of this world. A little light somewhere makes a brighter light everywhere." **(Xoliswa Qumana)**

"A witch cried out yesterday and a child died today. Who does not know that it was the witch who killed the child?" **(Yoruba Proverb)**

"The danger to our planet does not lie in man's determination to provide necessaries for mankind; the danger lurks around man's ambition for frills which he can live without." **(Rev Chidozie Ejimadu)**

"Kindness makes you the most beautiful person in the world. No matter what you look like." **(Pamela Mbatha)**

"Nothing is more confusing than being around someone who gives good advice but set bad example." **(Letwin Dadirai Mandishona)**

"Peace is the greatest weapon for development that any person can have." **(Nelson Rolihlahla Mandela"Madiba)**

"One of the biggest problems that money creates is, you never know whether you are loved or your money is being respected!!" **(Lilian Ngozi)**

"Never place all your hopes in one thing for "A pot trader whose fortunes are all invested in her clay pots is not much of a merchant." **(Igbo proverb)**

"It takes favour to succeed; it does not take labour to succeed." **(Pastor Ethel Onyanta)**

"As we grow up, we learn that even the one person who wasn't supposed to ever let you down probably will. You will have your heart broken probably more often than once and it's harder every time. You will blame a new love for something an old one did, you will cry because time is passing too fast and will eventually lose someone you love. So take too many pictures, laugh too much and love you've never been hurt because the sixty seconds you spend upset is a minute of possible happiness that you will never get back. Life is a small place, very little and quite fragile, so don't be afraid that it will end, be afraid that it will never begin and take a bound step forward and be ready to die with your decision." **(Raphael Ikechukwu Ogbuagu)**

"To get the best out of life, realize your past without regret, handle your present without confidence, and prepare for the future without fear." **(Elizabeth Lizzy)**

"One of the truest tests of integrity is its blunt refusal to be compromised." **(Professor Chinua Achebe)**

"If you want to go fast, walk alone; if you want to go far, walk together." **(African Proverb)**

"Love is practical, love is not mere wishful thinking, and it is not mere dishing out the word of God. It goes beyond that. Love cares, endures and does not react irrationally." **(Osadebe Ibegbu)**

"I was placed in solitary confinement for a year and ten months out of the period in which I stayed in prison, which was just over two years." **(Professor Wole Soyinka)**

"Durango died this morning. He did not say a word. He just woke up and died. Yesterday he bought one of the flashiest cars in the world. Day before yesterday he parked into a marble house in the West Indies. A day before that he married a girl every man desires called goddess." **(Digidi Dunhill)**

"Education is the most powerful weapon which you can use to change the world." **(Nelson Rolihlahla Mandela"Madiba)**

"No one was born perfect: Education and lots of practice provide you with essential skills.When the archer was born, he did not hold a bow." **(Ashanti proverb)**

"When you become a sign and a wonder, you live above situations and circumstances." **(Bishop David Oyedepo)**

"Sometimes saying SORRY is the most difficult thing on earth. But it's the cheapest thing to save the most expensive gift called Relationship." **(Hrh Frank Times)**

"Thoughts have power, thoughts are energy. You can make your world or break your world by your thinking. So be careful of negative thoughts, because it will disrupt the journey the Creator has put you on. Keep the positive energy flowing and never give up." **(Chika Nwankwo)**

"The more you look back, the less you get ahead. No man is rich enough to buy his past." **(Rev Elias Ndeda)**

"I am a black man inside and outside and you are white men on the outside, but inside, you are Africans like me." **(General Olusegun Obasanjo)**

"I want people to remember me as someone whose life has been helpful to humanity." **(Thomas Sankara)**

"Class, race, sexuality, gender and other categories by which we categozie and dismiss each other need to be excavated from inside." **(Dorothy Allison)**

"It takes information to be free from stagnation and deformation. If you are informed, you will be formed, and if you are well informed, you will be well informed. The amount of information you have on any issue of life will determine your accomplishment in it." **(Bishop David Oyedepo)**

"Disrespect has become so acceptable in our generation that so many blind eyes think showing respect is uptight and crazy. Which is SAD?" **(Letwin Dadirai Mandishona)**

"Our vision of the past can thwart our vision of the future." **(Ayanda Nkosi Ngcobo)**

"To me any soldier who doesn't want to be a general in the army is not a good soldier." **(Raphael Ikechukwu Ogbuagu)**

"When the mouse laughs at the cat, there is a hole nearby."
(African Proverb)

"We can re-dream this world and make the dream come real.
Human beings are gods hidden from themselves." **(Ben Okri)**

"If somebody who is wearing a red cap is denying you of what is
due to you and is calling another person who does not wear red
cap evil, but who is giving you in full what is due to you, who of
the two is evil?" **(President Goodluck Jonathan)**

"People looking for cheap popularity can afford to donate
thousands of dollars, pounds, rands, naira in the public to be
applauded while within their households there are children and
people starving to death from hunger and unable to go to school
because of lack of money what do we call this type of people
hypocrites, they say charity begins at home." **(Raphael
Ikechukwu Ogbuagu)**

"To ascend to the hill of the LORD, you need clean hands, pure
heart, not lift the soul unto vanity, & not swear deceitfully.
Fulfilling' these will make us eligible." **(Pastor Ethel Onyanta)**

"Be careful: Your kids will follow your actions, for they say,
"Where the sheep stands its kid stands" **(Ashanti proverb)**

"Luck is not a kingdom language; success is a reward for
diligence." **(Rev Elias Ndeda)**

"In my country, we go to prison first and then become
president." **(Nelson Rolihlahla Mandela "Madiba)**

"Don't waste words on people who deserve silence, sometimes
the most powerful thing you can say is nothing at all." **(Letwin
Dadirai Mandishona)**

"Destiny demands diligence. You cannot fulfil your destiny on
theory. Neither can you dream yourself to where you could be."
(Dr. Tunde Bakare)

"Champions are made through exercise. You will not become a champion by mere promise or wishes; you will only become one by exercising yourself in your field of sport. Likewise you must take great covenant steps in order to get to the top that God has planned for you." **(Bishop David Oyedepo)**

"Until you get comfortable with being alone, you'll never know if you're choosing someone out of love or loneliness." **(Pamela Mbatha)**

"Remember there are three poisons: greed, anger, and ignorance. Do not deny their existence but turn them around and you have generosity, compassion, and wisdom." **(Chika Nwankwo)**

"One good thing about evil is that it has two faces today you are the initiator, tomorrow you become a victim better desist from it." **(Chima Onyeagba Umealo)**

"Problems only emerge when there solutions for them. The role of leadership is to guide people towards those solutions." **(Walter Sisulu)**

"Life is not about what you have got but about what you have been able to offer to those who are in need." **(Raphael Ikechukwu Ogbuagu)**

"There are no mistakes, no coincidence. All events are blessing given to us to learn from." **(Sibongile Mthembu)**

"If you talk to a man in a language he understands, that goes to his head. If you talk to him in his language that goes to his heart." **(Chief Jonas Ndubueze Udeji)**

"The rich man's dog gets more in the way of vaccination, medicine and medical care than do the workers upon whom the rich man's wealth is built." **(Samora Machel)**

"Some people aren't worth your time or happiness. Love those who love you, leave those who curse you, pray for those who hate you." **(Letwin Dadirai Mandishona)**

"Some solutions take time and patience because "A tree that has twisted for thirty years cannot be straightened in a single day." **(Akan proverb)**

"Never explain yourself to anybody because the people who like us don't need it and the people who dislike us won't believe it." **(Contributed Lerato Princess Mofokeng)**

"Nothing stops us from having six Dubai in the six geopolitical zones of Nigeria if we have thinkers; if we have men who know how to think through and who can pre-engineer the whole process in a short while. "Dubai, once upon a time came, to Nigeria to borrow money. Once upon a time for three years, we paid the whole civil service fee of Trinidad and Tobago. There would be no Angola today if Nigeria did not sow a seed of $30 million." **(Dr. Tunde Bakare)**

"Religion is one of the biggest deceits to mankind. It is the same religion that the white-men used to enslave our ancestors in Africa. It is the same religion Islamist is using to kill millions of people. Let us go to worship houses to pray and worship God not the religious leaders. Our healing and solution to most of our problems lie with us." **(Olaniyi Abodedele)**

"We should never become despondent because the weather is bad, nor should we turn triumphalist because the sun shines." **(Thabo Mbeki)**

"You are either a blessing or a burden; an asset or a liability; a problem solver or a problem. It is all your choice." **(Johnny Muteba)**

"The majority in this country have not seen anything wrong with Zuma. I go with the overwhelming feeling of this country. If the majority say, 'Zuma, do this,' I will do it." **(President Jacob Zuma)**

"It is the story that owns and directs us. It is the thing that makes us different from cattle; it is the mark on the face that sets one people apart from their neighbours." **(Professor Chinua Achebe)**

"Think that feeling that if one believed absolutely in any course, then one must have the confidence, the self-certainty, to go through with that particular course of action." **(Professor Wole Soyinka)**

"Anger is a manifestation of a deeper issue... and that, for me, is based on insecurity, self-esteem and loneliness." **(Monyor Martin)**

"I do not want to be controlled by any superpower. I myself consider myself the most powerful figure in the world, and that is why I do not let any superpower control me." **(Idi Amin)**

"I do not know how I have come to live this long." **(President Robert Mugabe)**

"When what is in you comes on you, you cannot be intimidated by what is around you." **(Rev Elias Ndeda)**

"The fight for freedom must go on until it is won; until our country is free and happy and peaceful as part of the community of man, we cannot rest." **(Oliver Tambo)**

"No Matter how tough the situation is, no matter how much people try to put you down, just press on. Never buckle down. After the storm, you can look back at the situation and be proud of yourself that you stood tall. That is one lesson I have learned in life." **(Sampson Abosi Okorie)**

"Your failure won't hurt you until you start to blame them on others, Take action, and change your life." **(Sibongile Mthembu)**

"Relationship is nurtured and maintained and for it linger, a party sacrifices more to sustain it." **(Raphael Ikechukwu Ogbuagu)**

"I would rather have one rose and a kind word from a friend while I am here than a whole truckload when I am gone." **(Thumi Tshanyela)**

"South Africa is blessed to have women and men like yourselves who have little to give but give what you have with open hands and open hearts." **(Mangosuthu Buthelezi)**

"Most people don't actually know what they are looking for, and end up with the same people just with different names over and over again." **(Letwin Dadirai Mandishona)**

"Losing my life does not scare me, WASTING my life....now that's really scary!" **(Melicia Knowmyworth Dial)**

"You cannot produce what you don't have the talents or skills for because "The child of a snake is snake." **(Swahili proverb)**

"Let your giving be based on love. The truth is that you can give without love but you cannot love without giving." **(Robert Appiah)**

"Once a person is determined to help themselves, there is nothing that can stop them." **(Nelson Rolihlahla Mandela "Madiba)**

"Let all women be informed that lying in bed, naked, entangled with somebody, and screaming": Oh my God" "Oh my God" "Oh my God' will not be considered praying." **(Gauteng Love)**

"Stop celebrating the things you receive; start celebrating the things you give. It is in giving that you receive abundantly." **(Bishop David Oyedepo)**

"Gone are those days when a problem shared is a problem solved, nowadays a problem shared becomes the topic of discussion. At times you just got to carry your cross alone." **(Letwin Dadirai Mandishona)**

"The first entity you cannot fight is Almighty God and the second entity is the government. No matter how you interpret it, nobody can fight government successfully." **(Chief Diepreye Alamieyeseigha)**

"When you lack faith in the capacity of God and what He can do for you, you are finished." **(Dr. Richie Achukwu)**

"People put their trust in a lot of things. They find confidence in possessions, wealth, position and resources. But those who trust in the Lord will find safety and rest!" **(Lindiwe Kole)**

"It took the madmen of yesterday for us to be able to act with extreme clarity today. I want to be one of those lunatics. We must dare to invent the future." **(Thomas Sankara)**

"Do your little bit of good where you are; it's those little bits of good put together that overwhelm the world." **(Arch Bishop Desmond Tutu)**

"Salvation is by Grace, not by our might or power." **(Pastor Ethel Onyanta)**

"There is no duty we so much underrate as the duty of being happy." **(Raphael Ikechukwu Ogbuagu)**

"I will not say the fact that there are no European Union observers at an election means that it will not be fair and free." **(General Olusegun Obasanjo)**

"Desperation will always provoke revelation. When there is a genuine thirst to know, God promises that He would pour water upon the thirsty ground. Until there is a thirst, you don't have an access, because God does not waste His water, He pours it out upon the thirsty." **(Bishop David Oyedepo)**

"Give advice; if people don't listen let adversity teach them." **(Ethiopian Proverb)**

"If we were to make the conscious and frequent effort of treating others with consideration, the effects on us and on society as a whole would be amazing." **(Jason Chiwuzie Osuafor)**

"The gap between love and hate is so thin that when hate strikes it out weights the existed love, what a world." **(Sampson Abosi Okorie)**

"Better times will come. Do not let the pain of one season or misfortune to destroy the joy of the rest. Do not judge life with one difficult season. Persevere through the difficult patches, believing God and the better times are sure to come, it may tally or linger but it will come." **(Raphael Ikechukwu Ogbuagu)**

"The distance between who I am and who I want to be is separated only by my actions and words." **(Letwin Dadirai Mandishona)**

"When will the day come that our dignity will be fully restored, when the purpose of our lives will no longer be merely to survive until the sun rises tomorrow?" **(Thabo Mbeki)**

"Don't marry or go in a relationship for money, for "If you marry a monkey for his money, the money will go away & the monkey will stay the same." **(Egypt Proverb)**

"We have made other people rule and now I challenge the people today to rise up. Let the best, the brightest, the fittest and the most competent accept responsibility and let's put the thinkers into power." **(Dr. Tunde Bakare)**

"Blaming the west for slave trade, apartheid, senseless wars, economic sabotage and poverty in Africa without flushing out their agents amongst us is a white wash solution. It is the domestic rat in the house that told the wild rat in the forest that there is a fish in the cupboard! A saboteur is more dangerous than an enemy because you know your enemy but a saboteur is faceless." **(Jimmy Elozie)**

"If you benefit from people, others should benefit from you too for "He who eats another man's food will have his own food eaten by others." **(Swahili proverb)**

"Happiness is something that comes into our life's through doors we don't even remember leaving open." **(Sibongile Mthembu)**

"Oh, the most important thing about me is that my life has been full of changes. Therefore, when I observe the world, I don't expect to see it just like I was seeing the fellow who lives in the next room. There is this complexity which seems to me to be part of the meaning of existence and everything we value." **(Professor Chinua Achebe)**

"If your boyfriend isn't strong enough to pick you up and pin you against the wall, you have a girlfriend." **(Pamela Mbatha)**

"Never before in history has such a sweeping fervour for freedom expressed itself in great mass movements which are driving down the bastions of empire. This wind of change blowing through Africa, as I have said before, is no ordinary wind. It is a raging hurricane against which the old order cannot stand the great millions of Africa and of Asia, have grown impatient of being hewers of wood and drawers of water, and are rebelling against the false belief that providence created some to be menials of others. Hence the twentieth century has become the century of colonial emancipation, the century of continuing revolution which must finally witness the total liberation of Africa from colonial rule and imperialist exploitation." **(Kwame Nkrumah)**

"Everyone has three lives; a public life, a private life, and a secret life." **(Contributed by Tshwane Nicolette Monamane)**

"Nigerian parents are a funny. They'll beat their kids with the intent of making them cry and then start beating them to stop crying." **(Edith Okoroji-Akinsola)**

"There is no apology for love; jealousy is a freedom for fool." **(Chima Onyeagba Umealo)**

"When the missionaries came to Africa they had the Bible and we had the land. They said, 'Let us pray.' We closed our eyes. When we opened them we had the Bible and they had the land." **(Arch Bishop Desmond Tutu)**

"Saying that we are going to create a climate so that there is respect, there are no insults, there is proper decorum in which all members of the executive can come and answer." **(Deputy President Cyril Ramaphosa)**

"When love goes wrong a woman can do the unimaginable and unthinkable." **(Raphael Ikechukwu Ogbuagu)**

"Money is power but love brings happiness and peace." **(Chike Brown Osuji)**

"Never lose God in a moment of significance, nor forget the people that have made you great." **(Pastor Idah Peterside)**

"Diplomacy is the ability to tell someone to go to hell in such a way that they actually look up to the trip." **(Edith Okoroji-Akinsola)**

"Fear is the dark room where we develop our nagatives." **(Tumi Leeuw)**

"Responsibility is the price for greatness. No irresponsible person will ever become great; as it takes discipline to be distinguished. And one thing that is able to turn dreams into reality, and impossibilities into possibilities, is unequalled dedication." **(Bishop David Oyedepo)**

"In order to live, we must kill fear. This LIFE is about conquering one of the biggest things WE allow to destroy our quality on earth. When we regain power of the self - through mindfulness - we regain our ability to find our own inner joy and to bring about real change to this world." **(Dr. Carl Oshodi-Isibor)**

"People too weak to follow their own dreams will always find a way to discourage yours." **(Mamsie Phooko)**

"My stiffest earthly assignment is ended and my major life's work is done. My country is now free and I have been honoured to be its first indigenous head of state. What more could one desire in life?" **(Dr. Nnamdi Azikiwe)**

"The heaviest load that one can bear is a grudge against another person." **(Chidi Onuigbo)**

"Praying should be your first response not your last resort." **(Letwin Dadirai Mandishona)**

"I have no intention to inflict pain on Nigerians. To save Nigeria, we must all be prepared to make sacrifices." **(President Goodluck Jonathan)**

"We will be judged through our works more than our talks." **(Raphael Ikechukwu Ogbuagu)**

"If you don't proclaim your success in your privacy, you will never experience it publicly." **(Pastor Chris Oyakhilome)**

"The greatest kind of men are in their hollows waiting that one day their imaginations and ideals will be practically brought to the revival of mankind... but many dreams are cut short, basically because the necessities of our environment, the hardships that pervades us unequally; the poverty within the scarfolds of man's greatest form of ideals all these drag us to the baser part of our passion and avoid our dreams from coming to reality." **(Dr. Carl Oshodi-Isibor)**

"Many people are living an unhappy life because they are mindful of what others have and mindless of what they have." **(Pastor David Adeoye)**

"So many people out there are afraid to live their dreams. Just keep doing your best and the world will definitely notice. I always say, the toughest part about following your dreams is having the guts to go after them, once that is done, you are on the right track." **(Ntsako Mbhokota)**

"People will call you 100 times a day when they want to borrow money from you and won't call you the whole year when they owe you money." **(Edith Okoroji-Akinsola)**

"There are three enemies of personal peace: regret over yesterday's mistakes, anxiety over tomorrow's problems and ingratitude over today's blessings." **(Hugo Africa)**

"I smile when I feel like screaming, sing when I feel like crying, cry when I am happy, and laugh when I am afraid. I fight for what I believe in." **(Lerato Princess Mofokeng)**

"Bad chapters can still create a story that ends well." **(Letwin Dadirai Mandishona)**

"The fact that many people are doing foolish things does not make it right. Do the right thing and never follow the crowd." **(Dr. Tunde Bakare)**

"Ignorance is the cause of all chaos not knowledge." **(Raphael Ikechukwu Ogbuagu)**

"Everyone in the Middle East pretty much wants to come and be an American citizen, but pretty much everybody is angry with the U. S. foreign policy." **(Mohamed ElBaradei)**

"They haven't changed me, have they? They have not withered me. They have not made me senile yet, no. I still have ideas, ideas that need to be accepted by my people." **(President Robert Mugabe)**

"Don't search for heaven and hell in the future. Both are now present. Whenever we manage to love without expectations, calculations, negotiations, we are indeed in heaven. Whenever we fight, hate, we are in hell" **(Dr. Carl Oshodi-Isibor)**

"And gradually they're beginning to recognize the fact that there's nothing more secure than a democratic, accountable, and participatory form of government. But it's sunk in only theoretically; it has not yet sunk in completely in practical terms." **(Professor Wole Soyinka)**

"Adversity is part of life. It is like the rain. You cannot stop it but you can prepare for it. So, remember this: NEVER NEVER GIVE UP." **(Robert Appiah)**

"The ones who say you can't and you won't are probably the ones scared that you will." **(Letwin Dadirai Mandishona)**

"Positive thought creates around yourself an atmosphere propitious to the development of positive outcome that liberates your wellbeing." **(Raphael Ikechukwu Ogbuagu)**

"Your success in business isn't based on your ability to simply change it is based on your ability to change faster than your competitors." **(Phophi Rhinah Muguru)**

"Nigerians are just too religious. You ask someone in the elevator "Are you going down?" and they go "God forbid! I am going up in Jesus name" **(Edith Okoroji-Akinsola)**

"Motivation without inspiration is like a rocket shut into space without a direction. Inspiration is the seed." **(Hugo Africa)**

"No, no matter what I did, it was never enough for some, but for others, they knew I was the son of Gamal Abdel Nasser, the only true Arab and Muslim leader we've had since Salah-al-Deen, when he claimed the Suez Canal for his people, as I claimed Libya, for my people, it was his footsteps I tried to follow, to keep my people free from colonial domination – from thieves who would steal from us." **(Col Mohmmar Gaddafi)**

"You can unite but can never succeed in unifying peoples whom language has set distinctly apart from one another; the more educated a linguistic. Group becomes, the stronger it waxes in its bids for political self-determination and autonomy, unless it happens to be the dominant group." **(Chief Obafemi Awolowo)**

"Poor people talk about each other, they gossiping whilst Rich people talk to each and ask how did you do that? You are Poor because of what you say, not what you do." **(Dr. Richie Achukwu)**

"There is no difference between drunkenness and madness only that one last longer." **(Contributed by Linda Ejiofor)**

"When a man marries a woman only for her beauty, he misses all the things that make her a woman." **(Benin Proverb)**

"Life is a battle and you only have two options, either you run and hide or stand and fight." **(Ntsako Mbhokota)**

"In a war battle soldiers go first then the commanders come in to seal the battle." **(Raphael Ikechukwu Ogbuagu)**

"When an igbo man puts his arm and leg around you when you're sleeping. He's not cuddling, he is only making sure you don't steal and run." **(Igbo proverb)**

"Giving with love and compassion is one of the best communications and it will speak for you." **(Prince Ikpe Ekong)**

"Freedom is an education, knowing that you have the tools to make a life for yourself. Knowledge is the one thing no one can take from you." **(Samamina Mosese)**

"Pope John Paul II not only visited Nigeria twice but stood by the country in its fight against dictatorship and injustice." **(General Olusegun Obasanjo)**

"We live in crazy times. You can't tell a story without it feeling political." **(Johnny Muteba)**

"Time and health are two precious assets that we don't recognize and appreciate until they have been depleted." **(Letwin Dadirai Mandishona)**

"Be selective in your battles. Sometimes peace is better than being right." **(Contributed by Mamsie Afrolucious)**

"The word "Royalty" is just a privilege. If you were born Royal count yourself privileged." **(Contributed by Prince Divine Chike)**

"First impressions can mislead, for "A farmer does not conclude by the mere look of it that a corn is unripe; he tears it open to confirm." **(Tanzania Proverb)**

"Stories can conquer fear, you know. They can make the heart bigger." **(Ben Okri)**

"Mr. Brown had thought of nothing but numbers. He should have known that the kingdom of God did not depend on large crowds. Our Lord Himself stressed the importance of fewness. Narrow is the way and few the number. To fill the Lord's holy temple with an idolatrous crowd clamouring for signs was a folly of everlasting consequence. Our Lord used the whip only once in His life - to drive the crowd away from His church." **(Professor Chinua Achebe)**

"No better witnesses that your own eyes." **(Ethiopian proverb)**

"Poverty is not forceful; it sneaks in when you slumber and folds your hand." **(Rev Elias Ndeda)**

"Our true character is most accurately measured by how you treat those who can do nothing for you." **(Raphael Ikechukwu Ogbuagu)**

"An old woman is always uneasy when dry bones are mentioned in a proverb." **(Professor Chinua Achebe)**

"The greatest Achievers were once called unrealistic & too ambitious." **(Pallabo Safara)**

"Ignorance is not the same as illiteracy. Knowledge is not the same as literacy, or, even the same as the acquisition of educational certificates, or, academic ranks. Some of the most highly literate Nigerians, and the most highly educated, by virtue of their certificates and ranks, are some of the most ignorant over many crucial areas of natural and human existence and over our national life, like our geography, history, economy and politics." **(Yusufu Bala Usman)**

"You cannot carry out fundamental change without a certain amount of madness." **(Thomas Sankara)**

"I am wondering why some people waste time and energy on things that cannot bring any positive change in their lives nor to anybody in this planet. Leadership is a tricky thing as you must learn to be an obedient servant before you can be a great leader!" **(Jimmy Elozie)**

"Giving does not reduce you in any way, what leaves your hand does not leave your life." **(Rev Elias Ndeda)**

"But class is a not for me yes I am blessed. But God could have chosen anyone, so it is not because of my class it was only by his grace. So why would I want to outsmart God by bow want to think I am better than other people. I can't stop people to label me and I can't blame me either because the society we live in today makes things look that way and we automatically judge people by the way the dress; drive ,level of education, money. It's a status core in our today society." **(Phophi Rhinah Muguru)**

"If you can't behold you can't apprehend. The pursuit of destiny requires commitment and being spiritually responsible. A life of gratitude and thanksgiving is a life of continuous access to God. You have to be blind of your needs to find God, for your needs are in God. There is something great in you that without pressure it may die in you." **(Pastor Ethel Onyanta)**

"I have always admired men and women who used their talent to serve the community, and who were highly respected and admired for their effort and sacrifices, even though they held no office whatsoever in government or society." **(Nelson Rolihlahla Mandela"Madiba)**

"Before you jump to a conclusion, you should check to see how far you're going to fall if you're wrong." **(Letwin Dadirai Mandishona)**

"For every voice there is an invoice." **(Raphael Ikechukwu Ogbuagu)**

"You have freedom of speech, but freedom after speech I cannot guarantee." **(Idi Amin)**

"When we are comfortable and inattentive, we run the risk of committing grave injustices absent minded." **(Professor Chinua Achebe)**

"Learning is richer than praying; Learning has greater value than fasting. Learning is the master key of living." **(Bishop David Oyedepo)**

"Heroes will always be remembered, but legends will never die." **(Raphael Ikechukwu Ogbuagu)**

"What you see is what you make. What you see in a people is what you eventually create in them." **(Ben Okri)**

"Today we are entering a new era for our country and its people. Today we celebrate not the victory of a party, but a victory for all the people of South Africa." **(Trevor Manuel)**

"Negative and positive are most always based on perception and tend to rent space in our minds and largely dictate our reaction to situation." **(Sibongile Mthembu)**

"One of the most difficult things to do these days is to talk with authority on anything to do with African culture. Somehow Africans are not expected to have any deep understanding of their own culture or even themselves. Other people have become authorities on all aspects of African life." **(Steve Biko)**

"If I am not above the law, nobody in this country can then claim to be above the law." **(General Olusegun Obasanjo)**

"If you are neutral in situations of injustice, you have chosen the side of the oppressor. If an elephant has its foot on the tail of a mouse and you say that you are neutral, the mouse will not appreciate your neutrality." **(Arch Bishop Desmond Tutu)**

"Self Conquest is the greatest conquest. He who conquers others is strong but he who conquers himself is mighty." **(Rev Elias Ndeda)**

"Love is having all the reason to walk out of a relationship but you still hang on." **(Raphael Ikechukwu Ogbuagu)**

"It took me time and tears to be this relationship, so I can't destroy it because I don't build and destroy." **(Digidi Dunhill)**

"Only free men can negotiate; prisoner cannot enter into contract." **(Nelson Rolihlahla Mandela"Madiba)**

"Thoughts and ideas we do not see neither do we touch but thoughts have given birth to all that man has made physical today." **(Hugo Africa)**

"One, who makes a mistake and then gives an excuse for it, makes two mistakes." **(Rev Elias Ndeda)**

"To poison a nation, poison its stories. A demoralised nation tells demoralised stories to itself. Beware of the storytellers who are not fully conscious of the importance of their gifts, and who are irresponsible in the application of their art: they unwittingly help along the psychic destruction of their people." **(Ben Okri)**

"Determination of purpose is the starting point of all achievement. Life is what happens to you while you're busy making other plans." **(Obinna Nwizu)**

"What is democracy really, the government of the people, by the people and for the people, is the originators of this system really practicing what they want to impose on the world in general. Governments are been topped because they are termed undemocratic in well organised systems that have sustained the integrity of nations for decades." **(Raphael Ikechukwu Ogbuagu)**

"I was a good soldier in the British Army. I was born in a very, very poor family. And I enlisted to escape hunger. But my officers were Scottish and they loved me. The Scots are good, you know." **(Idi Amin)**

"I was loyal to my leader, the late great President Umaru Yar'adua. I am loyal to Nigeria, I don't claim to represent North, South or a Committee-I represent Nigeria. I am loyal to Nigeria's economy, I do not have accounts or property abroad, ALL my children live and school in Nigeria. I am loyal to my wife and friends. Can those who accuse me say the same?" **(President Goodluck Jonathan)**

"Don't expect loyalty when you can't provide honesty." **(Letwin Dadirai Mandishona)**

"Africa & its people" may seem too simple and too obvious to some of us. But I have found in the course of my travels through the world that the most simple things can still give us a lot of trouble, even the brightest among us: this is particularly so in matters concerning Africa." **(Professor Chinua Achebe)**

"If you have attended over 100 weddings and you are still single. Sister, you are no longer different from a canopy." **(Edith Okoroji-Akinsola)**

"Hatred kills more people every year than drugs and alcohol." **(Pastor Idah Peterside)**

"The only limitation you have to your ability and dreams is your mind. If you can think it then you can be it!" **(Dr. Lucas Moloi Caesar)**

"We have not yet arrived, but every point at which we stop requires a re-definition of our destination." **(Ben Okri)**

"You need to get to the point where God becomes your reason for a living, then things will start happening in your favour." **(Bishop David Oyedepo)**

"Love ceases to be a pleasure, trilling, excitement and adventurous when it ceases to be a secret." **(Raphael Ikechukwu Ogbuagu)**

"Love rumours. I learn a lot about myself that I didn't know." **(Letwin Dadirai Mandishona)**

"If you're not making changes in your life, you're not growing; you're only getting older. Growth is making positive changes." **(Pastor Chris Oyakhilome)**

"I have walked that long road to freedom. I have tried not to falter and made missteps along the way. However, I have discovered that the secret of climbing a great hill one only finds that there are many more hills to climb. I have taken a moment here to rest, to steal a view of glorious vista that surrounds me, to look back on distance I have come. But I can only rest for a moment, for freedom comes with responsibilities and I dare not linger for long. The walk is not ended." **(Nelson Rolihlahla Mandela"Madiba)**

"Marriage is a very sacred institution that must not be taken lightly, for they say, "To marry is to put a snake in one's handbag" **(Bantu proverb)**

"Tupac is dead and still releasing songs. So don't tell me you couldn't text me because your battery died." **(Pamela Mbatha)**

"All prejudices of yesterday should die with yesterday." **(President Goodluck Jonathan)**

"Your Success is not measured by what you have done, compared with what others have done; rather what you have done compared with what you should have done." **(Rev Elias Ndeda)**

"Style is about self expression, it should come from who you are or who you want to be." **(Letwin Dadirai Mandishona)**

"With realization of one's own potential and self-confidence in one's ability, one can build a better world." **(Monica Vink)**

"It is good to fight for someone that you love, but stupid to fight for someone to love you." **(Digidi Dunhill)**

"Personally, I believe in self-determination, but in the context of one South Africa - so that my self-determination is based in this region, and with my people." **(Mangosuthu Buthelezi)**

"Remember, the energy of the mind is the essence of life and a life lived for others, is a life worthwhile." **(Ekos Akpokabayen)**

"True charity & love lies in touching the head of an Orphan & in feeding the poor.... Here lies evergreen knowledge, in its practice rest the soul of Nature. This is Truth!!!" **(Dr. Carl Oshodi-Isibor)**

"Fellow Nigerians, when someone gives a huge sum of money (billions) to another person to pursue an ambition (political) - Is he making an investment or just being totally and unbelievably GENEROUS?" **(Hon Bukola Saraki)**

"Keep calm. Tension blocks the flow of thought and power. Your brain cannot operate efficient under stress; go at your problem easy like and you will find that you will overcome it." **(Raphael Ikechukwu Ogbuagu)**

"You must develop the habit of skepticism, not to swallow every piece of superstition you are told by witch-doctors and professors." **(Professor Chinua Achebe)**

"Isn't it funny how we'll trust man-made inventions with our lives & won't trust the God who created the man? Right. It's not funny." **(Letwin Dadirai Mandishona)**

"To run a marathon without preparation leaves your body feeling weak from head to toes, planning is important in all we do." **(Alicia Tobeka Gana)**

"You cannot run faster than a bullet." **(Idi Amin)**

"The Blackman shall be absolute and undisputed master in his own home, and shall enjoy unaffected and un-patronizing equality with the other races of the world." **(Chief Obafemi Awolowo)**

"I am in search for a world of contentment as opposed to a world of prosperity." **(Rev Chidozie Ejimadu)**

"Many today are dying in the valley of mediocrity because they are paying attention to what people say or what they might say." **(Pastor David Adeoye)**

"Form independent opinions on the basis of your own reason and experience; do not allow yourself to be led blindly by others." **(Chima Onyeagba Umealo)**

"The actions of older and more experienced people should not be taken for granted because "An old he-goat does not sneeze for nothing." **(Menu proverb)**

"Pop corns are prepared in the same pot, under the same heat, in the same oil but they don't pop at the same time. Do not compare yourself to others, your turn is coming." **(Pamela Mbatha)**

"The moment a lie is said, there are other backup lies to cover up for the initial lie thus forcing ourselves into uncompromising situation which in term affects our morality, ego and personality. The truth to all this is to be truthful and sincere from the onset." **(Raphael Ikechukwu Ogbuagu)**

"Something is profoundly wrong with the way we live today. For thirty years we have made a virtue out of the pursuit of material self-interest: indeed this very pursuit now constitutes whatever remains of our sense of collective purpose. We know what things cost but have no idea what they are worth. We no longer ask of a judicial ruling or a legislative act: Is it good? Is it fair? Is it just? Is it right? Will it help bring about a better society or a better world? Those used to be the political questions even if they invited no easy answers. We must learn once again to pose them." **(Trevor Manuel)**

"Towards back biting, bold people confront." **(Rev Elias Ndeda)**

"Good use of photography can given even poverty with all its rags, filth and vermin a measure of divines rarely noticeable in real life." **(Nelson Rolihlahla Mandela"Madiba)**

"Use your knowledge for good to preserve peace among men."
(Emperor Hailes Salassie)

"Don't make promises when you are in joy, don't reply when you are mad most importantly, don't make decisions when you are angry. They might hurt you for the rest of your life, so if you ask me, think twice act wise." **(Raphael Ikechukwu Ogbuagu)**

"This earth that we live on is full of stories in the same way that, for a fish, the ocean is full of ocean. Some people say when we are born we are born into stories. I say we're also born from stories."
(Ben Okri)

"A true friend knows your weakness but shows your strength, feels your fears but fortifies your faith, sees your anxieties but frees your spirit, recognizes your disabilities but emphasizes your probabilities." **(Sibongile Mthembu)**

"No problem is so deep that it cannot be overcome, given the will of all parties, through discussion and negotiation rather than force and violence." **(Nelson Rolihlahla Mandela"Madiba)**

"Respect yourself enough to walk away from anything that no longer serves you, grows you, or makes you happy." **(Melvin Udo Richmond)**

"BELIEVE that the best will HAPPEN every day. Be aware that even trials are gifts to make us strong enough to face life and hard times." **(Lindiwe Kole)**

"To remain neutral, in a situation where the laws of the land virtually criticized God for having created men of color, was the sort of thing I could not, as a Christian, tolerate." **(Albert Lutuli)**

"Don't ever get to a point in your faith where you feel like the power of prayer isn't powerful enough for your situation."
(Letwin Dadirai Mandishona)

"Where there is no accountability there will be no responsibility."
(Pastor Sunday Adelaja)

"I am not African because I was born in Africa but because Africa was born in me." **(Kwame Nkrumah)**

"Corruption is not the only problem with the Nigerian system. Attitude has become another nightmare facing our country and it is dragging it down the mould. Attitude to time, attitude towards life, attitude how we view our subordinate, attitude towards money, attitude to how we perceive power be it the president, state administrators ,chairpersons of labour and even captains of industries, and unless this attitude issue is redressed we may find our nation in a bigger dilemma than what we are complaining of corruption." **(Raphael Ikechukwu Ogbuagu)**

"As a former governor, they will think you have all the money in the world, so they will continue to bring their needs to you. Therefore, think towards entrepreneurship, so that you can still meet the needs of people round you." **(Dr. Orji Kalu)**

"Sometimes people mistake the way I talk for what I am thinking." **(Idi Amin)**

"If you want to make peace with your enemy, you have to work with your enemy. Then he becomes your partner." **(Nelson Rolihlahla Mandela"Madiba)**

"The faith of a person is not only proven by how far he/she can push ahead regardless of the odds; but also by how much prepared a person is to suffer for what s/he believes in." **(Mike Kokwana)**

"Love your parents as they are the main reason why you are here. I have learned that people will forget what you said, they will forget what you did, but they will never forget how you made the feel." **(Sampson Abosi Okorie)**

"The philosophy of Africanism holds out the hope of a genuine democracy beyond the stormy sea of struggle." **(Robert Sobukwe)**

"The significance of chieftaincy titles in the Igbo land and some quarters of the country have been widely defeated as hoodlums have been conferred with the most prestigious titles in the land while the main achievers that have touched life in all areas of ratifications have been neglected." **(Raphael Ikechukwu Ogbuagu)**

"The immediate present belongs to the extremists, but the future belongs to the moderates." **(Helen Suzman)**

"I detest racialism, because I regard it as a barbaric thing, whether it comes from a black man or white man." **(Nelson Rolihlahla Mandela"Madiba)**

"It pains me when we spiritualize marriage failures: we must leave the devil alone in his hidden place. He has no part in our marriage failures. Capitalism is the only driving force for most failed marriages. And no matter how your marriage issues are, they might not get attention except you are 'accidentally' a billionaire or a celebrity of substance." **(Chika Osueze)**

"They want to do to Libya what they did to Iraq and what they are itching to do to Iran. They want to take back the oil, which was nationalized by these country's revolutions. They want to re-establish military bases that were shut down by the revolutions and to install client regimes that will subordinate the country's wealth and labour to imperialist corporate interests. All else is lies and deception." **(Col Muammar Gaddafi)**

"As we judge others so are we judged by others? The suspicious will always be tormented by suspicion." **(Nelson Rolihlahla Mandela"Madiba)**

"If money fails to become a blessing to you, it becomes a curse be warned." **(Chief Chidozie Monty Osita)**

"There are attributes such as character, vision, courage, empathy compassion and many more attributes that you simply would not find in a classroom or in a school. They in the homes, in our communities and they are also in the value system of our society." **(Hon Babatunde Raji Fashola)**

"It is better to show who you truly are, in that way you will earn the respect you deserved." **(Letwin Dadirai Mandishona)**

"Statistics are like bikinis, they don't reveal everything." **(Steve Komphela)**

"In this present generation, people now tend to have more rights than obligations." **(Raphael Ikechukwu Ogbuagu)**

"All the Great things are simple, and many can be expressed in a single word: freedom, justice, honour, duty, mercy, hope, love." **(Monica Vink)**

"I believe that in each of us lives another new improved version waiting to come to life. Most of us die never realizing our full potential." **(Jason Chiwuzie Osuafor)**

"Never try to understand why some people hate you. The issue is theirs, not yours!" **(Letwin Dadirai Mandishona)**

"American parents will drop their kids off at school with much love...but Nigerian parents in the other hand will drop their kids off with Abuse." **(Chief Obi)**

"The patient dog eats the fattest bone "But in Nigeria, the patient dog starves while the most aggressive dog enjoys the juiciest bones and even stores (banks) excess bones it and its puppies won't eat in their lifetime." **(Chidi Onuigbo)**

"You have to see the invisible in order to do the impossible" **(Rev Elias Ndeda)**

"Eventually, you'll meet someone right for you. And whether you share a minute, a month, or a lifetime with them is uncertain. But the fact that you found that person, even if for a moment, means more than the lifespan life allows you to have with them." **(Hrh Frank Times)**

"It was unity we wanted, not rebellion. We had watched our leaders rape our country. The country was so diseased that bold reforms were badly needed to settle social, moral, economic and political questions. We fully realised that to be caught planning, let alone acting, on our lines, was high treason. And the penalty for high treason is death." **(Major Emmanuel Ifeajuna, on Nigeria civil war)**

"You can suppress but if other things that are supposed to be there are not there, you will only suppress, sooner than later, it will rear its ugly head again, and what should be done, we should remove its root, stem and branches and I believe that too can be done." **(General Olusegun Obasanjo)**

"If people say you are dictator... you know they are saying this merely to tarnish and demean your status, then you don't pay much attention." **(President Robert Mugabe)**

"It will take a lion heart to have a lion share." **(Pamela Nkenke Blessing)**

"The world will provide you with stones every day. What you build from them, is your choice, wall, road or bridge, you may even chose to do nothing. At the end of the day, the world will know you by what you did with it irrespective of the situation." **(Raphael Ikechukwu Ogbuagu)**

"Running away will never solve the problem because they say, "When you abandon your own hill, the next one you climb will crumble." **(Wolof proverb)**

"Sometimes in the heat of the battle we might lose perspective on who the real enemy is." **(Hrm Eze Akuenwebe Emechebe)**

"You can't steal anyone who wasn't ready to leave, and no one can be taken from you if they didn't want to go." **(Bontle Modise)**

"When you were single, you dated married men and now that you're married, you're saying you can't share your husband. You need deliverance; it is called law of karma what an irony of life." **(Rapahel Ikechukwu Ogbuagu)**

"Success Will Bring Back The People That Left During The Struggle. But Definitely Not As Friends Again But As FANS, Be Motivated, Be Inspired!!!" **(Chika Nwankwo)**

"One who thinks deeply can deal with any situation because "Only a wise person can solve a difficult problem" **(Akan proverb)**

"Success is a reward for diligence. Your input into life and work directly determines your output and quality." **(Rev Elias Ndeda)**

"Young people have to understand the purpose of entrepreneurship is not necessary to become rich but to create a livelihood." **(Tuming Lee)**

"A life without challenge is a life without strength." **(Raphael Ikechukwu Ogbuagu)**

"Resentment is like drinking poison and then hoping it will kill your enemies." **(Nelson Rolihlahla Mandela"Madiba)**

"We get comfort from those who agree with us, but we get growth from only those who disagree with us." **(Contributed by Bruno Ezeani)**

"Let nobody rig for me." **(President Goodluck Jonathan)**

"To answer oppression with appropriate resistance requires knowledge of two kinds: in the first place, self-knowledge by the victim, which means awareness that oppression exists, an awareness that the victim has fallen from a great height of glory or promise into the present depths; secondly, the victim must know who the enemy is. He must know his oppressor's real name, not an alias, a pseudonym, or a nom de plume." **(Professor Chinua Achebe)**

"One must never compare one's self to any other person because "What is bad luck for one man is good luck for another." **(Ashanti proverb)**

"I grew up in an atmosphere where words were an integral part of culture." **(Professor Wole Soyinka)**

"Every pioneer needs a passion. Pioneers cannot be satisfied with mere maintenance, for they have nothing yet to maintain. They create from nothing. The common people often view them as eccentrics – but their passion attracts other pioneers." **(Dr. Oby Ezekwesili)**

"In any country there must be people who have to die. They are the sacrifices any nation has to make to achieve law and order." **(Idi Amin)**

"The thing about friends is that unlike family we choose who we become friends with, and the truth of the matter is that good friends are actually hard to come by, that's why when we have good friends it's important that we treat then with compassion, respect and love they deserve." **(Kgomotso Matsunyane)**

"The greater part of progress is the desire to progress." **(Jason Chiwuzie Osuafor)**

"We must all try to move from mediocrity to excellence." **(Raphael Ikechukwu Ogbuagu)**

"I want to build a new Nigeria for generations that will come after us. Will you support me to achieve this great vision?" **(President Goodluck Jonathan)**

"It is safer and wiser to cure unhealthy rivalry than to suppress it." **(Chief Obafemi Awolowo)**

"There is prayer from your lips and prayer from your heart. Prayer from your lips can do a lot; but prayer from your heart is God moving." **(Pastor Chris Oyakhilome)**

"If you are a man and you do not have a mentor, your wife is in trouble." **(Major Prophet Uebert Angel)**

"My origin is my heritage; it is not by my choice but by divine pronunciation." **(Chima Onyeagba Umealo)**

"Always live life to the fullest with INTEGRITY, PURPOSE, LOVE and WISDOM. You will be remembered by the good things you did and NOT by your achievements." **(Obinna Nwizu)**

"In Nigeria, People are attracted more towards bad things because being good has been turned into a boring duty." **(Chika Nwankwo)**

"Behind every wealthy person there is a story. And the story is always a story of ENDURANCE." **(Robert Appiah)**

"For there to be a positive change in Nigeria, it's citizens needs to re-examines its priorities , which starts from our attitudes towards what we regard as important to mankind." **(Raphael Ikechukwu Ogbuagu)**

"Football is like putting your trust on a beautiful woman you have not married, hoping you can win." **(Pastor Idah Peterside)**

"Keep alight the flame which you received in C.K.C. Onitsha." **(Rev Nicholas Tagbo)**

"Arnold Schwarzenegger Only Spoke 700 Words in Terminator 2 and Was Paid $15M.... How much has your gossip fetched you? Kindly Mind Your Business!!" **(Letwin Dadirai Mandishona)**

"Let them shut down all the western embassies in Africa, they are control dens to spy, milk, bleed, steal from and enslave the Africans further." **(Mutongoi Maluki)**

"A jealous mind talks about others. A confident heart lifts others up." **(Contributed by Gontse Tau)**

"Don't let desperation push you to evil because "Even when the crocodile is in need, it finds its meals in the river, not in the forest." **(Akan proverb)**

"Making a change when you don't do anything about your life then your life will never change so when you want the world to be a better place take a look at yourself and then make a change within, the change starts with you." **(Raphael Ikechukwu Ogbuagu)**

"Stories are not always innocent; they can be used to put you in the wrong crowd, in the party of the man who has come to dispossess you." **(Professor Chinua Achebe)**

"Don't ask for trouble but if granted the opportunity to handle trouble, you must be eqiped and ready enough to take it up." **(Steve Komphela)**

"Your wealth is hidden in those things that come easy to you and for which people always seek your opinion." **(Dr. Richie Achukwu)**

"He who thinks he is leading and has no one following him is only taking a walk." **(African Proverb)**

'There is plenty of room at the top because very few people care to travel beyond the average route, and so most of us seem satisfied to remain within the confine of mediocrity." **(Dr. Nnamdi Azikiwe)**

"Acting is my source of income. I cannot abandon my career because I have to make a living. Being an actor, just like being a footballer, does not stop you from serving Christ. Christianity is not religion; it is a lifestyle; how you live and treat people, obey the word of God, etc." **(Eucharia Anunobi)**

"I have come to understand that patience is the product of trials." **(Hrm Eze Akuenwebe Emechebe)**

"Let's commit towards our common goal, a nation where all of us are winners. Let's build a nation of champions! Let's build a nation that Walter Sisulu can be proud of. When I see him in the next life, I need to take good news to him." **(Nelson Rolihlahla Mandela"Madiba)**

"You have to take big risk to get big reward and be ready to accept responsibility when it goes wrong." **(Raphael Ikechukwu Ogbuagu)**

"Sex is a duty if done with your wife/husband, an art if done with your lover, education if done with a virgin, business transaction if done with a prostitute, social work if done with a divorcee, charity if done with a widow/widower, sacrifice if done with your hands." **(Nthabi Nen maph)**

"Don't wait for something big to occur. Start where you are, with what you have, and that will always leads you into something greater." **(Jason Chiwuzie Osuafor)**

"Love hurts when you break up with someone, hurts even more when someone breaks up with you but loves hurts the most when the person you love has no idea how you feel." **(Hildah Mashaba)**

"Strength shows, not only in the ability to persist but the ability to start over." **(Ziphorah Mflathelwa)**

"My ambition is not worth the blood of any Nigerian." **(President Goodluck Jonathan)**

"Even the strongest person, has a moment of weakness. Even the most intelligent person, has a moment of foolishness. Even the most vibrant individual, has a dull moment." **(Mike Kokwana)**

"Experience has taught me that there is no one secret to success but multiple secrets. You just have to pick the one that works for you." **(Tuming Lee)**

"In every situation we find ourselves at times, it is for the better, in the beginning we may see it as bad but a closer look at it will bring out the bright side of it." **(Raphael Ikechukwu Ogbuagu)**

"The greatest injustice to one is being silent in the face of moral injustice." **(Chima Onyeagba Umealo)**

"When the middle is well and good, the past is repaired and the future is prepared." **(Young Kizzye)**

"The emperor would prefer the poet to keep away from politics, and his domain, so that he can manage things the way he likes." **(Professor Chinua Achebe)**

"In order for us to fight corruption, nepotism and influence of vested interests which has plagued Lagos, we must make ourselves accountable." **(Hon Jimi Agbaje)**

"Honest criticism is hard to take, particularly from a relative, a friend, an acquaintance, or a stranger." **(Contributed by Bruno Ezeani)**

"Sport can create hope, where once there was only despair. It is more powerful than governments in breaking down racial barriers. It laughs in the face of all types of discrimination." **(Nelson Rolihlahla Mandela "Madiba)**

"No frivolities, we should look for water that we can use to quench our thirst before we can look for palm wine that we can use for enjoyment." **(Yoruba proverb)**

"A real philanthropist is one who is more bothered by the number of children going to bed without food and those that cannot afford to go to school." **(Raphael Ikechukwu Ogbuagu)**

"You do not need to give them free money. Rather, you can give them opportunities in business where you have dominant shares, or link them with other colleagues and friends who equally have investments, if you don't do this, they will abuse you as a selfish man, who does not give opportunities to others." **(Dr. Orji Kalu)**

"Nigerians are very unique set of people, they always have this magnitude and aroma within them, that it is not yet over until it is over and that have given them edge in various aspects of life." **(Mmatshilo Motsei)**

"Every man or woman in this passing phase of humanity must strive to create his or her own world; with utmost peace, non violence and courage they must sincerely do so, creating the energy vortex of harmonic vibrates of light, reflection, serene thoughts and internal peace." **(Dr. Carl Oshodi-Isibor)**

"When you marry an illiterate woman, you make stupid decision like Jonathan." **(Professor Wole Soyinka)**

"The history of the civil war still evokes a two-sided argument. He is a hero to many people, though they would more readily talk about his gold medal than his involvement in the war. There are people who think he was unjustifiably executed and others who believe the opposite." **(Chief Emeka Anyaoku, On Major Emmanuel Ifeajuna)**

"Some problems can't be corrected overnight because "A tree does not grow bent for thirty years that one should expect to straighten it in one." **(Ashanti proverb)**

"Destiny is the picture you have in your own mind of what you're about and fully convinced that it will come true." **(Melvin Udo Richmond)**

"Success comes to those who still have hope although they've been disappointed, betrayed, and failed before." **(Letwin Dadirai Mandishona)**

"Regime change is a diabolical illegal policy of interference in the domestic issues of my country." **(President Robert Mugabe)**

"Raise Your Standards!!! Stop Praising Men And Women For Their Physical Appearance; Instead Praise Them For Their Value, Self Respect, Attitude And Self Worth!!!" **(Lindiwe Kole)**

"It's not the load that breaks you down. It's the way you carry it." **(Chika Nwankwo)**

"It is meaningless to say you worked for all you have got, some people work more than you yet they do not have a quarter of what you have got, does it mean they don't work hard? They do but it takes the special grace of God for us to succeed in life and if we are fortunate to see ourselves there, it is our obligation to take care of those around us; especially the people who brought us into the world." **(Sampson Abosi Okorie)**

"Stupidity is what we all have in common as human beings, but some people insist that improving it is their entitlement." **(Pete Edochie)**

"There are few true leaders amongst us, what we now have are opportunist who have taken advantage of the present situations to become overnight leaders, and all we have seen in their various leadership capacities are greedy and selfish bosses, who enjoy lording over their subjects as against the true leaders that lead with, compassion and zeal for the upliftment of mankind." **(Raphael Ikechukwu Ogbuagu)**

"To gossip about others is a sin, but to gossip about self is healthy and good." **(Nelson Rohohlahla Mandela"Madiba)**

"The secret of life is to have no fear... I do not tell lies about anybody. That's why i win all my fights." **(Fela Kuti)**

"Do not hustle with people who do not have the same drive and ambition as you do, people who have nothing to lose if the deal falls through. You must hustle with people whose hunger for success is similar to yours or even deeper. People who won't abandon you when the going gets tough." **(Gayton McKenzie)**

"Most important time to hold our temper is when the other person has lost it." **(Contributed by Bruno Ezeani)**

"Those who would manipulate the victims of terrorism for their own benefit are engaging in a similar kind of evil: Psychological terrorism." **(President Goodluck Jonathan)**

"Where there is no accountability, there will be no responsibility." **(Pastor Sunday Adelaja)**

"It would be remiss of me if I did not express my sincere appreciation to the leadership of the ANC who saw fit to trust me with the responsibilities of a member of the Executive. For this I thank President Jacob Zuma, current Deputy and former President Kgalema Motlanthe and former President Thabo Mbeki. My greatest honour, however, has been the incredible faith and confidence that Nelson Mandela had in my abilities and I hope that I was able to meet his expectations. My conduct and actions were, and remain, guided by his words and his example. I must thank the ANC for the opportunity to serve and flourish and assisted me to live out the values and the policies that the movement has always represented to me and to the people of the country." **(Trevor Manuel)**

"My past is my past, it made me who I am, I have no regrets, wouldn't change a thing. I just don't live there anymore." **(Letwin Dadirai Mandishona)**

"Dreams are eternal, you never stop dreaming, once you accomplish one dream, you still dream to conquer something else and you must just know that, no one in this world, no one, unless if it is your maker can take away your dreams. So keep at it!!!" **(Nandi Mngoma)**

"When the fool is told a proverb, its meaning has to be explained to him." **(Pete Edochie)**

"Yes, nothing will really ruffle me because I am willing and ready to serve but I am not desperate to serve. That is what keeps me going." **(President Goodluck Jonathan)**

"Time is the most precious element of human existence. A successful person knows how to put energy into time and how to draw success from time." **(Obinna Nwizu)**

"Having an honest man in this time and age is like finding a virgin in a maternity ward." **(Chima Onyeagba Umealo)**

"A smelling virginal is still far better than the neatest anus, let's call a spade a spade; homosexuality is a big no for Africa." **(President Robert Mugabe)**

"A society that does not value its older people denies its roots and endangers its future." **(Nelson Rohohlahla Mandela "Madiba)**

"Impossibility is the language of mediocre. All stars in any field of human endeavour are POSSIBILITITARIANS." **(Pamela Nkenke Blessing)**

"Life Is So Ironic. It Takes Sadness To Know What Happiness Is, Noise To Appreciate Silence and Absence To Value Presence." **(Contributor Elizabeth Lizzy)**

"An eror is an error if committed once and an error becomes suspicious if committed twice and thrice. But the minute it become more consistent, then it become deliberate." **(Steve Komphela)**

"Nigeria's politics has to mature. We have to realize that once elections are over, we must all accept the outcome and learn to work with each other. It is a big, big misconception that you have to like people to work with them or to build upon what they started. If man had kept reinventing the wheel, we would never have invented the plane." **(Ben Murray Bruce)**

"Even Britain is worried, they said their problem is that if one million Nigerians come to Britain, in 10 years, there will be 10 million Nigerians in Britain and they will rather keep us here." **(General Olusegun Obasanjo)**

"If your opponents are very fast on the counter and want space behind your defensive line, if you give them that space you are stupid." **(Monica Vink)**

"While revolutionaries as individuals can be murdered, you cannot kill ideas." **(Thomas Sankara)**

"Never do anything that might reflect badly on your school or family." **(Rev Fr Nicholas Tagbo)**

"Failure is simply the opportunity to begin again. This time more intelligently. Don't be afraid to fail because only through failure do you learn to succeed. Take chances, make mistakes. That's how you grow. Pain nourishes your courage. You have to fail in order to practice being brave. Keep trying and believe in yourself." **(Hrh Frank Times)**

"When you think negatively, you attract negativity. That is the awesome power of the mind." **(Letwin Dadirai Mandishona)**

"A kiss is a lovely trick designed by nature to stop speech when words become superfluous." **(Young Kizzye)**

"I have come to view challenges as my partner in growth, that aids me to reach my desired goals and calling in life." **(Raphael Ikechukwu Ogbuagu)**

"As a child, success meant scoring a on every exam, but now I take it to mean good health, close family and friends, achievement in my work, and helping others." **(Ahmed Zewail)**

"I know the road to development and modernization is difficult; I know that it is long and I also know that the next stages will be even tougher and longer. But I have faith in God, I believe in my people, in the wisdom of our leadership and the future of our nation. I am confident we will realize our goals. Our vision is clear, our road is paved and the clock is ticking. There is no more time for hesitation or half-baked goals or solutions. Development is an ongoing process and the race for excellence has no finish line." **(Hon Babatunde Raji Fashola)**

"Until a statement is challenged it becomes a fact." **(Dr. Richie Achukwu)**

"The real art of conversation is not only to say the right thing at the right time, but also to leave unsaid the wrong thing at the tempting moment." **(Contributed by Bruno Ezeani)**

"It should also be understood that apart from Floyd Mayweather (Jnr) and the late Italian American Rocky Marciano, there is no boxer that has not had his waterloo, his Nixon of sort nature has made life generally and boxing so. For a Tyson there is a Buster Douglas or Holyfield, for a Holyfield there is a Riddick Bowe or Michael Moore. For a Mohammed Ali there is a Ken Norton or a Joe Frasier and for a Joe Frazier there is a George Foreman and for a George Foreman there is a Mohammed Ali. For a Sugar Ray Leonard there is a Roberto Duran, For a Marvellous Hugler there is a Sugar Ray Leonard, For a Buster Douglas there is a Holyfield and Bone Crusher Smith, the list goes on and on." **(Raphael Ikechukwu Ogbuagu)**

"Humility is a great strength not a weakness." **(Lehoko Noe)**

"A horny Igbo girl's nipple can be used to crush diamond." **(Pete Edochie)**

"Do not allow erection to give you direction for whatever a man soweth he alone shall reap." **(Chima Onyeagba Umealo)**

"Live life as though nobody is watching, and express yourself as though everyone is listening." **(Nelson Rohohlahla Mandela Madiba)**

"Bad things will happen and good things too. Your life will be full of surprises. Miracles happen only where there has been suffering. So taste your grief to the fullest. Don't try and press it down. Do not hide from it. Do not escape. It is life too. It is truth. But it will pass and time will put a strange honey in the bitterness. That's the way life goes." **(Ben Okri)**

"There are three things the human brain cannot resist noticing Food, attractive people and danger." **(Letwin Dadirai Mandishona)**

"We have corrupted the Nigeria system and eventually the system turned around and corrupted us." **(Contributed by Matthew Okafor)**

"Lets us choose the harder right instead of the easier wrong." **(Rev Father Nicholas Tagbo)**

"The thought and fear of witches and wizard in Nigeria has crippled many from pursuing their goals and fulfilling their destiny's with God." **(Raphael Ikechukwu Ogbuagu)**

"When the son of a Hunter is afraid of the sound of a gunshot; his mother's faithfulness should be questioned." **(Pete Edochie)**

"My dreams have always been bigger than the contacts I have in my phone book." **(Tuming Lee)**

"You can never be promoted until your belief is tested." **(Contributed by Nomthandazo Ade Angwenya)**

"A clear vision of what you want, be it professional or personal, is the solid foundation around which a balanced life can be moulded." **(Dr. Martie Lancellas)**

"The key to turning your adversity into advancement is looking at it from God's viewpoint. No matter what may be the cause, make up your mind to learn from it." **(Hrm Eze Akuenwebe Emechebe)**

"The friends you surround yourself with can either break or bless your marriage." **(Isaac Kubvoruno)**

"It is, I think, enough for me to say that life itself is, from the cradle to the grave, a series of unbroken risks. I make no boast about this, but those who know me intimately will testify to the fact that I have never, at any time, shrunk from taking my full share of the risks which life, with its unending opportunities and vicissitudes, offers." **(Chief Obafemi Awolowo)**

"If I lose this election, of course I will go back to my village. The country is not my father's estate." **(President Goodluck Jonathan)**

"Your set time is coming for good or for bad but certainly for good for the man who wins is the man who thinks he can." **(Jason Chiwuzie Osuafor)**

"Be careful the devil doesn't always leave footprints for you to know where your troubles are coming from." **(Raphael Ikechukwu Ogbuagu)**

"Hustlers succed not because of anything, they succed despite everything due to their will power." **(Gayton Mckenzie)**

"But unless we are given the chance to think freely and we fail, other races should not conclude that we are inferior in intelligence. Every man is fundamentally the same irrespective of his racial inclination. God has been used as a tool to mentally enslave the People of Africa keeping us in perpetual paralysis development wise. This is the time of Awakening. Rise up Africa for this is the time." **(Hugo Africa)**

Hastings Kamuzu Banda letter of Apology to the people of Malawi.

"Systems of government are dynamic and they are bound to change in accordance with the wishes and aspirations of the people...During my term in office, I selflessly dedicated myself to the good cause of Mother Malawi in the fight against Poverty, Ignorance and Disease among many other issues; but if within the process, those who worked in my government or through false pretence in my name or indeed unknowingly by me, pain and suffering was caused to anybody in this country in the name of nationhood, I offer my sincere apologies. I also appeal for a spirit of reconciliation and forgiveness amongst us all...Our beautiful country has been nicknamed `**The Warm Heart of Africa**' and we have been admired for our warmth and spirit of hard work. This admiration calls not only for a need for us to look at our past and present and draw lessons from it, but there is even a greater need for us to look forward to the future in our endeavours to reconstruct and reconcile if we have to move forward at all.

Nigeria's Youth Forum was welcomed to address Nigerians in a meeting here in South Africa

The chairman, along with the Nigerian youth forum is extending their warm welcome to you all, his Excellency our Ambassador, our future president and every other protocol observed. This is our first meeting for the year, we are glad to have come this far despite all the troubling afflictions, discouragements, and challenges. I should say that behind every great accomplishment there should be perseverance, and in every vision there is a hurdle. The vision and purpose of the Nigerian youth forum is not a speculation. Despite all rough voyages, we still made an Amazon progress and overwhelming impact in our society.

As an organization that has the objective and vision, we have been able to foster peace and unity in the southern part of Johannesburg South Africa. It is important to have a goal and set an eye on the reward while pursuing it. Our motto is to encourage peace and unity in the society we live in, and we believe that unity establishes one and peace enables us to live in harmony. Our trust in God and our strength come from Him. We know and believe that God is and can never be mocked, for whatever a man soweth, so shall he reap, so let therefore depart from Evil.

In conclusion, the measure you use will be used back to you. The only poison you have is in your heart, only those who love God and the truth, will see his kingdom. No family is too poor, no house is too filthy, and no town is too remote, and no country is too ignorant to receive the good news that life could still be better. Ask yourself, what really matters in life?

What will matter is not what you bought, but what you build, it is not what you got, but what you give, what matters is not your success, but your significance; it's not what you learn but what you are taught. What matters in any act is integrity, commission; sacrifices that empower and enrich others.

Lastly, what will matter is not your competence but your character. It is not how many people you know, but how many will feel a lasting loss when you are gone. It is not your money; it is your memory of those who loved you and for the cause we have been fighting for, let us strive together to take Nigerian youth forum in South Africa to a new height in leadership as we give our future president of Nigerian union support for posterity and for generations to come.

Viva Nigerian youth forum, Viva Nigerian Union, Viva South Africa. "Hon Beltus Ikenna Nwanojuo." **(Chairman Nigerian Youth Forum South Africa)**

To honour my Mentor and principal, Christ the Kings College Onitsha, Anambra State Nigeria. Your impact and influence in our various lives that passed through you cannot be easily forgotten; hence I bring forth your favourite prayers for the school that has lived in our hearts and memories. CKC COLLEGE PRAYER –Rev Fr Nicolas Chukwuemeka Tagbo

Oh God Our Father, Thou Searcher of Men's hearts. Help us to draw near to Thee in Sincerity and truth. May our religion be filled with gladness and may our worship of Thee be natural.
Strengthen and increase our admiration for honest dealing and clean thinking and suffer not our hatred of hypocrisy and pretence ever to diminish. Encourage us in our endeavour to live above the common level of life .Make us to choose the harder right instead of the easier wrong and never to be content with a half truth when the whole can be one. Endow us with courage that is borne of loyalty to that entire in noble and worthy: Loyalty to our parents, loyalty to our class, loyalty to our College and loyalty to our country. Loyalty that scorns to compromise with vice and injustice and knows no fear when truth and right are in jeopardy. Guard us against flippancy and irreverence in the

sacred things of life. Grant us new ties of friendships and new opportunities for service. Kindle our hearts in fellowship with those cheerful countenances and soften our hearts with sympathy for those who sorrow and suffer. Help us to maintain the honour of our College untarnished and undiminished and to show forth in our lives the ideals of CHRIST THE KING COLLEGE: Bonitas, Disciplina Scientia, in doing our duties to Thee Oh Lord. To our College and to our country. All of these we ask in the name of our great friend and Master, Jesus Christ. Amen!!

Inspirational Quotes from Authors, writers and philosophers from the American Continent.

"It takes sacrifice to serve the need of other people; the sacrifice of our own pride and prejudice among other things." **(Stephen Covey)**

"The truth will set you free but first it will make you angry." **(John Maxwell)**

"The media is the most powerful entity on earth. They have the power to make the innocent guilty and make the guilty innocent, and that's power, because they control the minds of the masses." **(Malcolm X)**

"Good thinkers can always overcome difficulties including lack of resources." **(John Maxwell)**

"In order to make friends, one must first be friendly." **(Dale Carnegie)**

"It takes intelligence to make real comedy, and it takes a reality base to create all that little stuff I like to do that makes you giggle inside." **(Chris Tucker)**

"I failed in some subject in exam, but my friend passed in all. Now he is an engineer in Microsoft and I am the owner of Microsoft." **(Bill Gate)**

"In order to succeed, your desire for success should be greater than your fear of failure." **(Bill Cosby)**

"I am not sure what the future holds but I do know that I'm going to be positive." **(Nicole Kidman)**

"We cannot build our own future without helping others to build theirs." **(Bill Clinton)**

"Disappointment is the difference between expectation and reality." **(John Maxwell)**

"The best way to destroy an enemy is to make him a friend." **(Abraham Lincoln)**

"Life is most persistent and urgent .The question is what we are doing for others." **(Dr. Martin Luther King Jnr)**

"I am very proud to be black, but black is not all I am. That's my cultural historical background, my genetic makeup, but it's not all of who I am nor is it the basis from which I answer every question." **(Denzel Washington)**

"If you are going to achieve excellence in big things, you develop the habit in little matters. Excellence is not an exception, it is a prevailing attitude." **(Colin Powell)**

"Friendship is the hardest thing in the world to explain. It's not something you learn in school. But if you haven't learned the meaning of friendship, you really haven't learned anything." **(Muhammad Ali)**

"Before planning where you want to go, decide who you want to be." **(Alan Cohen)**

"It takes 20 years to build a reputation and five minutes to ruin it. If you will think about that you'll do things differently." **(Warren Buffett)**

"If a guy wants you for your breast, thighs and legs send him to KFC, you are not cheap value meat." **(Nicolas Cage)**

"Honesty is the first chapter in the book of wisdom." **(Thomas Jefferson)**

"A people without the knowledge of their past history, origin and culture is like a tree without a root." **(Marcus Garvey)**

"I believe there are many soul mates, because my soul has a lot of different facets and it needs a lot of different..." **(Cameron Diaz)**

"If your view is that immigrant are either fundamentally bad to the country or that we actually have the option of deporting 11 million immigrants, I reject that." **(President Barack Obama)**

"The real differences around the world today are not between Jews and Arabs; Protestants and Catholics; Muslims, Croats, and Serbs. The real differences are between those who embrace peace and those who would destroy it. Between those who look to the future and those who cling to the past. Between those who open their arms and those who are determined to clench their fists." **(Bill Clinton)**

"Money was never a big motivation for me except as a way to keep score. The real excitement is playing the game." **(Donald Trump)**

"Most people are too indifferent or lazy to acquire facts with which to think accurately. They prefer to act on opinions created by guesswork or snap-judgements" **(Napoleon Hill)**

"Every person has a C.E.O in their head and their heart. Depending on your vision, your C.E.O will be either your "Chief Excuse Officer" or your "Chief Expectation Officer" Show up "EXPECTING" to win in 2014... GAME ON!" **(Hasheem Francis, CEO Built to Prosper)**

"Success is not achieved by winning all the time. Real success comes when we rise after we fall." **(Muhammad Ali)**

"The ability to speak several languages is an asset, but the ability to keep your mouth shut in any language is priceless." **(Terressa Kennedy)**

"You can give a person knowledge, but you can't make them think. Some people want to remain fools, only because the truth requires change." **(Tony A. Gaskins Jnr)**

"When I am able to resist the temptation to judge others, I can see them as teachers of forgiveness in my life, reminding me that I can only have peace of mind when I forgive rather than judge." **(Gerald Jampolsky)**

"Do one act of kindness each day of the year and change 365 lives" **(Anthony Douglas Williams)**

"Love is a Virus. It can happen to anybody at any time." **(Dr. Maya Angelou)**

"Black people are the most talented people in the world." **(Jamie Foxx)**

"The LESS time you spend criticizing how others choose to live, the MORE time you can spend improving the quality of your life." **(Dodinsky)**

"Repetition can't transform lie into truth." **(Franklin D. Roosevelt)**

"In life you need either inspiration or desperation." **(Tony Robbins)**

"We all want progress, but if you're on the wrong road, progress means doing an about-turn and walking back to the right road; in that case, the man who turns back soonest is the most progressive." **(C. S. Lewis)**

"It's not whether you get knocked down; it's whether you get up." **(Vince Lombardi)**

"Alone we can do so little; together we can do so much." **(Helen Keller)**

"No matter what people tell you, words and ideas can change the world." **(Robin Williams)**

"In business, if you have courage, you can win. You don't have to be the fastest, or the smartest. You have to have tenacity, and also have the fastest and smartest work for you." **(Hasheem Francis, CEO Built to Prosper)**

"Never argue with stupid people, they will drag you down to their level and then beat you with experience." **(Mark Twain)**

"I try to be as honest and open as I am with everything that I do because it's just, um, It helps me, you know, like whether it's stand up or singing or act. I just try to stay true." **(Jamie Foxx)**

"Silence is golden when you can't think of a good answer." **(Muhammad Ali)**

"Check the records. There has never been an undisciplined person who was a champion. Regardless of the field of endeavour, you'll find this to be true." **(Zig Ziglar)**

"You will not value generosity until you value people." **(John Maxwell)**

"Doing business without advertising is like winking at a girl in the dark. You know what you are doing, but nobody else does." **(Stuart Henderson Britt)**

"One of the lessons that I grew up with was to always stay true to yourself and never let what somebody else says distract you from your goals. And so when I hear about negative and false attacks, I really don't invest any energy in them because I know who I am." **(Michelle Obama)**

"Each person must live their life as a model for others." **(Rosa Parks)**

"I define joy as a sustained sense of well-being and internal peace - a connection to what matters." **(Oprah Winfrey)**

"There is some good in the worst of us and some evil in the best of us. When we discover this, we are less prone to hate our enemies." **(Dr. Martin Luther King Jnr)**

"A word to the wise isn't necessary - it's the stupid ones that need the advice." **(Bill Cosby)**

"I just want to keep trying to surprise myself and I want to keep challenging myself." **(Jennifer Aniston)**

"Its fine to celebrate success but it is more important to heed the lessons of failure." **(Bill Gates)**

"Sometimes when I consider what tremendous consequences come from little things, I am tempted to think there are no little things." **(Bruce Barton)**

"Sir, my concern is not whether God is on our side; my greatest concern is to be on God's side, for God is always right." **(Abraham Lincoln)**

"I hope the millions of people I've touched have the optimism and desire to share their goals and hard work and persevere with a positive attitude." **(Michael Jordan)**

"Change is the law of life. And those who look only to the past or present are certain to miss the future." **(John F. Kennedy)**

"One of the ways to break down complex or difficult issues is to ask questions." **(John Maxwell)**

"You can't have empowerment without first having trust. If you don't trust the people you are working with or the person you have a relationship

Colin Powell philosophy

"The less you associate with some people, the more your life will improve. Any time you tolerate mediocrity in others, it increases your mediocrity. An important attribute in successful people is their impatience with negative thinking and negative acting people. As you grow, your associate will change. Some of your friends will not want to go on; they will want to stay where they are. Friends that don't help you climb will want you to crawl. Your friends will stretch your vision or choke your dream. Those that don't increase you will eventually decrease you."

Consider this

Never receive counsel from unproductive people. Never discuss your problems with someone incapable of contributing to the solution, because those who never succeed themselves are always first to tell you how. Not everyone has the right to speak into your life. You are certain to get the worst of the bargain when you exchange ideas with the wrong person. Don't follow anyone who is not going anywhere. With some people you spend evening, with others you invest it. Be careful where you stop to inquire for directions along the road to life.

Wise is the person who fortifies his life with right friendships. If you run with wolves you will learn how to howl, but if you associate with eagles you will learn how to soar to great heights. A mirror reflects a man's face, but what he is really shown by the kind of friends he chooses. The simple but true fact of life is that you become like those with whom you closely associate for good and the bad.

Note: Do not be mistaken. This is applicable to family as well as friends, yes do love. Appreciate and be thankful for your family, for they will always be your family no matter what. Just know that they are human first and though they are family to you, they may be friends to someone else and will fit somewhere in the criteria above.

"In prosperity our friends knows us, in adversity we know our friends" Never make someone a priority when you are only an option for them. If you are going to achieve excellence it is not an exception, it is a prevailing attitude" (Colin Powell).

Inspirational Quotes and philosophy from Authors, writers and philosophers from the European continent

"The great pleasure in life is in doing what people say you cannot do." **(Walter Bageholt)**

"The world is a dangerous place to live not because of the people who are evil but also because of the people who don't do anything about it." **(Albert Einstein)**

"To win takes a complete commitment of mind and body. When you can't make that commitment they don't call you a champion anymore." **(Rocky Marciano)**

"You shall know the truth, and the truth shall make you mad." **(Aldous Huxley)**

"Men occasionally stumble over the truth but most pick themselves up and hurry off as if nothing happened." **(Winston Churchill)**

"Good words are worth much and cost little." **(George Herbert)**

"Life is not meant to be easy, my child; but take courage -- it can be delightful." **(George Bernard Shaw)**

"Ferdinand was a great player, without a doubt the best centre-half I ever played with. I would say for a time as well he was the best centre-half in the world." **(Paul Scholes)**

"The best of men choose one thing in preference to all else, immortal glory in preference to mortal good; whereas the masses simply glut themselves like cattle." **(Heraclitus)**

"Every person has three characters; that which he exhibits, that which he has and that which he thinks he has." **(Alphonse Karr)**

"The secret of change is to focus all of your energy not on fighting the old, but on building the new." **(Socrates)**

"I feel the older I get, the more I'm learning to handle life. Being on this quest for a long time, it's all about finding yourself." **(Ringo Starr)**

"The most wonderful of all things in life is the discovery of another human being with whom one's relationship has a growing depth, beauty and joy as the years increase. This inner progressiveness of love between two human beings is a most marvellous thing; it cannot be found by looking for it or by passionately wishing for it. It is a sort of divine accident, and the most wonderful of all things in life." **(Sir Hugh Walpole)**

"One secret of success in life is for a man to be ready for his opportunity when it comes." **(Benjamin Disraeli)**

"There is no pillow as soft as a clear conscience." **(French Proverb)**

"Mediocrity knows nothing higher than itself but instantly recognizes genius." **(Sir Arthur Conan Doyle)**

"Patriotism is your conviction that this country is superior to all other countries because you were born in it." **(George Bernard Shaw)**

"Manchester United is the most romantic club in the history of world football. And that will never change." **(Sir Alex Ferguson)**

"To speak gratitude is courteous and pleasant, to enact gratitude is generous and noble, but to live gratitude is to touch Heaven." **(Johannes A. Gaertner)**

"Tell me who admires and loves you, and I will tell you who you are." **(Antoine de Saint-Exupery)**

"My Philosophy is it is none of my business what people say of me and think of me. I am what I am and I do what I do. I expect nothing and accept everything and it makes life so much easier." **(Anthony Hopkins)**

"Human nature will not easily find a helper better than love." **(Socrates)**

"Be master of your petty annoyances and conserve your energies for the big, worthwhile things. It isn't the mountain ahead that wears you out- it's the grain of sand in your shoe." **(Robert Service)**

"We can easily forgive a child who is afraid of the dark; the real tragedy of life is when we are afraid of the light." **(Plato)**

"There is only one corner of the universe you can be certain of improving and that is your life." **(Aldous Huxley)**

"One of the most beautiful qualities of true friendship is to understand and to be understood." **(Lucius Annaeus Seneca)**

"Genius could be the ability to say a profound thing in a simple way." **(Charles Bukowski)**

"Courage is what it takes to stand up and speak; courage is also what it takes to sit down and listen." **(Winston Churchill)**

"The service we render others is really the rent we pay for our room on earth." **(Sir Wilfred Grenfell)**

"Wisdom is one thing, to know how to make true judgment, how all things are steered through all things." **(Heraclitus)**

"Discovery consists of seeing what everyone has seen and thinking what nobody else has thought." **(Jonathan Swift)**

"As long as I have any choice, I will stay only in a country where political liberty, toleration, and equality of all citizens before the law are the rule." **(Albert Einstein)**

"If you want to build a ship, don't drum up the people to collect wood and don't assign them tasks and work, but rather teach them to long for the endless immensity of the sea." **(Antoine de Saint-Exupery)**

"Lost wealth may be replaced by industry, lost knowledge by study, lost health by temperance or medicine, but lost time is gone forever." **(Samuel Smiles)**

"A good decision is based on knowledge and not numbers." **(Plato)**

"Three passions, simple but overwhelmingly strong, have governed my life: the longing for love, the search for knowledge, and unbearable pity for the suffering of mankind." **(Bertrand Russell)**

"Courage is first of human qualities because it is the quality which guarantees the others." **(Aristotle)**

"Circumstances are beyond human control, but our conduct is in our own power." **(Benjamin Disraeli)**

"Everyone who wants to do good to the human race always ends in universal bullying." **(Aldous Huxley)**

"Men who wish to know about the world must learn about it in its particular details." **(Heraclitus)**

"If one does not know to which port one is sailing, no wind is favorable." **(Seneca)**

"Men are born ignorant, not stupid; they are made stupid by education." **(Bertrand Russell)**

"No man becomes rich unless he enriches others." **(Andrew Carnegie)**

"To maintain a joyful family requires much from both the parents and the children. Each member of the family has to become, in a special way, the servant of the others." **(Pope John Paul II)**

"An unexamined life is not worth living." **(Socrates)**

"Where there is laughter there is always more health than sickness." **(Phyllis Bottome)**

"We live in a world where we have to hide to make love, while violence is practised in broad day light." **(John Lennon)**

"Everybody is a genius. But if you judge a fish by its ability to climb a tree it will live its whole life believing that it is stupid." **(Albert Einstein)**

"You can't make the other fellow feel important in your presence if you secretly feel that he is nobody." **(Les Giblin)**

"Coward die many times before their death, valiant ever taste of death but once." **(William Shakespeare)**

"You cannot cross the ocean unless you have the courage to lose sight of the shore." **(Christopher Columbus)**

"A healthy attitude is contagious but don't wait to catch it from others. Be a carrier." **(Tom Stoppard)**

"Do not spoil what you have by desiring what you have not but remember that what you have was, once among the things only hope for." **(Epicurie)**

"The time you enjoy wasting is not wasted time." **(Bertrand Russell)**

"You may have to fight a battle more than once to win it." **(Margaret Thatcher)**

"Weakness of attitude becomes weakness of character." **(Albert Einstein)**

"The truth is incontrovertible. Malice may attack it, ignorance may deride it, but in the end, there it is." **(Winston Churchill)**

"I count him braver who overcomes his desires than him who overcomes his enemies." **(Aristotle)**

"Most people say that it is the intellect which makes a great scientist. They are wrong, it is character." **(Albert Einstein)**

"Curiosity will conquer fear even more than bravery will." **(James Stephens)**

"Life isn't about finding yourself. Life's about creating yourself." **(George Bernard Shaw)**

"I will always regard the 81 times that I played for England, with immense pride. These are all treasured memories that will last a lifetime." **(Rio Ferdinand)**

"No man was ever wise by chance." **(Seneca)**

"He who does not expect will not find out the unexpected, for it is trackless and unexplored." **(Heraclitus)**

"The world as we have created it is a process of our thinking. It cannot be change without changing our thinking." **(Albert Einstein)**

"He who has never learned to obey cannot be a good commander." **(Aristotle)**

"Friends show their love in times of trouble, not in happiness." **(Euripides)**

"Never frown because you never know who might be falling in love with your smile." **(Justine Milton)**

"In order to be irreplaceable one must always be different." **(Coco Chanel)**

Inspirational Quotes and philosophies from Authors, writers and philosophers from all continents of the world

"To lose patience is to lose the battle." **(Gandhi)**

"Faith keeps the person who keeps the faith." **(Mother Teresa)**

"We are formed and moulded by our thoughts. Those whose minds are shaped by selfless thoughts give joy when they speak or act. Joy follows them like a shadow that never leaves them." **(Buddha)**

"People take different roads seeking fulfilment and happiness. Just because they are not on your road doesn't mean they have gotten lost." **(Dalai Lama)**

"He who is contented is rich." **(Lao Tzu)**

"If we accept that a mother can kill even her own child, how can we tell other people to not kill each other? Any country that accepts abortion is not teaching its people to love, but to use any violence to get what they want." **(Mother Teresa)**

"Simplicity is the key to brilliance." **(Bruce Lee)**

"Three things cannot be long hidden: the sun, the moon, and the truth." **(Buddha)**

"Gratitude is the sweetest thing in a seeker's life - in all human life. If there is gratitude in your heart, then there will be tremendous sweetness in your eyes." **(Sri Chinmoy)**

"There is nothing more dreadful than the habit of doubt. Doubt separates people. It is a poison that disintegrates friendships and breaks up pleasant relations. It is a thorn that irritates and hurts; it is a sword that kills." **(Buddha)**

"Be content with what you have; rejoice in the way things are. When you realize there is nothing lacking, the whole world belongs to you." **(Lao Tzu)**

"There are two kinds of people; those who seek but cannot find, and those who find but still want more." **(Ali Abi Abi Talib)**

"Greatness is not achieved by never failing but by rising above every time we fail." **(Confucius)**

"An insincere and evil friend is more to be feared than a wild beast; a wild beast may wound your body, but an evil friend will wound your mind." **(Buddha)**

"A man who was completely innocent, offered himself as a sacrifice for the good of others, including his enemies, and became the ransom of the world. It was a perfect act." **(Gandhi)**

"Disappointment is often the breaking plaster which hides a golden future." **(Buddha)**

"Always be yourself, express yourself, have faith in yourself, do not go out and look for a successful personality and duplicate it." **(Bruce Lee)**

"The true democrat is he who with purely nonviolent means defends his liberty and, therefore, his country's and ultimately that of the whole of mankind." **(Gandhi)**

"They took away my dream of playing in a world cup final, but the dream of being world champion has not been ended." **(Neymar)**

"Do the difficult things while they are easy and do the great things while they are small. A journey of a thousand miles must begin with a single step." **(Lao Tzu)**

"A poor man is like a foreigner in his own country." **(Ali Abi Abi Talib)**

"You cannot overcome the enemy until you have healed in yourself that which you find despicable in them." **(Chinese Proverb)**

"If you find serenity and happiness, they may be jealous, but be happy anyway." **(Mother Teresa)**

"In the practice of tolerance, one's enemy is the best teacher." **(Dalai Lama)**

"Choose a job you love and you will never have to work a day in your life." **(Confucius)**

"The biggest disease today is not leprosy or tuberculosis but rather the feeling of being unwanted." **(Mother Teresa)**

"You can search throughout the entire universe for someone who is more deserving of your love and affection than you are yourself, and that person is not to be found anywhere. You yourself, as much as anybody in the entire universe deserve your love and affection." **(Buddha)**

"To see things in seed, that is genius." **(Lao Tzu)**

"A wise man can learn more from a foolish question than a fool can learn from a wise answer." **(Bruce Lee)**

"The general who advances without coveting fame and retreats without fearing disgrace, whose only thought is to protect his country and do good service for his sovereign, is the jewel of the kingdom." **(Sun Tzu)**

"The superior man understands what is right .The inferior man understands what will sell." **(Confucius)**

"Your worst enemy cannot harm you as much as your own unguarded thought." **(Buddha)**

"If you want others to be happy, practice compassion. If you want to be happy, practice compassion." **(Dalai Lama)**

"When you say yes to others, make sure you are not saying no to yours." **(Paulo Coelho)**

"Strength does not come from physical capacity. It comes from an indomitable will." **(Gandhi)**

"If you are depressed you are living in the past, if you are anxious you are living in the future, if you are at peace you are living in the present." **(Lao Tzu)**

"Even the rich are hungry for love, for being cared for, for being wanted for having someone to call their own." **(Mother Teresa)**

"I cannot think of any need in a childhood as strong as the need of a father protection." **(Sigmund Freud)**

"Before the throne of the Almighty, man will be judged not by his acts but by his intentions. For God alone reads our hearts." **(Gandhi)**

"It is poverty to decide that a child must die so that you may live as you wish." **(Mother Teresa)**

"He who wishes to secure the good of others has already secured his own." **(Confucius)**

"Let us touch the dying, the poor, the lonely, and unwanted according to grace we received and let us not be ashamed or slow to do this humble work." **(Mother Teresa)**

"A country where flowers are priced so as to make them a luxury has yet to learn the first principles of civilization." **(Chinese Proverb)**

"I am learning to understand rather than immediately judge or to be judged. I cannot blindly follow the crowd and accept their approach. I will not allow myself to indulge in the usual manipulating game of role creation. Fortunately for me, my self-knowledge has transcended that and I have come to understand that life is best to be lived and not to be conceptualized. I am happy because I am growing daily and I do honestly not know where the limit lies. To be certain, every day there can be a revelation or a new discovery. I treasure the memory of the past misfortunes. It has added more to my bank of fortitude." **(Bruce Lee)**

"People's hearts are like wild animals. They attach their selves to those that love and train them." **(Ali Abi Abi Talib)**

"When the character of a man is not clear to you, look at his friends." **(Japanese Proverb)**

"Where the heart is willing, it will find a thousand ways, but where it is unwilling, it will find a thousand excuses." **(Borneo Proverb)**

"Mistakes are always forgivable, if one has the courage to admit them." **(Bruce Lee)**

"Anger and intolerance are the enemies of correct understanding." **(Gandhi)**

"Doing good to others is not a duty; it is a joy for it increases your own health and happiness." **(Zoroaster)**

CHAPTER 3
CHOOSING A CAREER THAT GIVES YOU JOY

Just like knowing your calling or assignment on earth; picking a career can be one of the most difficult things to do. A lot of people have gone into careers because of what a friend is doing. Others are influenced by their parents, while some simply accept whatever is available and with time they become dissatisfied with their chosen career. One is supposed to choose a career that provides joy, passion, and satisfaction. It does not matter what you do in life. You may have a job that puts money in your pocket, lots of it perhaps, but until you discover your path in life you will never find fulfilment. Choosing a career that gives you joy, passion, and fulfilment is greater and more important than the acquisition of money.

Success is not a function of position or possession, but function of fulfilment in life. You can never be fulfilled until you locate and begin to pursue God's purpose for your life. Many stars have refused to rise because they have applied themselves to wrong purpose; they are busy doing what they are not created for, so they live a directionless life. Have you ever bothered to think of what you would have done if money wasn't an issue and asked yourself will this make me happy and give me fulfilment?

A job may earn you a living, but working is about purpose, your destiny and divine assignment in life. All your blessings and happiness are located in your chosen career, and until you find that path and begin to walk in it, life may be meaningless to you. No one ever finds fulfilment chasing shadows.

"Your work is going to fill a large part of your life, and the only way to be truly satisfied is to do what you believe is great work. And the only way to do great work is to love what you do. If you haven't found it yet, keep looking. Don't settle. As with all matters of the heart, you'll know when you find it." **(Steve Jobs)**

"From what we get, we can make a living; what we give, however, makes a life." **(Arthur Ashe)**

"Doing what you like with passion is not selfish, it is all about empowering the real you." **(Raphael Ikechukwu Ogbuagu)**

Countless people have settled for misguided careers; which in the long run bring bitterness, disappointment, and frustration. Emphasis should be placed in exposing the danger in choosing a career or profession simply because it is popular and financially attractive. Career choosers should be properly guided to enable them make the right decision. Most times, it takes guts, bravery, and courage to pursue profession or career that your heart craves for; that brings joy in your life. What is it that you seek? Intellect or wisdom? Status or happiness?

When our possessions posses us, we lose our real treasure - our life. Bear in mind that one man's success is another man's prison. We must stop being busy trying to be like someone else and find what truly makes us happy. Any professional without passion for his vocation is just - marking time and destined for mediocrity.

"Find something that you're really interested in doing in your life. Pursue it, set goals, and commit yourself to excellence. Do the best you can." **(Chris Evert)**

"Success is not the key to happiness. If you love what you are doing, you will be successful." **(Albert Schweizer)**

"If you want to be successful, it's just this simple. Know what you are doing. Love what you are doing. And believe in what you are doing." **(Will Rogers)**

"Doing what you love is the cornerstone of having abundance in your life." **(Wayne Dyer)**

"If you are not doing what you love, you are wasting your time." **(Billy Joel)**

"Don't aim for success if you want it; just do what you love and believe in, and it will come naturally." **(David Frost)**

"Courage is the most important of all the virtues, because without courage you can't practice any other virtue consistently. You can practice any virtue erratically, but nothing consistently with courage." **(Dr. Maya Angelou)**

"One isn't necessarily born with courage, but one is born with potential without courage. We cannot practice any virtue with consistency. We can't be kind, true, merciful, or honest." **(Dr. Maya Angelou)**

"Often the difference between a successful person and failure is not one that has better abilities or ideas, but the courage that one has to be bet on, one's idea, take a calculated risk and to act." **(Maxwell Maltz)**

"Anything you're good at contributes to happiness." **(Bertrand Russell)**

MANDELA TO NIGERIA

"YOU know I am not very happy with Nigeria. I have made that very clear on many occasions. Yes, Nigeria stood by us more than any nation, but you let yourselves down, and Africa and the black race very badly. Your leaders have no respect for their people. They believe that their personal interests are the interests of the people. They take people's resources and turn it into personal wealth. There is a level of poverty in Nigeria that should be unacceptable. I cannot understand why Nigerians are not more angry than they are.

"What do young Nigerians think about your leaders and their country and Africa? Do you teach them history? Do you have lessons on how your past leaders stood by us and gave us large amounts of money? You know I hear from Angolans and Mozambicans and Zimbabweans how your people opened their hearts and their homes to them. I was in prison then, but we know how your leaders punished western companies who supported Apartheid.

"What about the corruption and the crimes? Your elections are like wars. Now we hear that you cannot be president in Nigeria unless you are Muslim or Christian. Some people tell me your country may break up. Please do not let it happen.

"Let me tell you what I think you need to do. You should encourage leaders to emerge who will not confuse public office with sources of making personal wealth. Corrupt people do not make good leaders. Then you have to spend a lot of your resources for education.

Educate children of the poor, so that they can get out of poverty. Poverty does not breed confidence. Only confident people can bring changes. Poor, uneducated people can also bring change, but it will be hijacked by the educated and the wealthy give young Nigerians good education. Teach them the value of hard work and sacrifice, and discourage them from crimes which are destroying your image as a good people."

(Excerpts taken from a 2007 interview with Mandela conducted by Dr. Hakeem Baba-Ahmed)

"One of the penalties for refusing to participate in politics is that you end up being governed by your inferiors." **(Plato)**

"There is no reason why any Nigerian child, at this point in time, should not have basic education, food and nutrition, and not only Nigeria child, any Nigerian should not go to bed without food. We have the resources to achieve all that. If we are not achieving it, does not mean we don't have the resources, it is because we haven't managed our resources well." **(General Olusegun Obasanjo)**

Ironically I'm from Nigeria, a beautiful country blessed by God. This is a country that is commonly identified as the giant of

Africa; and is endowed with intelligent, enterprising, and good hearted people. Abuja is its federal capital. Naira is the official currency. The country is made up of three major tribes namely Igbo, Yoruba, and Hausa. The Igbo's are known to be very industrious and business minded. The Yoruba's are quiet educated and have a strong economic base. The Hausa's are also wealthy with political power. Administratively, the country is divided into 36 states, 774 local government areas, with over 250 languages. It is the most populous country in Africa with a population of over 170 million and is blessed with immense human and natural resources. It has a long history of ancient civilization and a rich cultural heritage that has attracted several tourists. It is said Nigeria is a nation blessed with some of the greatest talents ever known, yet most of these talents are stifled and untapped. Thus they die unnoticed, because of lack of professional/parental guidance and counselling. Nigeria is a great country where the best brains, plans and ideas lay waste in the graveyards.

"The problem with Nigeria isn't people, it's the structure! If we don't fix our structure, even an angel will have challenges leading Nigeria." **(Ben Murray Bruce)**

"Apart from Nigeria, I haven't heard of a country where a court has power to give injunctue stopping someone from been investigated." **(Ben Murray Bruce)**

A lot of people are misled, misguided, and frustrated to follow a career choice. Many go to their grave without knowing their calling and so end up making a wrong career choice. These are precipitated by several factors that have deluded people. Situations have forced us to go with these thoughts in our minds: the survival of the fittest. It is said put a Nigerian in any environment and he will survive and make real meaning out of life. It is a known fact that the greatest hindrance to fulfilling our callings, talents, lies with our corrupt politicians and leaders.* No nation succeeds without a leader.

In all cases, leadership is build either on consensus or the system allows the authority to evolve and flow naturally. But, whatever the case may be, such an authority automatically commands the respect and loyalty of all, failure of which sanctions are imposed, otherwise such a society is doomed. There is little or no developmental structure that is well equipped to recruit and bolster talent. Recent events in this country have given one a serious cause for concern. It is rather unfortunate that of our over fifty years of attaining nationhood, Nigeria is yet to achieve significant development even as we were compelled to watch in awe how our contemporaries overtook us on the way.

Paradoxically, Nigeria has all that it takes for a nation to assume its rightful position in a global scheme of affairs. Endowed with abundant human and material wealth in addition to a very fertile land suitable for all year round agricultural activities, we still could not exploit all these potentials for our own good. Ironically, individual Nigerians are rich while the country put together remains poor. We take pride in struggling for power mainly to steal and live in affluence and fashion simply because "once an opportunity is lost will never be gotten". And because we careless for the country that we do not have at heart, yet we wanted to be clever by half in trying to always remain relevant by making a lot of noise as if our individual antecedents have been forgotten by the very masses that we claim to represent.

Certainly, those societal ills and crimes could not have been caused in the last three years; neither could they have been solved at once. Indeed, if such ills were not inherent in us, and the society was okay, then Buhari could not have launched the War against Indiscipline and Corruption in 1985 or Babangida'sethical revolution, Abacha's failed Banks Tribunal or Obasanjo's EFCC. It baffles me to see people like Olusegun Obasanjo a one-time president raising his voice against corruption when he himself was part and still involved in the canworm eating deep into the fibre of the corrupt system Nigerian. Is he telling us he is innocent of the crime and faithful to the total upholding of the interest of Nigeria as a country? I do not think so he is part of the problem Nigeria has ever and and still having. I pray that the Almighty God will bless us further with Responsible, Responsive and God-fearing leadership. So that this truncate of dreams, ideas and lives called poverty will be eradicated from this country that is so blessed with abundance of natural resources in Jesus Mighty Name.

"Nigeria has no business with poverty. With our human and material resources, we shall strive to eradicate poverty from our country." **(General Olusegun Obasanjo)**

"Nigerian politics has been, since the military dictatorships, largely non-ideological. Rather than a battle of ideas, it is about who can pump in the most money and buy the most access." **(Chimamanda Ngozi Adichie)**

"A friend of mine attributed almost all our problems to corruption and unemployment, yet my experience after travelling to a number of European countries shows that they also have unemployment and corruption problems. But the difference is that in Africa we seem to measure everything in terms of ill gotten wealth. We worship money and political status. As such we elevate mediocrity into sainthood." **(Chika Osueze)**

"We have wasted resources and everyone that has been in charge of past budgets must be held accountable." **(Dr. Tunde Bakare)**

"Nigeria, the fundamental problem is still corruption; we have enough for our need, but not enough for our greed." **(Professor Wole Soyinka)**

"Don't be like Kenya and Nigeria where you have to dip into your pocket to get anything done." **(President Robert Mugabe)**

"Nigeria is a country where few people have turned themselves into mini gods and superstars that know it all, and have in turn used their positions and influence to oppressed and subdue mankind in all ratifications." **(Raphael Ikechukwu Ogbuagu)**

"The world will not respect Africa until Nigeria earns that respect. The black people of the world need Nigeria to be great as a source of pride and confidence. Nigeria love freedom and hates oppression. Why do you do it to yourselves?" **(Nelson Rolihlahla Mandela'Madiba)**

"Nigeria is among top 10 private jet owners in the world. Distribution of wealth, not poverty is our problem." **(President Goodluck Jonathan)**

"The greatest evil in our society may not be the Boko Haram or terrorist bombing the nation but the people who continue to milk the nation depriving the poor masses of their collective wealth but also ready to defend their evil." **(Osadebe Ibegbu)**

"The best way to fight corruption amongst our political class is very simple. Remove the immunity because majority of our politicians are reformed criminals." **(Chima Onyeagba Umealo)**

Embezzlement is the order of the day. According to World Bank report, over 80% of Nigeria's wealth is in the hands of 1% of its population. Where elected officials feel it is their birth right to loot fund meant for the development of the nation. While these embezzlers and their cronies live a life of comfort and extravagancy, with excess money starched away in foreign banks; they have done this at the expense of a nation in dire need of good employment opportunities, adequate power supply, good roads and drainages, affordable health care, affordable and improved educational system etc.

Corruption is our greatest problem. In Nigerian we are now being ruled by some money bags without vision or direction, people without day time jobs have become decision makers, money has given people with unimaginable character a bargaining power over the masses, my honourable comrade Collins Thomas Mgbo has this to say aboy Nigeria based leadership "We must learn to make distinction between people with money and rich people. In a society people with money are not always rich in all ramifications but rich people posse's wealth in different dimension ranging from rches in knowledge, riches in wisdom, riches in finance, and riches in moral inter alia. People with money are those who have money and that is all they have fullstop.

"Nigeria needs politicians for whom politics is a vocation not an occupation, who make money from their businesses not the public treasury." **(Ben Murray Bruce)**

"For Nigeria to make meaningful progress, our leaders have to be more interested in the price of leadership than in the perks of leadership." **(Ben Murray Bruce)**

He thus went further to say, in developed world , people who have money and fullstop, soldom show interest least publicly to occupy any public office, rather they encourage and in most cased sponsor those whom God has blessed with such talent and those who have disciplined themselves way enough tp attain certain hierarchical placement in a society, but it is ironical that countries like Nigeria we think that when a man has money , he governs everybody and everything with his money, Isn't that stupid enough? Infact he put it this way, I am beginning to wonder who is more stupid we the electorate who choses to chose empty head to lead us or the empty head who knows he is empty but still want to lead."

Personal to me this should be of high sense of concern to all well meaningful Nigerians that we have failed our generation, we have failed to take a bold stand against corruption, some of us are now deeply rooted in corruption that we have sold our consciences and birthrights to the highest bidder all these has indeed given rise to bad government, mismanagement of our resources, high level of corruption and abuse of power. From the executive, the legisture and the judiciary all are corrupt, majority of the members of the National Assembly live above the law in both misconduct and corruption and cannot in good conscience carry out oversight duties on any government ministry or department . Today, there is no institution of government that is not riddled with corruption, not even the military. As the people cry out, where then is the salvation. It is time the grounded comrades and revolutionaries begin to take a stand and say no to corruption and with the help of God we be overcome this canwarm that has eaten deep down into the fibre of our county. When the guard is the thief, only God can keep the house safe and secure. God will give us guards of integrity and honesty with the fear of God and genuine love of their people and their country.

"Nigeria is a dream nation lost for the love of money." **(Ifeanyichukwu Okonkwo)**

"Nigeria needs total cleansing. We need what happens in Ghana to happen in Nigeria to send a shock wave to the corrupt people in the country. The corrupt people will think of the grave consequences of their actions before they embark on corruption. The entire system is rotten. We need more than overhaul of the system. We need a constitution from the people; the one that is not imposed on them." **(Dr. Tunde Bakara)**

"Our value system have been side tracked from what you can offer, who you are, the potentials in you to how much do you have in your pocket, that has become the greatest nightmare that our beloveth country Nigeria has become." **(Raphael Ikechukwu Ogbuagu)**

"It was unity we wanted, not rebellion. We had watched our leaders rape our country. The country was so diseased that bold reforms were badly needed to settle social, moral, economic and political questions. We fully realised that to be caught planning, let alone acting, on our lines, was high treason. And the penalty for high treason is death." **(Major Emmanuel Ifeajuna, on Nigerian first Military coup)**

"People without day time jobs have hijacked the government machinery of Nigeria; hence there are so much crimes and corruptions in the country." **(Raphael Ikechukwu Ogbuagu)**

The consequence of this ineptitude is that we are ranked among the poorest countries in the world, where close to 80% of our population earn $2 a day. This has led to the emergence of radical groups such as MASSOB, MEND, MOSSOP, OPC, BOKO HARAM etc demanding for an equitable distribution of the nation's wealth. While some are demanding for an outright autonomy. The lessons for future leaders is to make a radical departure from corruption and other vices that have become the norm and help create leaders with a clear vision and the required commitment to move our nation forward. This brings me back to the message I am trying to preach in the chapter called; **Career Choice**. Our fature is in our hands basically the youths.

"The children of any nation are its future. A country, a movement, a person that does not value its youth and children does not deserve its future." **(Oliver Tambo)**

"I advise youths not to look at Nigeria from a pro PDP or APC perspective, but with a pro youth outlook. Your future is greater than a party." **(Ben Murray Bruce)**

By Muyiwa Adetiba; what are we without passion and compassion?

It is my passion for journalism that has kept me in the profession these past forty years, despite the common knowledge that it is not the most lucrative of professions. For me, I was being paid for what I would have done for free. This passion has gotten me interested in almost every aspect of journalism from basic reporting to publishing. It is this passion that has allowed me to make the sacrifices of detention, of police and security harassment, of court cases, of life and death in foreign countries, of precious family time that I have had to make. It is this passion that has seen me within a walking distance to the top of my chosen profession. Even today, after forty years, I am still in awe when I read some write-ups and marvel at the display of talent in the way words have been woven together .While it is true that most of us picked our professions without any serious mentoring many are doctors and engineers simply because they were good in the sciences many, it must be said, have developed the compassion and passion that made the inevitable odds around their jobs surmountable.

I know doctors who treat patients on compassionate grounds and lawyers who treat cases on 'pro bono'. I also have the story of a policeman who made a financial sacrifice to help me when I needed help that will forever live within me. This is why the recent news that the leadership of the Nigerian Medical Association refused to call off the strike of medical doctors even in the wake of the Ebola outbreak was very distressing. The fact that not one dissenting voice reportedly came up among the Executive was most upsetting. Their decision to continue with the strike was unanimous although prior to this, their President, Kayode Obembe, had resigned following disagreement with his colleagues over the strike. Where is their passion? Their compassion?

What makes them get up in the morning to go to work? Is it only the pay cheque? I couldn't imagine doing a job that I had no passion for. It is true that a lot is wrong with the Nigerian structure. A structure that allows a Local Government official to earn more than a University professor is dysfunctional. A structure that allocates so much of the commonwealth to the political class is doomed to fail. But I am resolved on my part to do my bit to make humanity better. The fact that the Jonathans, the Marks, the Tinubus and the like will not take their money to heaven gives me comfort. This is why it is confounding that professional doctors will ignore a clarion call to serve humanity on the grounds that the government is not serious. Members of 'Doctors without borders' are risking their lives because of the passion for the jobs not minding the working conditions or the pay cheque. Foreign care givers who come from more equitable societies are here risking their lives because of compassion.

"A clear vision of what you want be it personal or professional is the solid foundation around which a balanced life can be moulded." **(Dr. Martie Lancellas)**

"It's a tragedy anytime someone neglects his potentials and misses many of the possibilities that life has to offer." **(John Maxwell)**

"Everyone is gifted but some people never open their package." **(Anna La Torre)**

I am among many others who choose wrong careers. Fortunately it is never too late to make corrections, amendments, and ways to forge ahead. I was born multi talented and it baffles me now when looking back that all the things I derived joy in doing then I am not involved in any more.

Firstly, I was born a multi talented sports man gifted in sprinting, wrestling, football and boxing. However, what gives me the greatest joy was football (soccer). I was a very good football player and had often told myself that I was going to make a living through the beautiful game. I was a player as well as a good goal keeper. I stood my grounds in all department of the game back then and I could play as a midfielder and that gave me the name "Little Maradona" and in the defence I was called "Defence Minister and Dean of Defence." If I was ever told that I will not take football as a profession I wouldn't have agreed, it gave me so much Joy and I felt the passion in me whenever I played however the rest is history circumstance beyond my power has prevail that I have to watch from the sideline how wonderful they beautiful game can be. Anthony Ogbuagu my younger brother was also dealt the same bow by fate so I pray that my cousin Chike Akpua in the United States of America will feel the gap that we both left, and have started by signing for CD Mafra football club in Portugal. God will sustain this gifted young man that is so passionate about the round leather called soccer. Soccer has been in our gene my Uncle John Ogbuagu (Japan) played alongside Patrick Okala in Morning Star football club of Onitsha though on an amateur bases.

"Ignoring your passion is slow suicide. Never ignore what your heart pumps for you. Mold your career around your life style, not your life style around your career." **(Unknown)**

"We are all geniuses up to the age of ten." **(Aldous Huxley)**

Nevertheless, two factors had contributed in depriving me of a career opportunity in soccer. First, there wasn't enough support from my parents. My uncle and family members saw football as a sport for hooligans. Hence, most parents weren't supportive of their children involvement in the beautiful game. The second reason was a mysterious leg problem that was incurable for more than two and half decades. It started 1982 and got relieved in 2006, but still come on and off. Despite the setback in my football career, there are several gifted Nigerian footballers that are unable to show case their talent to the world due to family issues, and impediments within the football fraternity such as Godfatherism and nepotism (a.k.a. having the right contact). The so-called coach more often than not would want his percentage in your salary and earnings.

I won't fail to mention a few of my close friends and associates who have inspired me and others in the beautiful game. My childhood twin brothers, Fidelis and Felix Orere, late Christopher Obuh Onudu, Chidi Nwazwue, Emmanuel Apata. At secondary/high school level I had the likes of late Emeka Okoli(Mapito), Stanley Ukadike (Tension), Felix Obele (Oge Hard), John Kingsley, Emeka Nzegwu (Kpanla), Emeka Odili (Ufele), Dr. Ifeanyi Duaka, Geoffrey Ofoegbu (Enegwea), Chukwudi Egbo (Achumgbe), Ogbo Nwanze (Stopper), Godfrey Okoye (Goddy Nna), Tochukwu Onwe, Raphael Udoka Emeka (Sirralph), Okey Igbo, Chibuzor Ike (Magic leg) and finally Emmanuel Anayo Anaka (Montiny Yeye). Among the above mentioned persons it was Raphael Emeka Udoka and Chukwudi Egbo that played professional soccer. Raphael Emeka Udoka played for both Rangers International and Jasper United. While Chukwudi Egbo (Achumgbe) played for Julius Berger. Emeka Okoli, Ogbo Nwanze, Chibuzor Ike, Emeka Nzegwu, John Kingsley, and Godfrey Okoye played amateur level, Okey Igbo played for Premier football club in the 2 division while Stanley Ukadike, Geoffrey Ofoegbu, Felix Obele, Emeka Odili, Dr. Ifeanyi Duaka ended theirs at secondary senior teams level. However, the most talented of these lots was Tochukwu Onwe and

Emmanuel Anayo Anaka. They never played amateur or professional football but they were the best that Nigerian soccer lived to forget. Currently, they are both based in the United States of America. In the bigger scene the likes of Pastor Anthony Adiele (Wine wine), Emeka Nwobodo (Emeka Single), and Ndubuisi Ndah that both played for Enugu Rangers international, the bigger politics of Nigerian football didn't allow them and other good footballers to exploit their full potentials to their highest level.

They were frustrated as they did not have god-fathers. Pastor Anthony Adiele could only end his marvellous football adventure by playing for Julius Berger of Lagos. Emeka Nwobodo only got a call up to the Flying Eagles squad of 1987 but could not make the team, while Ndubuisi Ndah was only able to make it to the dream team Atlanta Olympic 1996 as an alternate player, they were among of the best players I have ever seen, their passion and zeal was astonishing from their days at Julius Berger, and the later two that played for Enyimba and Premier football club Onitsha respectively till the later they joined Rangers International football of Enugu.Nwobodo and Ndah been born leaders captaining their various teams from Enyimba football club, Premier football club and later Rangers International of Enugu.

I, myself went for a wrong career choice as well. I was to be a writer, Journalist, commentator, poet, you name it. But I followed the bandwagon and did Business Administration and Management in school. This was a decision that was largely influenced by following the trend among my friends and the negligence of my father who never wanted me to pursue higher education. He wanted me as the first son, to start making a living through craftsmanship such as carpentry or the servicing of auto mobile. Thanks to my God sent mother, through her I was able to acquire the little education I had. Back then in school I was very good in English literature as it was my favourite. I always made distinction. I was offered a provisional admission to study Mass Communication at Nnamdi Azikiwe University Awka or alternatively I would have studied law as I also had it as a nice course I could involve myself; however I went for my admission at Federal Polytechnic Oko to study business administration and management. I was indoctrinated that mass communication was a course basically for women. That was how I lost an opportunity for another profession I loved.

"If you've got a natural talent, I think it's fantastic. If I wasn't in retail, being a singer or a tennis player would be a better idea." **(Sir Philip Green)**

I also loved football commentary while growing up and as a young boy of Eight then, I could name all the green Eagles players, Brazilian, Italian, German and others, not to mention my flare for local teams and could mention the house hold names in teams like the Rangers International Of Enugu, IICC later Shooting Stars football club of Ibadan, Bendel Insurance of Benin, Stationary Stores, Sharks football of Port Harcourt, Spartans Later Iwuanuanwu Nationale, Abiola Babes, Flash Flamingos ,Leventis United to mention but a few. I had all the names of Our Eagles, flying Eagles and Eaglets from 1978 to the year 2008 before the interest in commentary started fading off I was also privileged to have followed the best football radio and television commenter's our country has ever produced from our great Ernest Okonkwo and Yinka Criag Walter Oyatogun all of blessed memory, Emeka Odikpo , Tolu Fataimgbo etc, at a stage I took my recorded commentary to Emeka Odikpo at the Radio Nigerian discussed with him and he encouraged me on my attributes and asked me to keep it up. For the love and flare I have for the of football as the chairperson of Westrand Brothers association I formed an amateur football team Westrand football club to keep body and soul together , I am also in collaboration with other Nigeria amateur teams owed and ran by Nigerians in South Africa like Genesis and Panorama football clubs.

Finally, I was a good entertainer. I acted dramas and made people laugh. Yet no one spotted or valued my talent let alone nurturing it. As I grew older that talent died and gave way to other ideas mostly as a result of the harshness and short sightedness from some of my uncles and guardians. Today the movie industry in Nigeria (Nollywood) and others all over the world is a very big money making machine. I hope parents/guardians will learn from my ordeal and identify the special skills and talent in their children and give them the necessary support. Of recent I had to be called up in the movie industry in South Africa where I made brief appearance as an extra in one of it most watched programmes isidingo.

"Choose a job you love and you will never have to work a day in your life." **(Confucius)**

"People with many interests live, not only longest but happiest." **(Anna La Torre)**

"Life is not about making the right decision; it's about how you deal with your decision." **(Roza Kaulitz Azman)**

"Some of the best music was composed by Beethoven who was deaf, some of the best poetry about nature was written by Milton, who was blind. One of the greatest leaders Franklin Roosevelt served from a wheel chair. Those who are born to achieve, turn scars into stars." **(Beware Kurdistani)**

"No matter how far you have gone on a wrong road, turn back." **(Turkish Proverb)**

"You are never too old to set another goal or to dream a new dream." **(C.S Lewis)**

It is not still late to turn around your situation. The important thing here is to realize you have made a mistake. And mistakes can be corrected or reversed if noticed. Great men like former President Nelson Mandela (Madiba), Arch Bishop Desmond Tutu, Dr. Don Mattera, former America President Abraham Lincoln, and a host of others achieved their dreams and aspiration in the later stages of their lives. That is to say, that if they could do it we can do it. All we need is the zeal and determination that through God all things are Possible. They say it is only the dead that do not have hope as far as I am alive I will keep trying, making mistakes here and there till I get to my destination. No matter where in life, and regardless of how old or young you are, it can be **"half time"** for you, where you can change your direction and reassess your career and focus on going back to a career that gives you joy, happiness, passion and a sense of fulfilment in life.

"With God, delay does not mean denial, He never fails, He is God of immediate not ultimate, and He will send fire that is meant to bless you not burn you, He will make you better not bitter. Arise and Shine." **(Raphael Ikechukwu Ogbuagu)**

"No matter how difficult the challenges, when we spread over the wings of faith and allow the wind of God's spirit to lift us, no obstacle is too great to overcome." **(Raphael Ikechukwu Ogbuagu)**

I have finally come to the decision of sticking to my God given career which is writing, poetry, commentary etc. I may not be proficient in the use of grammars, punctuations and other linguistic attributes. But I want to use this little gift of mine to touch souls, resurrect people, and give hope to the hopeless.

"A Healthy, supportive family is like a safe heaven in a storm." **(John Maxwell)**

"The family was ordained by God before He established any other institution, even before He established the church." **(Billy Graham).**

My mother Mrs. Christiana Adaeze Ogbuagu, my brothers Anthony Chukwuemeka and Leonard Chinedu Ogbuagu, my sisters Roseline Nnenna Molokwu, Florence Obianuju Ofoto, my uncles Justin Ogbuagu, John Ogbuagu, Clifford Ogbuagu, Emmanuel Ogbuagu and my aunts Mrs. Augustine Anyaji, Mrs. Florence Nnonye and Mrs. Josephine Akpua Thompson have been the pillars behind me. I wouldn't have attained this height without their support. When others gave up on me, because of my inability to parade flashy cars, expensive houses, and money my family stood by me. Though it may tarry I know I will surely be victorious in all my endeavours.

"One should guard against preaching to the young success in customary form as the main aim in life. The most important motive for work in school and in life is pleasure in its result and knowledge of the value of the result in the community." **(Albert Einstein)**

"Wars of nations are fought to change maps. But wars of poverty are fought to map change." **(Muhammad Ali)**

"To the youth of today, I also have a wish to make: be the scriptwriters of your destiny and feature yourselves as stars that showed the way towards a brighter future." **(Nelson Rolihlahla Mandela 'Madiba)**

"When all the talents in society are not fully developed, it is not the individuals that are adversely affected alone who suffer; the society as a whole suffers as well. Now, granting that every Nigerian is given an opportunity to develop his talents, it is imperative that he should also be given an opportunity to employ these developed talents. Full development of man and his full employment are not only social imperatives, but also inseparably inter-connected and complementary." **(Chief Obafemi Awolowo)**

A lot of skills, potentials and talents are wasted in the African Continent, I weep whenever I look at our African continent. It baffles me that this great continent which has most of the resources that the world exploits, is in perpetual poverty. Poverty is killing Africa, and there is no money to put food on the table for most families not to talk of sending kids to school to pursue their dreams and aspirations .It is an eye sore to see and hear the way the leaders of Africa embezzles funds meant for its citizens and developmental purposes for their personal luxury. We all need to stand and fight for what rightly belongs to us, we need to put our great continent Africa in prayers if not in the near future we won't have qualified doctors, engineers, lawyers, writers, administrators the list goes on.i wept for my beloved continent Africam many of our youths have died in the high see in their verge for better living conditions in Europe, our future leader and hope that will reenergize the continent are treated like slaves and the futhur of the upcoming generation has been placed in jeopardy.

With what is happening in the Arab region most African countries should have learnt their lessons, that youth unemployment, youth dissatisfaction and youth frustration were part of the causes of the so-called Arab Spring from which Libya and Egypt have not yet fully come out and which caused insecurity and instability in the whole of the Arab world. We must learn the right lessons and put in place, programmes that will address youth empowerment and youth employment, youth discontent and youth dissatisfaction and youth frustration to avoid youth anger and explosion generated there from. Companies, well meaning individuals, organizations and philanthropist in Africa should try and invest funds for developmental purposes and the nurturing of skills and talents in Africa as a whole, it should not always be what will I get from this, it should be what am I capable of doing that will leave a lasting legacy when I am no more. Nothing will unlock Africa's economic potential more than ending corruption.

"Upon the education of the people of this country the fate of this country depends." **(Benjamin Disraeli)**

"Education is an ornament for the prosperous, a refuge for the unfortunate." **(Democritus)**

"Education is our passport to the future, for tomorrow belongs to the people who prepare for it today." **(Malcolm X)**

"Higher education must be a right for all. Not just for wealthy family." **(Bernie Sanders)**

"Formal education will make you a living; self education will make you a fortune." **(Jim Rohn)**

"An educated, enlightened and informed population is one of the surest ways of promoting the health of a democracy." **(Nelson Rolihlahla Mandela'Madiba)**

"A child miseducated is a child lost." **(John F. Kennedy)**

"Education is the only foundation that can ensure the consistent growth of a nation. I have always believed that a nation will not become great by the minerals under her ground. Such will only come by developing the human resources of the country." **(President Goodluck Jonathan)**

"If a man neglects education, he walks lame to the end of his life." **(Plato)**

"In order to attain to the goals of economic freedom and prosperity, Nigeria must do certain things as a matter of urgency and priority. It must provide free education (at all levels) and free health facilities for the masses of its citizens." **(Chief Obafemi Awolowo)**

Education is very important in life hence children should be encouraged to go to school so as to be useful to themselves and the community. Education gives a lot of options in life, makes you fit into any environmental condition you may find yourself in life. It's like the water we drink every day. Parents, institutions and various governments should emphasis and encourage children on the need and importance of education. We must never mistake schooling for education. Education is largely a function of information, whereas schooling is a career. It is possible to spend years in school and still not be educated. Great minds are not born, they are developed, and every great mind is personally developed.

Nothing enhances dignity like information; your dream for transformation is rooted in information. Information makes the difference in school of success every successful leader is an avid reader. To be a leader means to be ahead, to see ahead, to see before, and to stay above others. I think one of the reason for the leadership problem in Africa today is because a lot of undeveloped minds are in charge , the people in charge are mostly uninformed, your level of information determined your speed and overall accomplishment that is why I call for proper education among the youth to foster a more better and coordinated Africa. While I believe that education opens doors to opportunity, I also strongly believe that the choice of subject and career one chooses is equally very important. Take the high unemployment rate in Nigeria, South Africa and Africa as a whole, it is not because they don't have qualifications in the form of degree and diplomas, they do, but unfortunately they have studied courses that the market does not require'. The market may be saturated with courses that the market does not require hence the need for proper guardian councillors and mentors to give youths the rightful directions. Self development is the qualification to life.

Formal education without informal education is disequilibrium of education. You can buy formal school certificate but you can't buy informal certificate. Someone can write formal school exam for you with excellent grade. Nobody will write formal life exam for you. Only you will develop yourself. Formal development is personal and is the ultimate key to life. A continent cannot walk into tomorrow with confidence, if it is guided by leaders with the insecurity's of yesterday. Our leaders need to change their attitudes and perceptions. Eighty Five percent of African youths don't know their calling neither do they choose careers that gives them joy or make them worthy of who they really are. When a nation wastes the minds of her youth by not providing them access to education, those youths will waste the nation. If a nation does not invest her wealth in educating her youths, that nation will invest the same wealth fight insecurity, lack of jobs, crimes verse vise among those same youth meaning it is pennywise pound foolish, the youth and education is the key for a nation survival.

It is also of important that educating our youth should not be a sole government responsibility. In Africa state owned schools are poorly run and underfunded and more and more people are spending their meagre resources to send their children to private schools. Many schools still teach a curriculum that went out of date 20 years ago. Men of means within their community pool resources and build these facilities and in that way the community is made more prosperous. And the more prosperous the community is the more secure the men of means within that community are. Almost 100% of Nigeria's elite achieved the success they have today because leaders like Chief Obafemi Awolowo, Sir Ahmadu Bello and Dr. Nnamdi Azikiwe ensured that they benefited from free education. Yet, after climbing up the education ladder, we have removed the ladder that got us there instead of perpetuating it. Without the effort of our heros past most of the benefits of education and facilitates we are enjoying at the moment are to their level of awareness for the need for education. Education is the only foundation that can ensure the consistent growth of a nation. I have always believed that a nation will not become great by the minerals under her ground. Such will only come by developing the human resources of the country.

"Any system of education which does not help a man to have a healthy and sound body and alert brain, and balanced and disciplined instinctive urges, is both misconceived and dangerous." **(Chief Obafemi Awolowo)**

"I call on our elites to show more concern to their places of origin. Help to educate the less privilege in your village/Community, if you can build a school, and then build one beside your mansion." **(Ben Murray Bruce)**

"I want to assure Nigerians that crude oil is not our black gold, the real gold of Nigeria her people and the can grow in value from the gold to diamond via education." **(President Goodluck Jonathan)**

"The Youth of a Nation are the trustees of posterity." **(Benjamin Disraeli)**

"Genius, when young, is divine." **(Benjamin Disraeli)**

"If you cannot build schools, then buy books for the children of the less privileged. If you cannot buy books, why not volunteer to teach in the local primary school in your village whenever you are home? You will 'oppress' the people more when you impart knowledge into their kids than you would with your latest SUV!" **(Ben Murray Bruce)**

"Almost everything that is great has been done by youth." **(Benjamin Disraeli)**

"Do not just wait until Ramadan or Christmas to give out food to the poor. Give them education and they will learn how to feed themselves." **(Ben Murray Bruce)**

With all the above wise words from men that have seen it all you would agree with me that the importance of education is a prority and necessity to the survival of our continent Africa, more educative and enlightenment programmes should be introduced on our big sreens at home, in office and every where for this meassage to go round. It would be a more bigger headache for citizen to understand government programmes, projects, measure and policies if they are not fully educated, how would they know that government would not function effeciantly and effectively if taxes are not paid, if roads are not maintained, to mention but a few all this will affect the service delivery by the government.

"Yes, stomach infrastructure is necessary, but even more necessary is brain infrastructure. Why? Because education is key. A hungry man is hungry for one day but an uneducated man is hungry forever." **(Ben Murray Bruce)**

"Today, Africa is a continent of COMPETING BEGGAR-NATIONs. We vie with one another for favours from our former colonial masters; and we deliberately fall over one another to invite neo- colonialists to come over to our different territories to preside over our economic fortunes ... Unless a beggar resolutely shakes off, and irrevocably turn his back on, his begging habit, he will forever remain a beggar. For, the more he begs, the more he develops the beggar characteristics of lack of initiative, courage, drive and self-reliance." **(Chief Obafemi Awolowo)**

AFRICANS MUST TAKE RESPONSIBILITY FOR THEIR BEHAVIORS

Real adults take responsibility for their behaviours; those who take responsibility for their behaviours learn from their mistakes and undertake to change them, to do the right thing; as long as one blames others for ones issues one is not going to change them; one gratifies ones ego's desire to seem perfect while behaving imperfectly and erroneously believing that other persons caused ones problems. Playing the innocent victim of Europeans Africans act as the worst enemy of Africa; they are not the victims of other persons; they are their own victimizers (playing other peoples victims is a means of garnering attention and sympathy; only children need that kind of pity; adults do not need other adults pity they just do the right things and leave them at that).White liberals condescending behaviour must now be dispensed with; Africans are adults and should not be treated with understanding that adults do not extent to their fellow adults.

Adults understand children misbehaving and forgive them but they insist that their fellow adults behave properly. In adult society we arrest, try and punish those who insist on antisocial behaviours. It is now time we began punishing Africans who engage in anti-social behaviours. Any and all acts of bribery and corruption ought to merit one a place in prisons; lock these criminals in government up and throw away the key (better still, use them to do hard labour, such as build canals in the Sahara desert, irrigate and plant trees in the desert). Africa the world is on our feet's and it is ours to take. Let us do the needful so as to put Africa in the map where it belongs the greatest continent ever.

"In Africa, people are now going into politics as the easiest way to make money as against the opportunity to serve the people, hence their motives is to empty the national treasury for their own personal pleasures and empowerment." **(Raphael Ikechukwu Ogbuagu)**

"The gap between rich and poor is widening dramatically. There's a hangar at the Cairo airport for private jets, billionaires are on the Forbes list, and Egypt's annual per-capita income is two thousand dollars. How can you sustain that?" **(Mohamed ElBaradei)**

"Africa is bloody messed up. Until and unless we invest in ourselves and stop talking about foreign investment, we will be elected into government, (not power) and we will drive black window tinted Mercedes Benz (and by so doing we make the Germans wealthy) until we wake up. Forget about a revolution." **(Mmatshilo Motsei)**

"We must start from simple promise that Africa's future is up to Africans. It will be the young people brimming with talent and energy and hope who can claim the future." **(President Barack Obama)**

"The roots of my family tree are in Africa," the first lady told the cheering crowd. "My husband's father was born and raised in Kenya. Members of our extended family still live there. I have had the pleasure of travelling to Africa many times over the years, including four trips as first lady, and I have brought my mother and my daughters along whenever I can." **(Michelle Obama)**

"Until such time that Africa does not depend on development finance from the so-called developed countries from the East or West, working on Africa's development will not differ from walking on a treadmill. You spend a lot of energy, you even break a sweat, but you are going nowhere." **(Mmatshilo Motsei)**

GADDAFFI'S LAST FORMAL SPEECH – THIS IS VERY MOVING!

In the name of Allah, the beneficent, the merciful...

For 40 years, or was it longer, I can't remember, I did all I could to give people houses, hospitals, schools, and when they were hungry, I gave them food. I even made Benghazi into farmland from the desert, I stood up to attacks from that cowboy Ronald Reagan, when he killed my adopted orphaned daughter, he was trying to kill me, and instead he killed that poor innocent child. Then I helped my brothers and sisters from Africa with money for the African Union.

I did all I could to help people Understand the concept of real democracy, where people's committees ran our country. But that was never enough, as some told me, even people who had 10 room homes, new suits and furniture, were never satisfied, as selfish as they were they wanted more. They told Americans and other visitors, that they needed "democracy" and "freedom" never realizing it was a cut throat system, where the biggest dog eats the rest, but they were enchanted with those words, never realizing that in America, there was no free medicine, no free hospitals, no free housing, no free education and no free food, except when people had to beg or go to long lines to get soup.

No, no matter what I did, it was never enough for some, but for others, they knew I was the son of Gamal Abdel Nasser, the only true Arab and Muslim leader we've had since Salah-al-Deen, when he claimed the Suez Canal for his people, as I claimed Libya, for my people, it was his footsteps I tried to follow, to keep my people free from colonial domination – from thieves who would steal from us.

Now, I am under attack by the biggest force in military history, my little African son, Obama wants to kill me, to take away the freedom of our country, to take away our free housing, our free medicine, our free education, our free food, and replace it with American style thievery, called "capitalism", but all of us in the

Third World know what that means, it means corporations run the countries, run the world, and the people suffer.

So, there is no alternative for me, I must make my stand, and if Allah wishes, I shall die by following His path, the path that has made our country rich with farmland, with food and health, and even allowed us to help our African and Arab brothers and sisters.

I do not wish to die, but if it comes to that, to save this land, my people, all the thousands who are all my children, then so be it. Let this testament be my voice to the world, that I stood up to crusader attacks of NATO, stood up to cruelty, stoop up to betrayal, stood up to the West and its colonialist ambitions, and that I stood with my African brothers, my true Arab and Muslim brothers, as a beacon of light.

When others were building castles, I lived in a modest house, and in a tent. I never forgot my youth in Sirte, I did not spend our national treasury foolishly, and like Salah-al-Deen, our great Muslim leader, who rescued Jerusalem for Islam, I took little for myself.

In the West, some have called me "mad", "crazy", but they know the truth yet continue to lie, they know that our land is independent and free, not in the colonial grip, that my vision, my path, is, and has been clear and for my people and that I will fight to my last breath to keep us free, may Allah almighty help us to remain faithful and free".

My brothers and sisters let's start loving more of each other and stop killing each other because Europe, America and other western world will never want to see sunshine of Africans.

"The highest patriotism is not a blind acceptance of official policy, but a love of one's country deep enough to call her to a high plain." **(George McGovern)**

Love for Our Continent Africa by Marianne Patricia Challens

If Africans from north to south ,east to west can love each-other then we can stand, Africa at the centre Africa heart of the world, God give us the heart to love ourselves, help us not to open doors to hatred that leadeth to death, Lord open our eyes to you world through your written word, widen our ears to hear all things from you , through this Holy word, your first love and only son Jesus Christ, help us to feel love for each-other, brother, sister mother and father, from coast to coast across every nation, through each and every home through rivers, seas that surround this beautiful continent, the wind, the clouds, the rain and sunshine ....pour out love that follows from one person to the another, For when we love, we live, we enjoy, we grow, we succeed, we excel, Jesus is love, he loves us just as we are each and every one of us, it's His love that sees us through, it's his love that sets us free, lets me in the rain let it rain love, peace, joy, happiness and growth in all our heart,

My Africans I love you all, love leads life.

Chapter 4
UPLIFTING YOUR SOUL AND WELLBEING
VOLUME ONE

This Chapter intends to affirm and stimulate positive thoughts as you read. It will intrinsically and extrinsically motivate you and enable you think rightly and seek better answers concerning your situation.

This Chapter will empower you! It will give you the ability to motivate others and bring hope to many, by extracting some of the uplifting words in this book and sharing them through e-mails, text messages, and social media, you can share on a daily basis to people who have lost hope. This will no doubt have a positive effect if received at the time of need.

Enjoy your reading!!

Promise to Yourself:

· To be so strong that nothing can disturb your peace of mind.

· To talk health, happiness, and prosperity to every person you meet.

· To make your friends feel that there is something in them.

· To look at the sunny side of everything and make your optimism come true.

· To think only of the best, work only for the best and to expect only the best.

· To forget the mistakes of the past and press on to greater achievement of the future.

· To wear a cheerful countenance at all time.

· To give much time to the improvement of yourself that you have no time to criticize others.

· To be too large to worry, too noble for anger, too strong for fear and too happy to permit the presence of trouble.

· To live in the faith that the world is on your side as long as you are true to God and the highest within you (Christian. D. Larson).

1. A morning is a wonderful blessing, sunny, stormy, cloudy, or windy. It stands for hope, giving us another start of what we call life.

2. Morning is God's way of saying one more time, live life, make a difference, touch one's heart ,encourage one's mind and inspire one's soul.

3. As God waters His creation may He also sprinkle His wonDr.ous blessing to you and your family forever Amen.

4. God determines who walks in your life, you decide who stays and walks out. Send this to people you never want to lose. I just did.

5. Trusting God may not necessarily make mountains smaller but it will definitely make climbing easier. May each new sunrise take you closer to your Dream.

6. Every sunrise is unique and everyday is a place you have never been before. Don't let anybody or anything spoil your day.

People usually change for two reasons. It is either they have learned a lot that they want to change or they have been hurt a lot that they need to change. Never take any one for granted.

Consult not your fears but your hopes and your dreams; think not about your frustrations but about your unfulfilled potentials. Concern yourself not with what you tried and failed in, but what is still possible for you to do.

7. The will of God will never take you where the grace of God can't keep you, where the arms of God can't support you, and where the word of God cannot free you.

8. Good friends care for each other. Close friends understand each other. True friends stay forever beyond words, time and distance.

9. God called us to be a light to those in darkness but sometimes He has to take us through our own darkness so we will learn to totally depend on His light.

10. Only you, a person can make you feel high, a person can make you feel low, but only you can decide which way you want to go, a person can hurt you mentally, a person can hurt you physically, but only you can place a limit on your abilities.

11. The weak can never forgive. Forgiveness is the attribute of the strong.

12. Always live your life smiling even when other people around you are crying.

13. Life is short, live it, love is sweet feel it, anger is injurious dump it, trouble are momentary face them, memories are forever cherish them.

14. Good morning, happiness is like a butterfly. The more you chase it, the more it will elude you. But if you turn your attention to other things it comes and softly sits on your shoulder. Don't seek happiness, happiness will find you.

15. As you step into this day may you step into abundant blessing, unmatched favour, unexpected breakthrough, divine connection, and overall success.

16. As I open my eyes, I hear birds singing announcing the beginning of a new day. That is when I know that Jesus has not failed me yet.

17. May your bed be guarded by angels, your sleeping face be light by a million stars. And may your pillow case be filled with pleasant dreams.

Never tell your problems to anyone except the one who really loves you; because 20% of people don't care and the other 79% of people are glad that you have problems. Tell God your problem He will listen.

18. God touch the people I care for, keep them safe and happy, remind them of your love, and bless them, especially the ones reading this message.

19. A friend is someone who sees your first tears drop, holds the second one, and makes sure that the third one never comes out. When I got enough confidence, the stage was gone. When I was sure of losing, I won. When I needed people most, they left me. When I wanted to dry my tears, I found a shoulder to cry on. When I mastered the skill of hating, somebody started loving me. That is life. Enjoy it.

20. People fail in life not for lack of ability or brain neither courage but simply because they have failed to organize their energy around a goal. Be grateful for all you have got. Be brave to face all kinds of challenges in life. Be passionate about what you do. Life comes in different forms, there are ups and down along the way. But faith is the key that make us strong and moves us forward. And having a goal is the way to turn your dream to reality.

21. I met peace, joy, love, and good health tonight. They needed a permanent place to stay. I gave them your address hope they arrive safely.

22. Giving someone a second chance is giving them a life time opportunity.

23. You cannot prevent the birds of sorrow from flying over your head but you can prevent them from building nests in your hair.

24. If you get a feeling that someone is watching you all the time don't worry I have asked the lord Jesus Christ to keep an eye on you, just because you are forever special.

25. God's favourite ring tones is your worship, please don't flash Him let it ring till He picks it, make sure you tell Him your needs and He will answer your prayers. Have a lovely day.

26. Today is a wonderful day to pray, to love, to care, to smile, to celebrate and to thank God for somebody as wonderful as you.

27. Life will never run out of mysteries, the more you want to understand it, the more it becomes complicated, so why worry, life will go on and on.

28. If the world was filled with people like you, then life would have been fair to all, if angels were elected I would always vote you to be my angel.

29. God opened His tap of blessing, some were collecting with cups, I laughed because I collected with a bucket, and I fainted when I saw you leaving with a tanker.

30. There were three angels in heaven the first was found in jail, another was found drunk in a bar and the sweetest of them was found reading this sms.

31. God gave us 86,400 valuable seconds each day, May I use just a few seconds to say thanks for giving me the gift of knowing someone special like you. Keep well and may God bless you always.

32. Special people and family are like jewel. We don't make them we find them. And if you are smart enough to know their value you keep them. You are in my jewellery box.

33. I made a list of friends and I smiled, a list of those I still have I smiled again, then a list of those I am keeping forever, I laughed because your name was still there.

34. Everything in life is temporary, night or day. Both sunrise and sunset are temporary. If things are going good enjoy, it won't last forever and if things are going bad don't worry because it won't last forever, either way everything will pass by.

35. Thought for the day: Good friends are hard to find, harder to leave and impossible to forget.

36. Friendship doesn't need everyday conversations, doesn't always require togetherness, and as long as the relationship is kept in heart true friends never grow apart. Thanks for being my friend.

37. Its not the presence of someone that brings meaning to life, but it's the way someone touches your heart that gives a beautiful meaning. Thanks for being that person to me.

38. I Wish I could be a dove to bring you peace, cupid to bring you love, an angel to bring you a miracle. All I am is a friend. I hope that brings you happiness.

39. Be strong and courageous; do not be frightened or dismayed for the lord your God is with you wherever you go. (Joshua 1:9).

40. I sent you a car, the car is loaded with blessing and love, happiness, joy, and peace. Please offload and return my car to me.

41. Smile today and know that God loves you; you are too blessed to be stressed and too anointed to be disappointed. Have a great day with God's love.

42. Trouble as light as air, love as deep as the ocean friends, as solid as diamonds and success as bright as gold these are all my wishes for u today and always.

43. Good morning, this morning when I woke and saw the sun above, I softly said, Good morning Lord, bless everyone I love right away. I thought of you and said a loving prayer that He would bless you specially, keep you free from problems and evil people, and take care of you. I thought of all the happiness a day could hold in store. I wished it all for you because no one deserves it more. I felt so warm and good inside. My heart was all aglow I know God heard my prayers for you. He hears them all you know!

44. Every single smile can touch someone's heart. May you have plenty of reasons to smile today and may you be the reason for someone else to smile too.

45. May each new day be more pleasant than the previous one. May your hopes and dreams for the future become reality. Make use of every opportunity that comes your way and remember that your character determines your destiny. May the joy of this special day last forever and God bless you.

46. Do you know that there is good in every unfortunate situation? Look for it, adversity reveals genius, prosperity conceals.

47. Never take someone for granted. Hold every person close to your heart because you might wake up one day and realized that you have lost a diamond while you were too busy collecting stones.

48. When I pray I don't see God but I know He listens. When I send sms or messages I don't see you but I know you read them with a smile .

49. Never blame a day in your life, good days gives you happiness. Bad days gives you experience both are essential in life. All are God blessing.

50. Let joy be the hallmark of your life. Happiness depends on happenings; joy depends on daily adventures, good and bad. Embrace every occurrence with joy.

51. God never takes a day off to love, to care and guide us in every moment in our lives. May His presence be with us this day and always.

52. Morning doesn't mean getting up and walking again, it rather means God loves you so much to let you live and see another day.

53. Eyes are looked upon as the window to the soul. Then a smile must be a doorway to the heart, just smile, and take intensive care of yourself.

54. Good morning, this is the angel wake up centre. We are waking all God's favourite because somewhere someone needs your wonderful smile today.

55. Dear Lord please look after the people I love and keep them safe just for me. Remove all burdens on them, especially this one because he/she is too precious and we can't afford to lose him/her. Amen.

56. Nothing splendid has ever been achieved except by those who dare believe that something inside of them is superior to circumstances.

57. Friends are forever like the stars that kept blinking in the sky. Though we might be far apart, but I know you are still near to me whenever I look up.

58. Close your eyes and let me pray for you. God protect this wonderful brother/sister of mine who is not closing his/her eyes while I am praying for him/her and is smiling before I even say Amen.

59. For the world you are someone, for someone you are the world. Life can give you thousands of reasons to cry but you give life thousands of reasons to smile.

60. Good night, may the lord grant you enough strength and wisdom to face the challenges of tomorrow.

61. God has spared us another day with our loved ones. Let us go into this day with wisdom, courage, and strength. Let our dream become realities.

62. Did you get the bag this morning; I left on your doorstep full of prayers, hugs, love, smiles, and blessing?

63. Every life in this world is written by God own hand. That is why I am thankful because as He wrote my life story he included you in it as my friend.

64. Morning greetings don't only say good morning it has a silent message. I remembered you when I woke up. Take care and have a great day.

65. I received a shocking email that says all people who love sex were found dead on their bed this morning. Please call if you are alive I am worried.

66. She came at night, explores my body, got on top of me, and touched me. She bit and sucked; when she was satisfied she left. I was hurt. Bloody mosquito hhhhaaa.

67. To those I have wronged, I ask for forgiveness. To those that God have used in giving me a better life I say thanks. I appreciate and wish you the very best of everything.

68. May the Almighty, whose arms protect, whose help assures, whose wisdom guides, whose words comfort and whose love endures bless and keep you safe this day.

69. Let the beauty that is in God recharge your spirit, purify your mind, touch your soul, and give you joy, happiness and a healthy life.

70. Before I sleep, I pray that God may keep you safe, warm, help you grow wiser everyday that you may find success in everything you do.

71. Without your permission I asked God to protect you, prosper you, bless you, pamper you, guard, and shower you with His divine mercies. Hope you don't mind.

72. Bed time is a wonderful opportunity to pray, to sleep, to rest to dream and to thank God for all the blessing we received.

73. If a kiss was a rain drop I did send you showers, if a hug was a second I did send you hours, if smiles were water I did send you sea, if friendship was a person I did send you myself.

74. Trusting in God won't make mountain smaller but will make climbing it easier. Do not ask God for a lighter load but ask Him for a stronger back.

75. In the end we will remember not the words of our enemies, but the silence of our friends.

76. You are so amazing, in you God implanted love, through you love shall be shared, may you be His messenger and distribute love and joy this beautiful day.

77. A simple friend thinks the friendship is over when you have an argument; a real friend knows that it is not a friendship until after you have had a fight.

78. True happiness consist not in the multitude of friends but on the worth and choice.

79. Grace functions without struggle; favour makes a man receive without asking. These gifts shall never depart from you. You are graciously favoured.

80. The road to success is not straight. There is a curve called failure, but if you have faith as your insurance and Jesus as your driver you will be successful.

81. Hugs are fat free and sugar free, they make you happy, so here is a big hug especially for you. Have a blessed day.

82. The nicest place to be is in someone's thoughts, the safest place to be is in someone's prayers, and the best place to be is in God hands. Stay in God's hand.

83. Mountains hide people I love, value and care about, distance pushes them away, but thought brings them close to me. You are always remembered.

84. Nobody goes to the stream early and brings dirty water. As you wake up today may your life be clean, clear, and calm like the early stream.

85. As vehicles queue up in filling station so shall angels queue to refill your life with blessings. May your prayers never enter voicemail. May you never run out of God's credit!

86. The only people you need in your life are the ones that need you in theirs. Nothing last forever so live it up, drink it down, laugh it off, avoid the bullshits, take chances, never have regrets, because at one point everything you did was exactly what you wanted.

87. Ask and it will be given to you, seek and you will find, knock and the door will be opened to you. (Matthew 7:7).

88. To have God in our life doesn't mean sailing on a boat with no storms, it means having a boat that no storm can sink.

89. Each person comes into this world with a specific destiny. He/She has something to fulfil, some message has to be delivered, and some work has to be completed. You are not here accidentally, but you are here meaningfully. There is a purpose behind you. The whole intent is to do something through you. So appreciate what you have, work if you have to. Do whatever you got to do.

90. There are only two people who can tell you the truth about yourself. An enemy who has lost his temper, and a friend who loves you dearly. So don't be bothered about people as those two kinds of creatures are in every part of the world.

91. There are things that you cannot recover in life.1.The stone-after it is thrown. 2. Words after it's said. 3. The occasion after it's missed. 4. The time after it is gone.

92. You try, you failed, you try, you failed, you try, you failed, and the only true failure is when you stop trying.

93. It is not how much you do that counts but how much love you put in the doing.

94. When the world puts you on your knees you are in a perfect position to pray.

95. A smile is an inexpensive way to improve your looks, if something makes you cry build a bridge and get over it.

96. Good morning, no one will manufacture a lock without a key. Similarly, God won't give problems without solutions, so go fearless, and face it.

97. Our best friends are those who bring out the best in us.

98. Our business in life should not be to get ahead of others but to get ahead of yourself, to break your own record.

99. In playing ball, and in life, a person occasionally gets the opportunity to do something great. When that time comes, only two things matter: being prepared to seize the moment and having the courage to take your best swing.

100. Relationships have to be worked on in order for them to succeed. You can't put your relationship on autopilot and expect everything to turn out okay. You have to stay connected. Falling in love is easy; staying in love is a challenge!

101. May there always be work for your hands to do.

102. May your purse always hold a coin or two.

103. May the sun always shine on your window pane.

104. May a rainbow be certain to follow each rain.

105. May the hand of a friend always be near you.

106. May God fill your heart with gladness to cheer you.

107. To create a beautiful future, think thoughts of goodness, speak good and kind words, and make sure your actions come from goodness.

108. Know your limits then ignore them.

109. The Tongue is one of the most powerful forces on earth. Learn how to use it.

110. For every minute you are angry with someone you lose 60 seconds of happiness that you can never get back.

111. Sometimes the one's you don't want in your life are always there but the ones that matter are sometimes too busy.

112. The greatest gift you can give someone is your time because when you are giving someone your time you are giving them a portion of our life.

113. You may find people who can share your dreams and goals but hoping that they will be identical to us is unrealistic.

114. As diamond is singled out among precious stone, gold stands out even in metals, so shall you be singled out for honour this period and God's people around the world.

115. I lean back today and closed my eyes. I thought of people that I love. I am now sending you powers and asking God to bless you because I care.

116. God has His eyes on you. His hand over you, His spirit, and peace inside you, His love, and angels around you. Whoever touches you; touches the apple of His eyes.

117. When you feel bad for not having what you wanted; just sit tight and be happy because God has thought of something better to give you.

118. I wanted to be the first to wish you good morning. I hope you are having a good one, if not, be encouraged by the fact that while you were sleeping God was watching over you and still is.

He has not changed His mind about you and His strength, love, peace, and wisdom are available for you to face each challenge this day.

119. Grace is an ocean of favour that has no shoreline. It's the fastest ladder to success in life. May that grace envelop your every being and qualify you for a miracle.

120. No matter how softly you whisper a prayer. God surely listens, understands, and knows the hopes and fears you keep in your heart; for you are the twinkle sheep of His eyes.

121. Life is a book with many chapters, some tell tragedy, others triumph, some chapters are dull and ordinary others intense and exciting. The key to being a success in life is to never stop on a difficult page, to never quit on a tough chapter God's champion have courage to keep turning the pages because they know a better chapter lies ahead and with God nothing is impossible.

122. A relaxed mind, a peaceful soul, a joyous spirit, a healthy body, a heart full of love, all of this and my prayers for you today.

123. Never waste an opportunity to say I love you to someone you really love, it's not every day you meet a person with the magic to make you fall in love.

124. Look outside, it's so pleasant, the sun is smiling at you, trees dancing for you, birds singing for you because last night I asked them to wish you good morning.

125. Life is like an undersized blanket, you pull it up your feet sticks out. You cover your feet, your shoulder gets cold. But if you have learned to bend your knees in prayers you will be covered from head to toe and still have enough room to cover all those you love.

126. It is said to hear of angels is a blessing, to see one is a gift, to touch one is a life experience, so how God must have loved me to let me have you as a friend.

127. God isn't Eskom but He lights up your way. He isn't Telkom but He communicates, He isn't MTN, Vodacom, or Cell C but His network is available all the time. May the same God be with you.

128. Someone loves caring for you, watching you, and protecting you. Guess who? It is God!! He is the best.

129. Eight things God does in psalm 107: He redeems gathers, delivers, leads, satisfies, saves, heals, and blesses.

130. A beautiful life does not just happen; it is built daily in prayers, humility, sacrifices, and love. May a beautiful life be yours always!

131. We crossed each other's path not because you need someone like me but because God knows I will never survive without a special person like you.

132. I have a special breakfast for you, a glass of care, a plate of love, a spoon of peace, a fork of hope, and a bowl of prayer.

133. In time of need, it is good to know that one has friends who comfort and remind us that God and His love will never end.

134. A smile to end the day, a prayer to bless your sleep, a song to lighten your dreams, a cheer to praise His presence, a peaceful night to you.

135. If you don't trouble, your trouble will trouble you. Hand them over to God.

136. Elephants don't pray to be big; birds don't pray to fly because they are naturally destined to be great in the sky. Trust in God.

137. One loyal friend is worth ten thousand relatives.

138. A friend walks in when the rest of the world walks out.

139. Misfortune shows those who are not really friends.

140. I belief in Angels, the kind heaven sends. I am surrounded by angels but I call them my best friends.

141. Between a thousand yesterday and a million tomorrow there's only one today and I wouldn't let this day pass without saying good morning.

142. Forget the things that made you sad, remember the things that made you glad. Forget the friends that proved untrue remember those who stuck by you. Forget the troubles that have passed your way. Remember the blessing and miracles every day. May you complete old dreams and start new ones and have safe trip through life's journey.

143. Life is more meaningful if you have plenty of cash Christ, assurance of salvation and holiness. May you never run out of cash for the rest of your life. God bless your family over the festive period.

144. Be joyful in hope, patient in trouble and persistence in prayers. May you know Him in all things.

145. When you were born you were crying, while everybody around you was smiling. Always live your life smiling even when others around you are crying.

146. Thank God for leading me down a path filled with people like you who make every step I take the reason to take another.

147. Let me guess what you are doing. Reading a book? No' Listening to music? Neh, watching TV? Nah caught you! Missing me and reading my sms? Neh' Now you are smiling.

148. One of my angels will be arriving soon to give you a hug so if you hear a crash on your window don't get scared she is still learning to fly.

149. This morning I send my care through nature and my wishes in the wind, when you hear the song of birds and the coolness of wind just know it is me saying Good morning.

150. Life is not about the people who act true in your face it is about the people who remain true behind your back.

151. Lord will make you an instrument of His peace. Where there is hatred let me sow love. Where there is injury pardon. Where there is sadness, joy, and He will never let you down.

152. Tomorrow is not to make promise to anyone. If today is all I get I will like to say how much I appreciate you and what a privilege it is having you in my life. Thanks for being that wonderful friend that you are.

153. A smile is a sign of joy, a hug is a sign of love, and a laugh is a sign of happiness. Knowing someone like you is a sign of God being very good to me.

154. What could you want that forgiveness cannot give? Do you want peace? Forgiveness offers it all. Do you want happiness, a quiet mind, a certainty of purpose, and a sense of worth and beauty that transcends the world? Do you want care and safety and warmth of sure protection always? Do you want quietness that cannot be disturbed, a gentleness that cannot be hurt, a deep abiding comfort, and a rest so perfect it can never be upset? All this forgiveness offers you. Whoever that want peace can only find it by complete forgiveness.

155. If you can read this message you are more blessed than over two billion people in the world that cannot read at all.

156. A friend is that someone who sees your first tears holds the second one and makes sure that the third one never comes out.

157. If you woke up this morning with health without illness you are more blessed than the millions who won't survive this week.

158. Life is bliss, taste it. Life is a dream, realizes it. Life is a challenge, meet it. Life is a duty, complete it. Life is a promise, fulfil it, Life is sorrow, overcome it. Life is song, sing it. Life is a struggle, accept it. Life is tragedies confront it. Life is an adventure, dare it. Life is luck make it. Life is too precious, do not destroy it. Life is life, fight for it.

159. If you have never experienced the danger of battle, the loneliness of imprisonment, the agony of torture or the pangs of starvation you are ahead of 20 million people around the world.

160. If you attend a church meeting without fear of harassment, arrest, torture or death you are more blessed than almost three Billion people in the world.

161. If you have food in your refrigerator, clothes on your back, and a roof over your head, a place to sleep, you are richer than 75% of this world.

162. If you have money in the bank, in your wallet and spare change in a dish somewhere, you are among the top 8% of the world wealthy.

163. If your parents are still married and alive you are very rare.

164. If you hold your head with a smile on your face and truly thankful, you are blessed because majority can, but cannot.

165. If you can hold someone's hand hug them or even touch them on the shoulder; you are very blessed because you can offer God's healing touch.

166. Stop worrying about who stepped on your small toes, who broke your heart, who wasn't there for you, who cursed you and forth. Be glad you are alive today and you have a chance to pick up the pieces.

167. To have joy one must share it. Happiness was born a twin.

168. When you talk like God and think like God. God shows up in your words. Then whatever you say comes to pass.

169. Don't waste time agonizing over what or might not work. Instead invest your time in effort that will enable you to know exactly what works.

170. Do not look back and grieve over the past, for the past is gone. Do not be troubled about the future for it has not come yet. Live in the present and make it so beautiful that it will be worth remembering.

171. Pain is temporary but quitting is forever.

172. There is always a way to create value. Success belongs to those who seek opportunity and take actions that create new and useful value. Whether the situation is gloomy or bright, there is always a way to add more positive value to it. With vision, commitment, focus, persistence, and sustained effort, opportunity turns into achievement.

173. The world changes quickly and tactics that once was successful may no longer be as effective. Yet there are new and existing opportunities for real. Solid value never goes out of style. There is always work to be done and there are always problems to be solved. Where there are challenges begging for solutions, an opportunity to offer real improvement to change life's for the better. Get in the habits of adding values and you will be in habits of creating success.

174. People will not bear it when advice is violently given, even if it is well founded. Hearts are flowers they remain open to softly falling dew, but shut up in the violent downpour of rain.

175. I made a list of all special people in my life, I wrote in pencil but when I came to your name I used a permanent ink because I decided to keep you in my heart forever God bless you .

176. Our future depends on many things, but mostly on you.

177. What you meditate on day and night controls your life. Let the word of God do it.

178. The God that gave you the lion and the bear shall also give you Goliath.

179. Whatever you give to life it gives back to you. Do not hate anybody the hatred which comes out of you will someday come back to you. Love others and love will come back to you.

180. Our goals can only be reached through a vehicle of a plan, in which we most fervently believe and upon which we must vigorously act.

181. Being different does not mean being outrageous or strange. It means being exceptionally unique. So let's stop trying to mould ourselves on other people controlling them or changing them to be what we want them to be.

182. For different individual to live together on this earth in harmony, we need to make some little adjustment for other people. It doesn't mean we are giving up our individuality.

183. In the word of Henley "I am the master of my fate, I am the captain of my soul. Live your live full of potential with love and consideration for others.

184. Learning how to adapt and adjust to the needs and desires of others means that we put away our selfishness in exchange for a higher and better purpose.

185. When we encounter conflicts with our loved ones, it should not feel like it's the end of the world, it should be a reminder of how different we are and how wonderful it is to be unique.

186. Life is about our relationship with others. A life lived entirely alone would be unbearable for most of us. In almost every aspect of our lives we need to interact with people whether it is work, home, family or even our friends.

187. Living a Joyous life involves cultivating positive relationships and choosing to cut off those that are harmful to us or make us feel bad ourselves.

188. Remember that within the best and most fulfilling relationships differences are unavoidable. Great minds work, and may think alike but they can never be exactly the same. In fact, the world would be less interesting if people were exact copies of each other and think in the same way all the time.

189. The Almighty made us unique from the moment we were conceived from our character down to our fingerprints. When we interact with other people it's important to recognize and celebrate our own uniqueness. In spirit it is impossible to always agree with someone. There will always be some little difference.

190. Bending just little to consider or accommodate other people will definitely maintain the harmony in our relationship. The sooner we accept that we are all individuals who happen to be different the better.

191. God did not plan that you should succeed alone. What you lack is always housed in someone else. When you pray today ask God to direct you to someone He has chosen to make an impact in your life. No man is an island.

192. Through Prayers God hear more than you say. He answers more than you ask. He gives more than you desire much more than you deserve. May God richly be with you.

193. You cannot make someone love you. All you can do is be someone who can be loved. The rest is up to them.

194. There will be good days, and there will be bad days. There will always be times when you want to turn around pack it up and call it quits. Don't give up at that time. DONT quit it's an opportunity to prove your worth!

195. Before this day slips over, I want to take time to say good night. I pray that God will Keep you in His care, shower you with blessing and envelope you in His love.

196. A relaxed mind, a peaceful soul, a joyful spirit, a healthy body, and a heart full of Joy are my wishes for you.

197. If you do not put your hands on it and get to work, you won't attract God's blessings.

198. When our praise goes up the blessing of God comes down. Good morning praise the lord always in good and bad times.

199. My friend there can be no conquest without combat. No triumph without trials, no testimony without testing.

200. Prayer can go where we can't go. Through prayers we can be with those we care for without being there. I may be far away but my prayers are with you.

201. You owe me 75 cent because I had to phone heaven to thank God for creating such a sweet and adorable person like you. Remain blessed.

202. Did you know that those who appear to be very strong in heart are real weak and most susceptible?

203. Did you know that those who spend their time protecting others are the ones that really need some -one to protect them?

204. Did you know that the three most difficult things to say are.1. I love you. 2. I am sorry. 3. I need help?

205. Did you know that it is easier to say what you feel in writing than saying it to someone directly? Did you know that it has more value when you say it to their face?

206. Is it true that those who dress in red are more confident in themselves?

207. Is it true that those who dress in yellow are those that enjoy their beauty?

208. Did you know that those who dress in black are those who want to be unnoticed and need your help and understanding?

209. Always have this in your mind any time you obey God you move a step higher in glory. Enjoy your day.

210. Do you know that when you help someone, the help returns in two fold?

211. Did you know that if you ask for something in faith your wish are granted?

212. It depends on whose hands it is. So put all your concern, your worries, your fears, your hopes, your dreams, your families, and your relationships in God's hand; because in His hands everything and anything is possible.

213. The devil does not chase empty vessels. You are loaded that's why he is after you. Please remain strong.

214. Like the sun shines in the morning may this brighten your day and remind you that you are thought of in a very warm way.

215. I sent angels to come and watch you but they came back early. I asked them why they came back they smiled and said we' Angels don't watch other angels they only give them a kiss and come back.

216. If you compare yourself with others you may become vain and bitter for always there will be greater and lesser persons than yourself.

217. Strength does not come from winning. Your struggle develops your strength, when you go through hardships and decide not to surrender that is strength.

218. The person who loves you a lot will always do two things extremely for you. Silently caring for you and openly hurting you to make you perfect.

219. Respect the emotions in someone heart, rather than expressions on someone face because expression is just a formality but emotions are reality.

220. To get something you never had, you have to do something you never did. When God takes something from your grasp, He is not punishing you, but merely opening your hands to receive something better. The will of God will never take you where the grace of God will not protect you.

221. Learn to love the people who are willing to love you at present. Forget the people in the past thank them for hurting you which let you to love people you have right now.

222. It takes more courage to reveal insecurities than to hide them, more strength to relate to people than to dominate them, more manhood to abide by thought-Out principles rather than blind reflex .Toughness is in the soul and spirit, not in muscles and an immature mind.

223. The most beautiful people we have known are those who have known defeat, known suffering, known struggle, known loss, and have found their way out of the depths. These persons have an appreciation, sensitivity, and an understanding of life that fills them with compassion, gentleness and a deep loving concern. Beautiful people do not just happen. Please be strong it will be well.

224. Success and excuses do not talk to each other. If you give excuses, forget about success. If you want success, don't give excuse. Believe me you can make it by His grace and focus.

225. Content makes a poor man rich. Discontent makes a rich man poor. Chose which is better for you and your health.

226. God made relatives. Thank God we can choose our friends. I bless the name of the lord the day I found you as a friend.

227. Some people, no matter how old they get, never lose their beauty and nature, they merely move it from their faces to their heart. You are one of such people. God bless you.

228. Have fun, explore life, and unchain yourself from the shackles you have inherited. Develop your own thought and beliefs. Live in love and never let fear be the reason behind your action or inactivity.

229. God's word is bound to work when you declare it. The life we live is a life of joy, a joy that must be expressed. We must let people know that we have a God who is alive and He has given us the victory. Our mouth must be filled with laughter, not the kind that mocks people but the laughter of joy in appreciation of what God has done for us. Even when you cannot see those great things, go ahead and express joy.

230. A sweet relationship is life pillow, when tired, sleep on it when sad drop a tears on it, when angry punch it and when happy hug it. You have been this and more to me thanks for been there always.

231. God answers in three ways. He says yes and gives you what you want. He says no and gives you something better. He says wait and gives you the best.

232. Today will never come again. Be a blessing; be a friend, encourage someone. Take time to care, let your word heal not wound.

233. It is never God's intention to make us become failures. However, He sometimes allows us to fail in order to bring to us success tomorrow. God has planted in our every defeat the seeds of our future success. Our every failure can be a stepping-stone to our success. Therefore when you fail, humble yourself in repentance, surrendering to His will and His goal for your lives. Memory verse: Matthew 7:24~27.

234. They love you, but they are not your lover, they care for you, but they are not your family. They are ready to share your pain, but they are not your blood relation. They are.... FRIENDS! A true friend...scolds like a DAD. Cares like a MOM. Teases like a SISTER. Irritates like a BROTHER, and finally loves you more than a LOVER.

235. Teach me to do your will, for you are my God, may your gracious spirit lead me on a level ground (Psalm 143 verse 10).

236. Wisdom produces ideas, ideas produces money, and money produces wealth. This is my prayers for you this day and forever. Amen.

237. Steps to a happy life 1. Don't stress yourself with useless people who don't deserve to be an issue in your life. 2. Never invest too much emotion at one thing because if you do, you will end up hurting yourself. 3. Learn to live your worries because God will take care of everything .4 Trust and have faith.

238. Life is very short, so break your silly ego, forgive quickly, believe slowly, love truly, laugh loudly and never avoid anything that will make you smile.

239. When I woke up this morning lying in bed, I was asking myself, what are the secret of success in life? I found the answer right there in my room. The fan said be cool, the roof said aim high, the window said see the world, the clock said every minute is precious, the mirror said reflect before you act, the calendar said be up to date, the door said push hard for your goals carry a heart that never hates, carry a smile that never fades carry a touch that never hurt. God bless you all.

240. Your body is what makes you sexy. Your smile is what makes you pretty, but your personality is what makes you beautiful.

241. Never leave a true friend or a relationship for few faults. Nobody is perfect, nobody is correct at the end. Affection is always greater than perfection. Life is short so break the rules. Forgive quickly. Love truly, laughs loudly and never avoids anything that will make you smile.

242. Dear God, I know that I'm nowhere near perfect. I know I don't pray every night. I know I lose my temper sometimes, but thank you for loving me every way and letting me see another beautiful day.

243. I might not be someone's first choice, but I am a great choice. I may not be rich, but I am valuable. I don't pretend to be someone I am not, because I am good at being me. I might not be proud of something's I have done in the past, but I am proud of who I am today. I may not be perfect but I don't need to be. Take me as I am, or watch me walk away.

244. The Journey of Life "Do not shut love out of your life by saying it is impossible to find. The quickest way to receive love is to give love; the fastest way to lose love is to hold it tightly. In addition, the best way to keep love is to give it wings, Do not dismiss your dreams as be without dreams, is to be without hope, to be without hope is to be without purpose. Do not run through life so fast that you forget not only where you have been but also where you are going. Life is not a race, but a journey to be savoured each step of the way.

245. When you are passing through the challenges of life, your attitude should be "God I know that you are going to turn this around and use it for my good. God, I believe that you're going to bring me out stronger than ever before.

246. I learned the hard way that I cannot always count on others to respect my feeling, even if I respect theirs. Being a good person doesn't guarantee that others will be good people too. You only have control over yourself and how you choose to be as a person. As for others, you can only choose to accept them or walk away.

247. Always remember that your present situation is not your final destination. The best is yet to come.

248. Never go to sleep angry because you never know if the person you are mad at will wake up the next morning. Always forgive someone. You never know if you will speak to them again. Get over it. Always forgive you may not forget. But it's better than knowing you will never get to tell them you are sorry, or that you still love them, it might be too late.

249. Sometimes, no matter how hard you try to be good, other people will always see your flaws. Just remind yourself that you don't live to please people, but to please God and feel in peace with yourself.

250. You don't stop being God's child when you mess up. God knows your heart and he loves you. Be blessed and have a wonderful day.

251. The most splendid future will always depend upon the necessity to release the past, you cannot move forward in life unless you learn from your past mistakes and move on.

252. Ten ways to love. *1.* Listen without interrupting (Proverb 18) *2.* Speak without accusing (James 1: 19) *3.* Give without sharing (Proverb 21: 26) *4.* Pray without ceasing (Colossians 1:9) *5.* Answer without arguing (Proverbs 17:1) *6.* Share without pretending (Ephesians 4: 15) *7.* Enjoy without complaint (Philippians 2:14) *8.* Trust without complaint (Corinthians 13: 7) *9.* Forgive without Punishing (Colossians 3:13) *10.* Promise without forgetting (Proverb 13: 12)

253. I met this guy who has a motto he lives by every day. He said "Listen carefully and live by those four rules: Drink, Steal, Swear and Lie. I was shaking my head 'No', but he then told me to listen while he explained his four rules. So here they are.

1. "Drink" from the everlasting cup" every day.

2. "Steal" a moment to help someone that is in worse shape than you are.

3. "Swear "that you will be better person today then yesterday.

4. And last, but not the least, when you "lie" down at night than God you live in a country where you have religious freedom. I am not as good as I should be; I am not as good as I could be. But thank God am I am better than yesterday.

254. Those who love you are not fooled by your mistakes you have made or dark images you hold about yourself. They remember your beauty when you feel ugly, your wholeness when you feel break, your innocence when you feel guilty and your purpose when you are confused.

255. Don't be a beggar of love, be a donor of love. Beautiful people are not always good, but good people are always beautiful.

256. Talking about our problem is our greatest addiction. Break the habit. Talk about your Joy.

257. When a train goes through a tunnel and it gets dark, you don't throw away the ticket and jump off. You sit still and trust the engineer. Trust God today no matter how dark your situation. God says "you are coming out"

258. Never push a loyal person to the point where they no longer give a damn.

259. The saddest things about betrayal is that it never comes from your enemy, it comes from friends and loved ones.

260. Remember happiness starts with you, not your relationship, or your friends, or your job but you.

261. If someone wants you in their life, they will put you there. You shouldn't have to fight for a spot.

262. Some people don't love you; they don't even care about you. They just want to stay connected to you. They love the benefits, so they do the minimal. A little phone call here and there, just checking on you. What they are really doing is maintain the connection, so when they need / want they have a way in.

263. Spend your time on those that love you unconditionally. Don't waste it on those that love you when conditions are right.

264. You don't have to feel guilty about removing toxic from your life. It doesn't matter whether someone is relative, romantic interest, employer, childhood friend, or even a new acquaintance. You don't have to make room for people who cause you pain or make you feel small. It's one thing if a person owns up to their behaviour and makes an effort to change. But if a person disregard your feeling, ignores your boundaries, and to treat you in a harmful way, they need to go. **(Danielle Koepke)**

265. I will leave the world and never come back, you will cry when you see my number, you will miss me when situation won't be able to hear my laugh and voice again. There will be no more me to irritate, tease, and make you laugh and say sorry stupidly. Tears might flow out your eyes but I will be gone long and forever, so enjoy my silly stupid company as much as before I close my eyes forever.

266. People say "find good people and leave the bad ones" But I say find the good in people and ignore the bad in them because no one is perfect.

267. Respect is earned, Honest is appreciated. Trust is gained. Loyalty is returned.

268. Anybody can love your looks, but it's your heart and personality that makes someone stays with you.

269. Life has knocked me down a few times, it has shown me things I never wanted to see, I have experienced sadness and failure. But one thing for sure, I always get up.

270. Don't let the size of where you are coming from confuse you with the size of where you are going. David was an errand boy the day he defeated Goliath and became a national hero. Stop judging your purpose with your pains. While Joseph was still a prisoner, he was comforting other prisoners because he knew where he was going. Be determined in the face of uncertainties and the cloud of limitations will soon clear.

271. No matter how hard your life may be right now! Just remember one thing there's only one person who can make it easy for you who can make the impossible possible for you. Just put your trust in His hand put all your trust in Him. Friends will love you for what you are and what you have but not for who you really are! But God loves the inner person in you and He wants you the way you are never doubt His love for you!

272. Every night, someone thinks about you before they go to sleep, at least fifteen people in this world loves you. The only reason someone would ever hate you is because they want to be like you. There are at least two people in this world that would die for you. You mean the world to someone, someone that you don't even know exists love you. When you make the biggest mistakes ever, something good comes from it. When you think the world has turned its back on you, take a look. Always remember the compliments you have received, forget the rude remarks so if you think this is true with you there are your friends who need to be told how special they are send this message to them, make someone's day , help get a smile on someone's face, help someone out , remember that you are loved my friend.

273. I was dying to finish my high school and start college, and then I was dying to finish college and start working, then I was dying to marry and have children and then I was dying for my children to grow old so I could go back to work but then I was dying to retire and now I am dying and suddenly I realized I forget to live. Please let this happen to you appreciate your current situation and enjoy each day.

274. Everything happens for a reason. People change so you can learn to let go. Things go wrong so that you can appreciate them when they are right. You believe lies so that you will eventually learn to trust no one but yourself, and sometimes good things fall apart so that better things can fall together.

275. Every test in our life makes us bitter or better, every problem comes to break us or makes us. The choice is ours whether we become victim or victor.

276. Give but don't allow yourself to be used. Love, but do not allow your heart to be abused. Trust, but do not be naive. Listen to others, but do not lose yourself.

277. Sometimes, people haven't apologized because they are ashamed. Forgive them anyway, Sometimes you have to be okay with a sorry you never got. Forgiveness unblocks your blessing. Do it you are worth it.

278. Never help an ungrateful person get to their feet it is like telling a wolf that you are a sheep.

279. I've come to realize that only people I need in my life are the ones who need me in theirs even when I have nothing else to offer but myself.

280. God, thank you that I am not defined by the mistake I made yesterday, thank you for setting me free.

281. A strong person is not the one who doesn't cry. A strong person is the one who cries and shed tears for a moment, then gets up and fights again.

282. Bible aren't allowed in school any more but are encourages in prisons. If kids were allowed to read it at school they may not end up in prisons.

283. The best kind of people is the ones that comes into your life, and make you see the sun where you once saw clouds. The people that believes in you so much, you start to believe in yourself too. The people that love you, simply for been you, they are once in a life time kind of people.

284. Spirituality is not a religion, being spiritual just means you are in touch with your own self.

285. God doesn't call the qualified. He qualifies the called.

286. I regret nothing in my life even if my past was full of hurt, I still look back and smile , because it made me who I am today .

287. Women are like police; they have all the evidence in the world, but will want a confession. What an irony.

288. When you are tempted to give up your breakthrough is probably just around the corner

289. Nobody can take away your pains, so don't let anyone take away your happiness.

290. Forgiveness is not something we do for other people. We do it for ourselves to get well and move on. Stop holding grudges.

291. Never allow yourself to be so desperate that you end up settling for less than what you deserve.

292. To be grateful is recognising the love of God in everything He has given us. Every breath we draw is a gift of His love.

293. Heart gift. It' not the things that can be bought that are life's richest treasure, it's just the little "heart sifts' that money cannot measure. A cheerful smile, a friendly word, a sympathetic nod are priceless little treasures from store house of God. They are things that can't be bought with silver or gold, for thoughts fullness, kindness and love are never sold. They are the priceless things in life for which no one can pay and the giver finds riches recompenses in giving them away.

294. The world is full of miracle to those who recognise them, But we have to look the right direction way since God sometimes will disguise the. He shines His light in places where we d' least expect Him to and often does the opposite of what we think He'll do. He has a way of bringing out the best within the worst, the moment we stop worrying and choose to put Him first, and if we do, He'll pull us through and help us find the door that opens to the very things that we'd been looking for. Sometimes things happen that are hard to understand, but I believe that faith will see you through. Please know my thoughts and prayers are with you.

295. God has blessed me. I have seen better days, but I also have seen worse. I do not have all my wants, but I do have all my needs. I woke up with a few aches and pains, but I woke up! My life may not be perfect, but I Thank God it is good.

296. To achieve your dreams remember your ABC's Avoid negative sources, people, things and habits. Believe in yourself

Consider things from every angle don't give up and give in Enjoy life today, yesterday is gone, and tomorrow may never come. Family and friends are hidden treasures, seek them and enjoy their riches. Give more than you plan to. Hang on to your dreams. Ignore those who try to discourage you. Just do it. Keep trying no matter how hard it

297. Like the waves in the ocean, our lives have good times and bad... Sometimes things are calm and other times it's a horrible storm, but one thing remains the same, God will smile down on us and the sun will shine again.

298. Create a room to be hurt with the truth than allowing to be comforted with a lie. The truth hurts for a while, but a lie hurts forever. The choice is yours."Lots of love"

299. Life is always full of ups & downs, so why are you worried when you are at the bottom? Because the next place is up. Sorrow is a fruit; God doesn't allow it to grow on a branch that is too weak to bear it.

300. Remember, just because someone has broken off with you does not mean that no one in the world wants you or that you are not worthy person. You may be tempted to bask in your own misery and pain while trying to enlist the sympathy of friends but a better course of action is to put the past behind you and leave it there. Dwelling on the past will only lead to self-pity and depression. Pity parties are lonely affairs.

301. GOD didn't Promise days without Pain, Laughter without sorrow, Sun without rain, but He did Promise strength for the day

302. People that gossip have not discovered who they are. You are interested in others because the only thing you know is others. You don't know who you are. Michael Faraday was said to forget to eat his breakfast, lunch and his wife in anger will clear the table. When he comes to the table to eat, he won't see any food. And he would say, "poor me, I forgot that I have eaten my lunch" The reason was because he was too engulfed in his research that he never had time for himself. When you have discovered who you are, you won't have time for who others are. Gossip is where idle minds get their medals

303. Never search your happiness in others, which will make you feel alone, Rather search it in yourself; you will feel happy even when you are left alone. The heart that cares too much for others is always misunderstood. The heart that acts like caring is always understood. Very sad but a stunning fact of life. In life, most people help us when it suits them. Very few help when it suits us. Let's make those few our friends and be those chosen few to others. Don't let the world CHANGE your smile. Make your smile CHANGE the world. We always feel that life of others is better than ours but we are also "others" for someone else. 90% of the problems are due to the tone of voice. It is not what you say, but how you say it, that creates the problem.

304. Many times in my life I've come through the storm and rain and times after times in my life I've overcome heartache and pains, but I always kept my faith in God cause I knew somehow He 'd make a way, kept trusting , kept believing and always pray

305. How to begin: Rebuilding life from within. Love yourself, unconditionally. Release your bottled up emotions. Avoid living beyond your means. Nurture your inner strength. Stop apologizing for being you, surrounding yourself with positive people.

306. Blessing for my friends. May you always have happiness to keep you smiling , trails to keep you strong, success to keep you confident , faith to keep you going , and belief each day is a gift.

307. When God has a plan for your life, I don't care how much you murmur and complain and kick and fuss and scream and yell. When you know that God has a plan for your life, He got you tied up... I serve a God who will tie you up when you're acting crazy, tie you up, while you're trying to do your own thing, tie you up while your temper is raging, and tie you up, when your ambition is out of control. Sometimes, God will tie you up till the time is right. Nothing will work, your money won't work, your career won't work, the boyfriend will leave, and the house will sell, because when God has you tied up, He's not going to let you get away. He'll say, be still and see the salvation of the Lord.

308. NO ONE KNOWS WHAT YOU ARE CAPABLE OF EXCEPT YOURSELF! People will judge you by HOW you look. And by WHAT you have. But please, fight on! Fight for Your place in history. Fight for your glory. NEVER EVER GIVE UP!

309. People who are living just to impress must be really very poor inside, because only people suffering from inferiority complex want to impress others. A really superior person never compares himself with anybody else because he knows he is incomparable & he knows others are also as incomparable as he is. He is neither superior nor inferior! Street Hustlers Believe with all of your heart that you will do what you were made to do! We are all born to be great! Nobody Supernatural! Don't allow anyone to "boh boh" you! Do what you know how to do best and Put all Faith in GOD!! May God bless us all?

310. Relationship between two people should be like the relationship between the hand and the eye. I don't know if you have ever noticed that if the hand gets hurt, the eye cries, and if the eye cries, the hand wipes its tear.

311. There is no divine seed that will not announce itself on earth in due season. Therefore, any man who lacks the principle of kingdom investment is prone to be infested by poverty. Right where you are, people who have doubted your ability to influence destiny or even succeed in life shall be positively influenced by you in this last period of the year because it is not over until it is over.

312. Never make a decision when you're angry. Smart, careful men/Women realize they must have a clear head to think. When you're angry, it's your boiling bloodlines that speak for you, not your logic. Control your emotions. This is one of the most important rules there is. When you're angry, you make threats you often can't deliver on, or decisions you come to regret. Don't say I didn't warn you

313. Whenever you make a mistake or get knocked down by life, don't look back at it too long. Mistakes are life's way of teaching you. Your capacity for occasional blunders is inseparable from your capacity to reach your goals. No one wins them all, and your failures, when they happen, are just part of your growth. Shake off your blunders. How will you know your limits without an occasional failure? Never quit. Your turn will come

314. Lord, I bring to you my burdens and you know my situation you know I can't make it without you. Comfort my heart, give me strength, and help me to carry on. At my lowest, God is my hope. At my darkest God is my light. At my weakest God is my strength. At my saddest God is my comforter in Jesus Name I pray Amen.

315. We all need someone to whom we are accountable and who will correct us when necessary. Many gifted people with bright future before them, and many who already attained a great measure of success, have crashed and burned unnecessary .Why? They were too proud to agree they needed help. Memory Proverb 1 verse 5.

316. Give, but do not allow yourself to be used. Love, but do not allow your heart to be abused. Trust, but do not be naive. Listen to others do not lost yourself.

317. The danger to our planet does not lie in man's determination to provide necessaries for mankind; the danger lurks around man's ambition for frills which he can live without.

318. Once there's a price for a particular commodity, this simply means the commodity has essential value. The bible says in 1 Corinthians 7:23 that, "You were bought with a price, do not become slave of men" Understand that before Jesus came to pay the price, other sacrifices were made but it couldn't match up the kind of value, dominion, authority, influence, power, you have. To really understand your worth and what you carry, you must know it took the blood of Jesus to bring back the original dominion God gave to man.

319. Don't despise the days of small beginnings. Our rewards come from obeying the specific callings He's placed on our lives, not from jealously trying to achieve things that you think will impress people. Don't let jealousy grow in you. Trust God to place you where you need to be.

320. A lot of people think God won't use them until every area of their life is perfected. That type of thinking keeps people from allowing God to use them. He uses us in spite of us, not because of us.

321. Have you found yourself in a situation that you never expected you would be in and you're stressed out of your mind? You may feel your whole world is crashing in on you and that you've lost everything. You are just plain tired. Don't panic and don't quit! You're still here in your right mind. Everything else is a bonus.

322. Let's face it, we can all be self absorbed from time to time. And it's easy to get wrapped up in your own personal goals and ambitions. But when you turn your attention away from yourself and focus on what you're able to offer to others, you'll find that you're full of good ideas, gifts and talents. By helping others, you'll see you have a lot to offer and this will make you feel more confident in yourself.

323. Everyone is good at something. It's time to give credit where credit's due, starting with yourself. Think about all the things you're good at and celebrate your victories, big and small. Remember the things you have achieved in your life and the obstacles you've had to overcome. Rather than focus on what you don't have, highlight your talents and give power to the positive aspects of who you are. Give yourself permission to take pride in your accomplishments.

324. The Best Way To Judge People Is To Love Them. You Are Not Called As A Spiritual Detective. Stop Finding The Faults And

Flaws Of People As If There Is A Reward For It. You Are Commanded By God To Love People And Not Judge Them because It Was The Side Of Jesus That Was Pierced And Not Yours. Grow Up And See People The Way God Sees Them And You Will Deal With Them Kindly! Jesus Is Lord.

325. THINKING CORNER: When you listen to my pain and frustration with tender-hearted compassion, it strengthens my faith more than quoting a million Bible verses would do. I know the spiritual truths already, that God cares and will guide me.

I need to experience God's love and compassion through your caring and listening and ministry of presence. I need God in your flesh to hug me, cry with me, and assure me of your concern, love, and support. I do need your prayers for me and with me, but to be there with me is the best answer to prayer.

326. Love can heal a wounded soul. We all have scars from our past. Scars on wrists and throats can be healed with time but there are some scars which are much deeper than those on the body. They are the scars on our hearts, minds and on our souls which take a long time to heal. Embrace people who love you because love has an amazing power to heal and bring radiance in our life.

327. A man doing a right thing in a wrong place will never get a right result. Divine placement is a necessary factor for achieving divine destiny.

328. God's Unique Love. A relationship with God is like no other relationship you may have experienced. God has a unique kind of love for you. It is unconditional (not based upon meeting certain conditions). God loves you because He loves you.

329. Sometime, no matter how hard you try to be good, other people will always see your flaws. Just remind yourself that you don't live to please people, but to please God and feel in peace with yourself. My name they call me by my brothers Odiraa Chukwu Mma meaning what is good in the sight of God.

330. No matter how big your house is. How recent your car is. How big your bank account is. No matter how expensive the food you eat it is. No matter how costly your designer shoes and clothes are. No matter how beautiful fully figured or how handsome muscular you are. No matter how expensive your casket will be. We are all going 6 feet underground and our grave is still going to be the same size. Stay humble.

331. You are where God wants you to be at this very moment. Every experience is part of His divine plan.

332. Never compare your journey with someone else's. Your journey is your journey not a competition.

333. God is the best listener; you don't need to shout, nor cry out loud because he hears even the very silent prayers of a sincere heart.

334. There are some people who put you down in life, mock your dreams, and challenge your personality, they look like winners. But in actual fact, they are only voicing out their insecurities and jealousy. Do not let them down. Believe and accept yourself and hold onto what you believe in.

335. 12 step to self care.

1. If it feels wrong, don't do it

2. Say"exactly"what you mean

3. Don't be a people pleaser

4. Trust your instincts

5. Never speak badly about yourself

6. Never give up on your dreams

7. Don't be afraid to say no

8. Don't be afraid to say yes

9. Be kind to yourself

10. Let go of what you can't control

11. Stay away from drama and negativity

12. Love everyone and don't be a judge to characters' you never know what the other person is going through and if you were in that person shoes you may be worst

336. Tips for a great life:
1- Forgive everyone who did make you cry in the past.
2- Forget them totally
3- Forget everyone who did hurt you and disrespected... your person.
4- Find new awesome friends no matter how far away they might be.
5- Never accept your ex-back into your life
6- Avoid mixing with people who knows your value but accepts to only Drag and abuse it.
7- Always learn to look forward
8- Be real and never anything fake.
9- Stay away from a cheating and an unfaithful partner.
10- If staying with someone makes you poorer, leave at once.
11- Find your Dream-likes.

337. Nothing in life is worth fighting for. Your best cloths is someone's rag, your bank account balance is someone's offering in church. Every single harlot you see in a hotel or on the street at night was at a point in time a virgin. So what is the squabble all about? Life is too small to feel big or that you are better than anybody. "We are all naked to death" says Steve Jobs. Nothing can save us from it. I hate to see people who brag about wealth, beauty, intelligence, level of education, fame and material possessions. There's nothing you've achieved in life that no one else has never gotten. There is one thing that is worth bragging which is "Life in God Almighty" So, be good to your fellow man and always make friends.

Always remember that people you trample upon on your way up a ladder will be the same you will pass on your way down. So cause no problem for others because if you do, they will become your very problem one day. Finally, even banana stem will one day become dried leaves. Please don't be selfish, share this message with family/friends as we are all one way or the other guilt. If one day you feel like crying, call me, I don't promise to make you laugh but I can cry with you, if one day you want to run away don't be afraid to call me, I promise to be there running beside you. But if one day you call and there's no answer, come to me perhaps I need you. One day, one of us will not be here and then it will be too late to say I care, I love you. Tears may flow but I will be long gone. So forward to everyone you care for. I just did to my lovely and God sent family/friends. Send to your best friends no matter how often you talk or how close you are, let old friends know you haven't forgotten them and new friends know you will never.

338. Twenty good reasons to Worship God
1. He forgives my iniquities
2. He heals all my diseases
3. He redeems my life from destruction
4. He crowns me with loving kindness
5. He satisfies my mouth with good things
6. He executes righteous and justice for the oppressed
7. He makes His ways known
8. He is merciful
9. He is gracious
10. He is slow to anger
11. He will not strive with us
12. He will not keep his anger forever
13. He does not punish us according to our iniquities
14. He shows great mercy to those who fear Him
15. He removes our transgressions from us
16. He has pity on us
17. He remembers we are dust

18. His mercy is everlasting

19. He blesses our children and grandchildren who obey Him

20. He rules over all and His throne is established

339. When someone undermines your dreams, predicts your doom, or criticize you in any way, remember, they are telling you their story not yours.

340. 7 things to give up

1. Pleasing people

2. Doubting yourself

3. Negative thinking

4. Fear of failure

5. Criticizing yourself

6. Saying yes when you want to say No

7. Procrastination.

341. Dear God, if I hurt others give me the strength to apologize. If people hurt me, give me the strength to forgive.

342. The last wish of Alexander the great. On his death, Alexander summoned his army generals and told them his three ultimate wishes.

1. The doctor should carry his coffin.

2. The wealth, he has accumulated (Money, gold, precious stones) should be scattered along the procession to the cemetery.

3. His hands should be let loose so that they hang outside the coffin for all to see. One of his general who was surprised by these unusual requests asked Alexander to explain. Here is what Alexander had to say;

4. "I want the best doctors to carry my coffin to demonstrate that in the face of death, even the best doctor in the world have the power to heal."

5. "I want the road to be covered with treasures so that everybody sees that material wealth acquired on earth will stay on earth.

6. I want my hands to be swing in the wind, so that people understand that we come to this world empty handed and we leave this world empty handed after the most precious treasure of all is exhausted, and that is: Time. We do not take to our grave any material wealth. Time is our most precious treasure because it is limited. We can produce more wealth, but we cannot produce more time.

343. "Don't waste time or energy on people who talk "about you" ...but won't talk "to you"!

344. I stopped explaining myself when i realized people only understand from their level of perception.

345. Don't waste words on people who deserve your silence, sometimes the most power thing you cn say is nothing at all.

346. Truth is: People that are jealous of you don't even realize you don't have it all together. They are actually jealous of struggling wrapped in your strength.

347. Growth is painful. Change is painful, but nothing is as painful as staying stuck somewhere you don't belong. Mandy Hales

348. Everyone deserves to be loved for who they are. Bruce Jenner

349. Most relationship fails because we spend too much time pointing out each other's mistakes and not enough time enjoying each other's company

350. Before you speak, before you write, before you spend, earn. Before you criticize wait, before you pray forgive, before you quit try. Your words, your Dreams, and your thought have the power to create condition in your life. What you confess brings possession. If you keep saying you can't stand your job you might lose your Job. If you keep saying you can't stand your body your body can become sick.

If you keep saying you can't stand your car your car could be stolen or just stop operating. If you keep saying you're always broke guess what you will always be broke. If you keep saying you can't trust a man or a woman you will always meet someone in your life to hurt and betray you. If you keep saying you can't find a job you will be unemployed. If you keep saying you can't find someone to love you will never find love believe me our very thought will attract more experience to confirm your beliefs. Turn your thought and conversations around to be more positive and power packed with faith, hope, love, and action.

Don't be afraid to believe that you can have what you want and desire. Watch your thoughts they become words, watch your word they become actions, watch your action they become habits, watch your habits they become character, watch your character it becomes your destiny. So to prevent obstacles get out of your own way, enjoy every minutes you live. Don't be too busy today, please share this inspiring message (Anonymous).

CHAPTER 5
DOES LOVE EXIST ANY LONGER?

Are we still living in a world where love is the principle upon which the other commandments of God are established? Are we still in an age where the true meaning of love is the reason behind the creation of this beautiful world by God for us to enjoy and live in harmony? Love dwells in a place where there is peace, joy, laughter, good health, hope, and faith. It dwells in a place where we could be our brother's keeper for real, not because of what we may stand to gain or what people can offer us, but because of the word. **LOVE** is the greatest commandment. I wonder how many of us can boldly say we love God whom we do not see, while we despise the people we see on a daily basis. This explains why forgiveness is a big problem amongst us as we carry grudges even into our graves. Yet every day we ask God to forgive us our trespasses while we can't forgive those who have offended us consciously and unconsciously. We were all humans until race disconnected us, religion seprated us, politics divided us and wealth classified us.

"A new command I give you; love one another. As I have loved you so you must love one another." **(Jesus Christ)**

"To be brave is to love unconditionally without expecting anything in return." **(Madonna)**

"Live in harmony with one another; be sympathetic, love as brothers, be compassionate and humble." **(1 Peter 3:8)**

"Love one another and help others to rise to the higher levels, simply by pouring out love. Love is infectious and the greatest healing energy." **(Sai Baba)**

"There is no surprise more magical than the surprise of being loved: It is God's finger on man's shoulder." **(Charles Morgan)**

"The good life is one inspired by love and guided by knowledge."
(Bertrand Russell)

"You and I must make a pact, we must bring salvation back. Where there is love, I'll be there." **(Jackson Five)**

"We are all visitors to this time, this place. We are just passing through. Our purpose here is to observe, to learn, to grow, to love and then we return home." **(Unknown)**

God created this beautiful world and gave us dominion over it. More so, He gave us the liberty to multiply and enjoy it. Sadly, it has been turned into a battle field, where anger, greed, envy, betrayal, frustration, Sodomy, cruelty, and wars are our lot. We have seen on a global scale where super powers fight themselves (e.g. World War1, World 11, The Cold War between the U.S. vs. U.S.S.R), continent against continent, country against country (e.g. Iraq vs. Iran, Britain vs. Argentina in the fork land war, Iraq vs. Kuwait, Nigeria vs. Cameroon in the battle for Bakassi Peninsula etc), citizens of a country fighting among themselves (e.g. the Rwanda genocide, the civil wars in Mozambique, Somali, Liberia, Sierra Leone, Ivory Coast, Syria etc), religions among one another (e.g. Sunni Muslims vs. Shia Muslims in Iraq, Boko Haram in Nigeria vs. Christians) church pastors against each other, pastors vs. members, family members against one another, brothers against their sisters, and parents against their children.

Very few people feel enough love in their lives. The world has become a rather loveless place. We can hardly even imagine a world in which all of us were in love all the time, with everyone. Very few of us were taught that we're essentially good. Very few of us were given sense of unconditional approval, a feeling that we're precious because of what we are, not what we do. We were raised by people who were raised the same way we were. What we lost was a sense of our own power. And what we learned was fear, fear that we weren't good enough, just the way we are. Thought separated from love is a profound miscreation. It's our own power turned against ourselves. The moment the mind first deviated from love an entire illusionary world came into being.

"Be of good cheer about death and know this as a truth, that no evil can happen to a good man, either in life or after death." **(Socrates)**

"Love is a miracle it is the only gift that makes you richer the more you give it out. Share love today and enrich your soul." **(Unknown)**

"Love is the greatest thing that can happen to anybody which should be shared and reciprocated." **(Unknown)**

"Love recognizes no barriers, it jumps hurdles, leap fences, penetrate walls to arrive at its destination full of hope." **(Dr. Maya Angelou)**

"Love and time, those are the only two things in all of life and all over the world that cannot be bought but spent." **(Unknown)**

"People are made to be loved and things are made to be used. The confusion in this world is that people are being used and things are being loved." **(Anna La Torre)**

"Love takes up where knowledge leaves off." **(Thomas Aquinas)**

"What we once enjoyed and deeply loved, we can never lose, for all that we love deeply becomes a part of us." **(Helen Keller)**

"Love and desire are the spirit's wings to great deeds." **(Johann Wolfgang von Goethe)**

"Love without truth is blind 'truth without love is empty." **(Joseph Cardinal)**

"Love means to commit yourself without guarantee." **(Anne Campbell)**

"To fear love is to fear life, and those who fear life are already three parts dead." **(Bertrand Russell)**

This brings me back to the point I am trying to emphasize in this chapter **Love.** I have taken my time to resight various quotes, wise words that talks about what love means, which talks about the benefit of true love in our society, which helps us to know that when God created this world from the word go he did with the word Love on his lips, the assurance that the world can be a better place for all if love becomes our watchword. Where we can loves one another not because of what we stand to gain from the other person be it materially, financially or sexually but spreading love in truth and in spirit becaue our creator is love himself.

There have been a lot of misconceptions on the real meaning of love. Love has lost its bearing in this present generation of ours. This chapter is the core reason for my writing this book and basically the title of my book "Hard Lessons of Life and Self Healing" originates from it. I and my immediate family have tested the worst form of misfortune from the very people we have given all our love, have fought for, prayed for, but rather we were paid back with evil, persecutions, animosity, and a host of others. I asked myself where it went wrong. Was it the beautiful clothes? Was it the shops? Was it the cars? Was it the houses? I could not really trace where the problems emanated from. There were times I wondered if the devil has succeeded in turning my lovely family tree into a graveyard where bitterness has become the order of the day.

If there was real love, there would be no war because we would not fight. There would be no hunger because we would feed each other. There would be no environmental breakdown because would love our children, our planet and ourselves too much to destroy it. There would be no prejudice, oppression, or violence of any kind. There would be no sorrow. There would only be peace. Most of us are violent people not necessarily physically, but emotionally. We have been brought up in a world that does not put love first, and where love is absent, fear sets in. Fear is to love as darkness is to light. It is a terrible absence of what we need in order to survive. Fear is the root of all-evil. It is the problem with the world. Our worldly problems are actually just symptoms of the real problem, which is always a lack of love.

"The touchstone of what is good, be it thought, or word or action, is LOVE. We are to love our neighbours as ourselves. That is the law and the prophets. Anything therefore - any thought or word or action - which falls short of LOVE is evil, and holds within itself the germ of its own eventual and inevitable destruction."
(Chief Obafemi Awolowo)

I grew up in a very lovely family surrounding, where love, unity, progress, fairness was the order of the day. There was always joy in proclaiming that I am from Ogbuagu Family. We usually visit one another, but today that spirit of love no longer exists. In its place, rivalry and witch-hunting has taken over. Where does this leave the new generation who are unaware of where this bad habit came from? I was born from a poor family background by very loving parents Chief and Mrs. Clement and Christiana Ogbuagu from Abagana in Anambra State. My parents lived in peace and harmony, worked hard and grew from strength to strength. They grew from being nobody to somebody in our local community and business community. They prospered and were known by the business name Menchristy and Sons Enterprises.

Our house played host to most of my paternal/maternal relatives. Those who were not related to us were also accepted, sometimes to the disapproval of my father who was trying to be cautious. But with the understanding and backing of my hard working mother, who is God sent we were able to bridge the gap; by way of showing love to all and restoring unity among our family members and friends.

After staying in this Cruel World of Love. I've learned that: Promises are not CONTRACTS. Kisses are not ASSURANCES. Sweet words are not GUARANTEES. Big Hugs are not BONDS. And nothing is Permanent in this Life..."One Day he's Mine...The Next Day he's Gone. Last Night she was Sweet. The Next

"Morning she's Insensitive."Loving Someone Is Not Always About "Fairy tales"& "Fantasies "it's About Truth and Realities that you face." **(Unknown)**

"Life is a game of football and we are the ball. Never mind the kicks of the people because without kicks we may not reach the goals." **(Atuh Kakkar)**

"Life is the greatest teacher; a teacher teaches a lesson and then takes the test. But, life takes the test and teaches us a lesson." **(Vibhuti Sareen)**

"The difference in life and school is, in school the teacher teaches you then you take the exams, but in life you take the exams, first that will teach you a lesson." **(Ravin Harshad Patel)**

From my little experience on earth, I have come to realize that some people are so cruel, manipulative, and wicked. It is written in the bible that God regretted creating man because of his wickedness. Wickedness does not come from God. God is the centre point of love and unity. My family tribulations aside, I have witnessed a hell of things from friends and people I have loved and cared for; who turned around and stabbed me in the back. I have never had a friend or friendship that is willing to die or sacrifice for me just as I do to anybody I call my friend. I always put my head on the block and sacrificed even my comfort to see that everything goes well. This has made me to ponder, if it is by chance, destiny, or hereditary that we're being rewarded with evil for the good things God has used us to do. It baffles me that the more I'm hurt as a result of my good gestures, I still want to do more.

I recall my mother telling me I have been betrayed time and again by the same people I fought for, yet I have not learnt my lesson. I have used the little resources God has Bless me with to harbour, clothe, and feed strangers or people I hardly know. However, the moment such people secure a job or have access to other means that improves their well being they consider you as a fool, as a stepping stone for their survival. Life can be cruel. In life, I've lived, I've loved, I've lost, I've missed, I've trusted, I've made mistakes, but most of all I've learned. So the problem with the world is that we have strayed from God, or wandered away from love. According to A Course in Miracles, this separation from God first happened millions of years ago. But the important revelation, the crux of the Course, is that in reality it never actually happened at all. The miracle, a shift from fear to love, works to an invisible plane. It transforms the world at the Causal level. Anything else is just a temporary palliative, a fix but not a healing, a treatment of the symptom but not cure. Let's ask for a new world.

Let's ask for a new life. Until that point, I was hiding from my love, and so resisting my own life. The return to love is hardly the end of life's adventure. It's the real beginning, the return to who you are, the perfect you isn't something you need to create, because God already created it. The perfect you is the love within you. Your job is to allow the Holy Spirit to remove the fearful thinking that surrounded your perfect Self. Taking responsibility for our lives, then, means taking responsibility for our thoughts, and praying to God to "save" our lives, means praying for Him to save us from our own negative thoughts. In asking the Holy Spirit to help us, we are expressing our willingness to perceive a situation differently. The purpose of life is to grow into our perception. Once we call on God, everything that could anger us is on the way.

Why? Because the place where we go into anger instead of love, is our wall. Any situation that pushes our buttons is a situation where we don't yet have the capacity to unconditionally love. It's the Holy Spirit's job to draw our attention to that, and help us move beyond that point. When we surrender to God, we surrender to something bigger than ourselves to a universe that knows what it's doing. Surrender means, by definition, giving up attachment to results. To place something in the hands of God is to give it over, mentally, to the protection and care of the beneficence of the universe.

"People are often unreasonable and self centred, for them anyway. If you are kind, people may accuse you of ulterior motives. Be kind anyway. If you are honest, people may cheat you. Be honest anyway. If you find happiness, people may be jealous. Be happy anyway. The good you do today may be forgotten tomorrow. Do good anyway. Give the world the best you have and it may never be enough. Give your best anyway. For you see, in the end, it is between you and God. It was never between you and them anyway." **(Mother Teresa)**

"Betrayal; feeling betrayed by love one is painful, feeling that your privacy, trust and relationship were not valued by other person is difficult to bear. In the end betrayal is about learning not to idealize external sources learn the lesson, grow forgive one another and move on." **(Unknown)**

"I have found that helping people to develop personal goals has proven to be the most effective way to help them cope with problems. Observing the lives of people who have mastered adversity, I have noted that they have established goals and sought with all their effort to achieve them. From the moment they decided to concentrate all their energies on a specific objective, they began to surmount the most difficult odds." **(Ari Kiev)**

"I have been stabbed in the back by those I needed most. I have been lied to by those I love, and I have felt alone when I couldn't afford to be. But at the end of the day I had to learn to be my own best Friend." **(Unknown)**

"A lie can travel half way around the world while the truth is putting on its shoes." **(Charles Spurgeon)**

South Africa is a beautiful and conducive country to live. I firmly believe in the fundamental human right of individual is it male or female? The rainbow nation basically is ruled by women indirectly, whatever the woman says stands whether it is true or false in the area of fundamental human right .A lot of innocent men have been jailed for rape, abuse, harassment and intimidation offences in some instance were never committed just because the women laid a complained the other party is never given a fair hearing on what really happened. We have seen situation where a wife have accused the husband for rape, a situation where daughters have false fully accused their fathers or step fathers of rape through the instruction of their mothers to settle grievances not putting into consideration the outcome as they are bent on settling scores.

There have also been situation where great men have been accused, blackmail by women for money or favours as in the case of Comrade Zwelinzima Vavi or has been used to settle political scores like in the case of president Jacob Zuma to mention but a few, never the less I am not taken away the fact that men do rape but my argument is that not all of those cry for rape are indeed true. I am a huge crusader against women abuse and I believe our women need all the protection in the world however all this should be done with care against the oppression of the men folks. This brings me to my own story.

"Our lives are not determined by what happens to us but how we react to what happens, not by what life brings us but the attitude we bring to life." **(Wade Boggs)**

What is rape? Rape is a type of sexual assault usually involving sexual intercourse, which is initiated by one or more persons against another person without that person's consent.

Consensual Sex

1. (Law) *Law* (of a contract, agreement, etc.) existing by consent

2. (Law) *Law* (of a sexual activity) performed with the consent of all parties involved

3. (Life Sciences & Allied Applications / Physiology) (of certain reflex actions of a part of the body) responding to stimulation of another part.

"Rape is a serious allegation and it is supposed to be taken VERY seriously but so is falsely accusing someone. When someone rapes a person they go to prison. THAT should also happen to the person that has wrongfully accused an innocent victim. They are not ONLY destroying innocent people's lives they are ALSO making it hard for the MEN and Women to find justice when they have been raped." **(Camille Cosby)**

I was false fully accused of rape by a girl I never knew that I helped while stranded. She said she was dumped by her boyfriend as she told me. After we talked, I took her to my house, after asking her some question like who her next of kin were, she told me she had no parent but a grandmother who stays in Alberton one of the subdues in Johannesburg, that she has a three years old son with the boyfriend and that they live together that the boy has paid her laboola, the problem was that the boyfriend was accusing her of having affairs and that the boyfriend threaten to kill her and brought her to a place she is not familiar with, I asked her how old she was she told me twenty.

She spent two days in my house I gave her all the comfort you can imagine, she was in the liberty of using my phone to make calls here and there, bought food for her, cold drinks in sympathy that I was helping a person in a helpless situation not knowing I was jeopardizing my name and my brand which has taken me five to six years to build. After the second day I told her it was time for her to leave believing her stress level would have been over and that she is in the right frame of mind to take a direction on the next step of action etc. I was tempted after the first day, though being human with blood running down my vein not water, but with her stressed mood I could not do anything by the special grace of God. I asked that I drop her at a convenient place where she told me she will get a taxi to where the said a person she has been in touch with can pick her up.

After dropping her on my way to Johannesburg town where I was buying fuel I was approached by a police car. In the car was her boyfriend and a woman who later claim to be her mother.

What a surprise I was taken to the police station, where I waited in view for them to find her as I was more than confused at this stage as I was being told she was abducted by me, you cannot abduct someone and give them your phone to be making calls here and there. A person can't be abducted when all the people living in the house with you are aware she is with you as she moves freely from the room to the bathroom and kitchen and also I left her one evening and went out to buy medication for my leg with the room door widely opened. This to me then sounded like a joke.

After waiting for about more than an hour came in the girl with the father or mother's boyfriend, what a big sigh of relief for me that at least she was found and that I was free to go. One of the biggest problem was the language barrier as I was not hearing what was been said at the police station.

They took her to a room where I didn't know what transpired in this instance language also became a barrier, only to get the greatest shock of my life that she said she was raped by me which to me and God Almighty never happened. I spent the worst three nights of my life in a holding cell in Florida Police station for an offence I never committed. This event still got me wondering what the world has turned into, has it now become a crime to help people in need. Maybe I have been used as a settling point between an aggrieved and negligence mother and a runaway daughter to mend their differences, also a bitter boyfriend thinking a foreigner (kwerekwere) as we are called, has enter his comfort zone also makes the battle ground for such accusation deadlier.

The said boyfriend that abandoned her was never brought into the picture. The most surprising part of it is that I don't even know her name as all this was happening. Some people even without hearing my side of the story have concluded that I was guilty; even some I called my friends doubted my innocence, for a few that know the real Ikechukwu, and what he stands for said the Ikechukwu I know will never do this irrespective of the situation he finds himself. A girl that could lie even to the extent that she does not have parents and that she has a three year old son looking for sympathy from a stranger could as well lie over what did not happen. A case that was opened and not followed was just meant to punish a person because of hatred of his nationality, however the Man above is never asleep. He once again came on board and the rest is history to Him be the glory, also special thanks to advocate Issac Mokgobi of Mokgobi attorneys.

"Justice will overtake fabricators of lies and false witnesses." **(Heraclitus)**

"When we think we have been hurt by someone in the past, we build up defences to protect ourselves from being hurt in the future. So the fearful past causes a fearful future and the past and future become one. We cannot love when we feel fear. When we release the fearful past and forgive everyone, we will experience total love and oneness with all." **(Gerald G. Jampolsky)**

"Forgiving is so simple. It is literally just a decision. No justification or cause has to happen, and forgiving does not have anything to do with accepting the other person's behaviour, approving of it, justifying it, rationalizing it, or understanding it. Forgiveness is just a spiritual power in dropping the weight of negativity, of negative emotion and energy around you. It's time to just let it go." **(Brendon Burchard)**

"Real love, I've learned, is a very, very strong form of forgiveness. I don't think people yearn for love because they hate staying home." **(Dr. Don Mattera)**

"Vengeance is mine, sayeth the Lord," means, "Relinquish the idea of vengeance." God balances all wrong, but not through attack, judgment or punishment. Contrary to how it feels when we're lost in the emotions that tempt us to judge, there's no such thing as righteous anger." **(Marianne Williamson)**

"Whatever has been broken or lost, can only be repaired and found again by telling the story of what happened. Telling your story is part of the process of forgiving." **(Arch Desmond Tutu)**

"Forgive is the highest most beautiful form of love. In return, you will receive untold peace and happiness." **(Robert Muller)**

"Forgiveness eliminates the negative thoughts and emotions which create negative effects in your life. When you learn to forgive, you no longer have reasons to be angry. You see. You hear. You intuit. You forgive. You move on. It is really quite simple." **(Iyanla Vanzant)**

"Forgiving is rediscovering the shining path of peace that at first you thought others took away when they betrayed you." **(Dodinsky)**

"One forgives to the degree that one loves." **(Francois de La Rochefoucauld)**

"Forgiveness is the final form of love." **(Reinhold Niebuhr)**

"Forgiveness is the highest level of human performance; it is divine, refreshing, liberating and amazingly rewarding." **(Elozie Jimmy)**

"The willingness to forgive is a sign of spiritual and emotional maturity. It is one of the great virtues to which we all should aspire. Imagine a world filled with individuals willing both to apologize and to accept an apology. Is there any problem that could not be solved among people who possessed the humility and largeness of spirit and soul to do either -- or both -- when needed?" **(Gordon B. Hinckley)**

There is this Igbo adage "Adi gi amu aka ekpe na nka" which says meaning you don't beginning to learn how to use your left hand at an old age, in essence it means what I didn't do as a youth in the madness of my Juvenile delinquency I cannot do now that I am adult and have built a little profile for myself Rape or forcing myself on a women was not part of me. The rest has become history and has now formed part of my hard lessons in life I have come to learn through experience. What happened and how the case went is still a mystery, the divine intervention by God's power and His grace was still on play. Was it xenophobia? Wickedness, hatred, or been mean that I can't still answer.

I was told not to hurt the heart of the one I love so much. But when I was so busy taking care of that heart, I never noticed my own was bleeding. People can be thoughtless or just plain mean. So you must be able to look inside for strength, and when that strength fails, you can also look above, to God, the ultimate source of strength and love. I really draw a lot of strength from God in that situation as it would have been a breaking point for me. Love is all about forgiveness. **Deuteronomy 26:16-19; Matthew 5:43-48** if you took forgiveness seriously yesterday, then loving will be easy today.

Otherwise, it'll prove impossible, because Jesus doesn't ask us to love our families and friends. He commands us to love our enemies! Start by praying for them daily. Whoever said revenge is sweet never tasted the sweetness of forgiveness. Love is living your own life, but sharing it. And this requires constant forgiveness. It's making a million mistakes and turning them into learning experiences. Love is patience, optimism, and sometimes it's a simple hug when there is nothing left to say.

"Karma' No need for revenge. Just sit back and wait. Those who hurt you will eventually screw up themselves and if you're lucky, God will let you watch." **(Dr. Farrah Gray)**

"My trust in a higher power that wants me to survive and have love in my life is what keeps me moving forward." **(Kenny Loggins)**

"Forgiveness is about empowering yourself, rather than empowering your past." **(T.D.Jakes)**

"Until we have seen someone's darkness we don't really know who they are. Until we have forgiven someone's darkness, we don't know what love is." **(Marianne Williamson)**

"There is knowledge you only get through experience." **(Osadebe Ibegbu)**

"Life is very interesting. In the end, some of your greatest pains become your greatest strengths." **(Drew Barrymore)**

"As time goes on, you'll understand. What lasts, lasts; what doesn't, doesn't. Time solves most things. And what time can't solve, you have to solve yourself." **(Haruki Murakami)**

"The most valuable things in life are not measured in monetary terms. The really important things are not houses and lands, stocks and bonds, automobiles and real estate, but friendships, trust, confidence, empathy, mercy, love and faith." **(Bertrand Russell)**

"The truth is you will overlook a lot of things in your path if you keep ignoring who really you are. There is an abundance of love within you. Let it flow." **(Dodinsky)**

"Nothing hurts a good soul and kind heart more than to live amongst people who can't understand it." **(Ali Bin Abi Talib)**

"There are no regrets in life, just lessons." **(Jennifer Aniston)**

Nonetheless, I am not bitter or aggrieved. Though being mortals we sometimes ask ourselves why us? It is also amazing how I have survived, especially when I do not have a regular paying job. God has been good to me and has used some people to bless me while I wait for the fulfillment of my destiny. I would not fail to thank my in-laws Mr. Henry and Vincent Molokwu, Sampson Okorie, UcheChukwu Amah, Chukwudi Ogbodo, Patrick Egbobe, Donatus Oguama, Michael Emetuche, Matthew Okafor, Tony Uba, Chief Onyeka Oguegbo, Nwabueze Ngigi Nwaobele, Emeka Otalor, Ngozi Ogbuji, Abraham Oganbor, Chidi Madubugwu, Okwuchukwu Eze, Chijoke Omanukwue, Ikem Nwankwo, Joseph

Kingsley, Emeka Ezinteje, Ms. Nomhle Makabane, Ms. Phindi Mahwayi, to mention but a few that have played a remarkable role in my life. It is obvious that I'm not suitable to any form of illness. That alone is a miracle and I'm grateful to God for that. I still believe in love as it's still the main reason for our existence. We should try as much as we can to avoid jealousy, greed, anger, and acrimony. We should pray for God's grace without which we are powerless.

"I've been absolutely terrified every moment of my life and I've never let it keep me from doing a single thing I wanted to do." **(Georgia'O'Keeffe)**

"The truth is, unless you let go, unless you forgive yourself, unless you forgive the situation, unless you realize that the situation is over, you cannot move forward." **(Steve Maraboli)**

"Find a place inside where there's joy, and the joy will burn out the pain." **(Joseph Campbell)**

"They can betray me, but I choose not to betray my peace of mind." **(Dodinsky)**

"The adventure of life is to learn. The purpose of life is to grow. The nature of life is to change. The challenge of life is to overcome. The essence of life is to care. The opportunity of like is to serve. The secret of life is to dare. The spice of life is to befriend. The beauty of life is to give." **(William Arthur Ward)**

"Hate, it has caused a lot of problem in this world, but it has not solved one yet." **(Dr. Maya Angelou)**

"Hatred stirs up dissension, but love covers over all wrongs." **(Proverbs 10:12)**

"Hatred does not cease by hatred, but only by love, this is the eternal rule." **(Buddha)**

"Hating people because of their colour is wrong. And it doesn't matter which colour does the hating. It's just plain wrong." **(Muhammad Ali)**

"Bitterness is like a cancer, it eats upon the host, but anger is like a fire, it burns it all clean." **(Dr. Maya Angelou)**

"I have been thinking about Hate, wondering how useful it is in our lives. We hate people, they do not go away. We hate the weather, it stays the same. We hate people's opinions, but ours are not necessarily right. We hate being sick, but we make little effort of being well. We hate it when we get weak or down, but we cannot be strong or up all the time. We hate our habits, but we do not change them. We hate governments, but we elect them. We hate violence, but we do not cultivate peace in our lives. We hate it when people hate us, but we fail to love them. We hate certain countries with a passion, but we are passionate about their goods. We go out of our way to buy labels and models that are made in the very countries that we hate. Does it make sense?" **(Mmatshilo Motsei)**

"Darkness cannot drive out darkness, only light can do that. Hate cannot drive out hate only love can do that." **(Dr. Martin Luther King Jr)**

"Whatever you give to life, it gives back to you, do not hate anybody. The hatred which comes out from you will someday come back to you. Preach and practice love all the time, it will add value to your wellbeing." **(Raphael Ikechukwu Ogbuagu)**

"Love is like a tree send it's root down deep so when the storms abound and winds of adversity blows, it shakes and bends and goes with the flow; but doesn't break or fall and during times of drought it drives its root down deeper. So whatever comes and goes, summer, winter, spring or fall, the good times and the bad it stands the test of all." **(Unknown)**

"I have no regrets in life. I think that everything happens to you for a reason. The hard times that you go through build character, making you a much stronger person." **(Chacha Pepe)**

What is love?

Love is patient, Love is kind, and love is not jealous or boastful. It is not arrogant or rude. Love does not insist on its own way, it is not irritable or resentful, it does not rejoice at wrong but rejoices in the right. Loves bears all things, believes all things, hope all things, and endures all things. Love is real. It's an eternal creation and nothing can destroy it.

"What is Love? Love is the absence of judgement." **(Dalai Lama)**

Five Bible Passages That Show Us What True Love Looks Like
1 Corinthians 13
1 John 4:16-18
Romans 12:9-13
1 John 3:10-17
Matthew 22:34-40

Ten ways to Love

1. Listen without interrupting **(Proverbs 18)**

2. Speak with accusing **(James 1:19)**

3. Give without sparing **(Proverb 21:26)**

4. Pray without ceasing **(Colossians 1:19)**

5. Answer without arguing **(Proverb 4:15)**

6. Share without pretending **(Ephesians 4:15)**

7. Enjoy without complaint **(Philippians 2:14)**

8. Trust without wavering **(Corinthians 13:7)**

9. Forgive without punching. **(Colossians 3:13)**

10. Promise without forgetting **(Proverb 13:12)**

"Until you find real love. You then realize that you have been loving the wrong persons.' a poor man doesn't know that his poor until a rich man arrives." **(Phophi Rhinah Muguru)**

"In real love you want the other person's good. In romantic love, you want the other person." **(Margaret Anderson)**

"It takes no time to fall in love, but it takes you years to know what love is." **(Jason Mraz)**

"When you care deeply about a person, you tend not to see the person's faults like others would because "Love is blind" **(Mende proverb)**

"Love is not a matter of what happens in life. It's a matter of what's happening in your heart." **(Ken Keyes)**

"Love without action is meaningless and action without love is irrelevant." **(Deepak Chopra)**

"Love does not harm to its neighbour; therefore love is the fulfilment of law." **(Romans 13 verse 10)**

"Love is sweet when it's new. But it's even sweeter when it's true! Wait for what's real!" **(Paula White)**

"True Love cannot be found where it does not exist, nor can it be denied where it does." **(Torquato Tasso)**

"Immature love says: 'I love you because I need you.' Mature love says 'I need you because I love you." **(Erich Fromm)**

"Love is a fruit in season at all times, and within reach of every hand." **(Mother Teresa)**

"Love is a force more formidable than any other. It is invisible - it cannot be seen or measured, yet it is powerful enough to transform you in a moment, and offer you more joy than any material possession could." **(Barbara de Angelis)**

"Be generous. Give to those you love; give to those who love you, give to the fortunate, give to the unfortunate - yes, give especially to those you don't want to give. You will receive abundance for your giving. The more you give, the more you will have." **(W. Clement Stone)**

A lot of names have been given to Love. There are different types of love. There is love for the wrong reasons, the list goes on. I want to list some so-called love.***Love for money**. This is good. It is good to have money but it becomes a problem when your love for money supersedes that for human being and for God. Money is meant to serve you and not you serving money. People have gone out of their way to do the most unlikely things to make money. Risk has been taken, and people are even killed for this purpose to fill the veil of being in the class of the rich. Money is a blessing to humanity. Do you love money?"The love of money is the root of all evil" The secret of making money is hidden in the Bible money code; in the book of proverb chapter 14; vs. 15 King Solomon said, "The naive believe everything but a wise man looks well into a matter" he used this ancient code/wisdom to become the richest man ever lived. Looking well into a matter involves study, homework, countless hours of research, and risking real money in trial and error tests.

This wisdom will help you avoid get-rich-quick -schemes that can snare even the most successful people. Jesus Christ revealed this code again in the parable of the talents in the book of Matthew chapter 14, the unfaithful servant representing those that are afraid of investing their money for fear of losing it. This is pure love of money as we saw in vs. 29 that what he has was taken from him and given to the one that has more. Money is simply a medium of exchange, a way people do business with one another, a neutral concept. It is how people go about getting money and how they use it after they have gotten it that makes all the difference. Anything that is not love is an illusion. Remember this, and you will be at peace.

"Many relationships are not based on love, they are based on money. However those relationships which are based on love are challenged by the absence of money. Many people find themselves in this state of absence of money, yet they are spiritual, they know that life and love cannot be contained by material. But that does not make it easy to meet and enjoy each other's company as they would have wished. Faith doesn't always fill up the cars with petrol. But it fills up the soul with love. But that does not help the situation either. The least people can do is keep sending positive vibes to each other." **(Mmatshilo Motsei)**

"Love is not patronizing and charity isn't about pity, it is about love. Charity and love are the same with charity you give love, so don't just give money but reach out your hand instead." **(Mother Teresa)**

Love for power. This is another phenomenon people are obsessed with. People will do anything to find themselves in a leadership position just to boost their ego and enrich themselves. People are attracted to you if you are in position of power or authority pretending they love you. Power should be used to better situations of people and the community not for personal or selfish purposes, people have joined various set of cults to acquire power both physical, and spiritual, some sacrifices' with human blood to strengthen their power , the list of what people can do to get this power is unimaginable. The fact remains that human being like power in any form; however the problem becomes what one is ready to do to acquire that power. We all need grace in gracing this consuming factor of life.

"The day the power of love overrules the love of power the world will know peace." **(Gandhi)**

"Nearly all men can stand adversity, but if you want to test a man's character give him power." **(Abraham Lincoln)**

"Let us make no pretense about it, every human being loves power; power over his fellow men in the state, or in business enterprises; or failing that; power over his wife and children, and over his brothers, sisters, and friends, or, in the case of children, power over his playmates. Of these categories of power, the desire for power over one's fellow men is the strongest." **(Chief Obafemi Awolowo)**

"The love of liberty is the love of others; the love of power is the love of ourselves." **(William Hazlitt)**

"Love someone out of admiration for who they are, not out of what they will do for you. Real love stubbornly endures. Conditional love always FINDS a reason to die." **(Chika Nwankwo)**

Love for cars; there are people that cars drive crazy no matter how much it is they want to drive it and can do anything in their capacity to have it, some even buy such cars even when it is above the level of the live hood.

"There is no disguise which can hide love for long where it exists, or simulate it where it does not." **(Francois de La Rochefoucauld)**

"People put their trust in a lot of things. They find confidence in possessions, wealth, position and resources. But those who trust in the Lord will find safety and rest!" **(Lindiwe Kole)**

Love for houses.

Love for fashion (designer wears, shoes, clothes etc)

Love for sex

"Love is something far more than desire for sexual intercourse; it is the principal means of escape from the loneliness which afflicts most men and women throughout the greater part of their lives." **(Bertrand Russell)**

Love for fame among others.

"The greatest happiness of life is the conviction that we are loved; loved for ourselves, or rather, loved in spite of ourselves." **(Victor Hugo)**

"Love does not obey our expectations, it obeys our intentions." **(Lloyd Strom)**

"Love is friendship that has caught fire. It is quiet understanding, mutual confidence, sharing and forgiving. It is loyalty through good and bad times. It settles for less than perfection and makes allowances for human weaknesses." **(Ann Landers)**

The above stated categories of love are good except when one is obsessed to the extent of getting them at all cost. We can't deny that we have neglected the "true love" God established from the inception of creation. This is what some referred to as the "**Agape Love**". **Agape love** is selfless love of one person for another without sexual implication (especially love that is spiritual in nature). Some defined it as the love of God or Christ for mankind. It is the evil prevalent on earth that makes us to think love exist in different levels. It is for these reason scholars have classified love into three major levels namely: **Eros love, Philos love and Agape love.**

Eros love is simply erotic love, based on the strong romantic feeling towards another. While **Philos love** is based on friendship between two people who share a mutual give and take relationship. But **Agape love** is the original and only true form of love. It is an unconditional love. It transcends the other types of love. It is pure and undiluted. It cuts across races, colours barriers, language limitations and other social constraints that have inhibited true love.

"You will find out as you look back upon your life that the moment when you have truly lives are the moments when you have done things in the spirit of love." **(Henry Drummond)**

"Love should make you feel free, not like a prisoner. You shouldn't have to cut off good friends and family for your relationship. Love should be pure, not toxic. Make sure you know what you have." **(Tony Gaskins)**

"Falling out of love is chiefly a matter of forgetting how charming someone is." **(Iris Murdoch)**

This brings to mind the popular saying that "you should do unto others as you will have them do to you." Philosophers have classified this saying as **"the golden rule"** It is appalling that regardless of the principle underpinning the **"golden rule"** people have failed to use it as moral compass to love one another. We live in a society that oppress, humiliate, abuse, and kill people with impunity. It is imperative therefore that we change our ways. We shouldn't allow the love for money, material possession, beauty, and political position over ride the relevance of true love in our society. When we get caught up in material goods and surface beauty and when we let other people determine our value, we give up too much of ourselves and risk letting our blessing go to waste. Love is the key word, we should first of all love ourselves in midst of all the troubles we pass through, this gives us an edge in life to overcome our troubles and obstacles.

"Love isn't about making things perfect. It's about accepting someone for who they are, learning to love their fault." **(Anna La Torre)**

"Love didn't hurt you! Someone that does not know how to love hurts you then you are confused the two. Love isn't pain." **(Tony A.Gaskin Jr)**

Institutions that Love should be preached

"All major religious traditions carry basically the same message that is love, compassion, and forgiveness. The important thing is they should be part of our daily lives." **(Dalai Lama)**

"Love and compassion are necessities, not luxuries. Without them humanity cannot survive" **(Dalai Lama)**

"There is no religion that was founded on intolerance - and no religion that does not value the sanctity of human life." **(Mohamed ElBaradei)**

"God did not create religion. God created man. Man created religion." **(Anthony Douglas Williams)**

"No that is fine, but also tells them that there is no religion in this world higher than compassion." **(Dr. Don Mattera)**

"Morality is doing what is right no matter what you are told. Religion is doing what you are told no matter what is right." **(Lilian Ngozi)**

Churches and Mosque

Churches and mosques are some of the biggest religious institutions that have failed to preach the real meaning of love. We are told the church is the dwelling place of God, where love, peace, joy, and tranquillity prevail. But some churches have failed to meet these objectives. Rather than preach salvation and love among people, some churches are busy fighting for members and the expansion of their branches. The multitude of churches in all nooks and corners of cities and towns is not making any much difference to the lives of people. Besides, internal politics is entrenched in the church to the extent that special recognition is often given to the rich. Everything is centred on money.

Without money you are no body in the kingdom of God in this new generation missionaries, your getting deliverance, one and one prayer session with your pastor or even miracle is centred on your contribution to the up growth of the church where is this leading us to, out of the presence of God who is our strength and our fortress in Him we trust. Favouritism is preeminent not minding that we are all equal before the Lord. There is rancour and bitterness among members, there is discrimination, the list goes on and on. Churches no more based their preaching is on love, peace and salvation but on the external riches of what they stand to get from its members.

"Religion has been the great and best weapon to destroy a nation throughout the ages. It has separated people and nations leading them to wars." **(Bishop Edir Macedo)**

"Religion is just mind control." **(George Carlin)**

"The true followers of the lord Jesus are naturally loving and respectful toward others, regardless of their skin colour, sex, race, or religion." **(Bishop Edir Macedo)**

"In fact, I thought that Christianity was very a good and a very valuable thing for us. But after a while, I began to feel that the story that I was told about this religion wasn't perhaps completely whole, that something was left out." **(Professor Chinua Achebe)**

"To say that religion exist to connect man to God is lie. If it were true, the world would be in perfect peace and harmony. In fact, religion has kept people away from God and sometimes unconsciously, it has destroyed them." **(Bishop Edir Macedo)**

"One of the truly bad effects of religion is that it teaches us that it is a virtue to be satisfied with not understanding." **(Richard Dawkins)**

"Religion has all too well blinded the eyes of mankind by turning historical facts into fantasies in order to stimulate and strengthen an emotional faith." **(Bishop Edir Macedo)**

"Religion does three things effectively divide people, control people and delude people." **(Mary Alice McKinney)**

"Even though I am a believer, I am not Christian. I am opposed to institutionalised religion. But I believe in the Higher Being that resides in the centre of my mind." **(Mmatshilo Motsei)**

"Religion is one of the biggest deceits to mankind. It is the same religion that the white-men used to enslave our ancestors in Africa. It is the same religion Islamist is using to kill millions of people. Let us go to worship houses to pray and worship God not the religious leaders. Our healing and solution to most of our problems lie with us." **(Olaniyi Abodedele)**

Having said this there are still some churches and Mosques that have gone its way to preach love, unity, forgiveness, harmony, among its members and everybody they come in contact with. I encourage more of such preaching, our lord will be very happy when he sees us living side by side with love which is the main base of which he created this world.

Schools

During our days as kids, schools used to be the epic centre for good behaviour and love. There was love among students. People could share their feelings and their belongings together without hassles. But times have changed; our schools are now bedevilled with in-house fighting, racial discrimination, greed, jealousy, and so many other bad habits. Teachers should teach contemporary students and children how to love and what love truly means. The School is the secong home many kids know and passes through in essence it is a key instrument that the true meaning of loved can be shared.

"If you're not willing to learn, no one can help you. If you're determined to learn, no one can stop you." **(Hasheem Francis, CEO Built to Prosper)**

Homes

The home is the first institution and breeding ground every child grows and learns from. It is the sole responsibility of the parents to raise their children in a conducive environment that is primarily governed by love.

The absence of true love, tolerance, and the spirit of forgiveness among people have led to the high rate of divorce cases in our present generation. This has deprived many children of the stability and genuine affection they deserve in their upbringing. This explains why there is a high rate of moral decay among children, which has adversely affected their lives. It must be emphasized that all children need the love of both parents while growing up. Nevertheless, Parents still owe it to God and their children for proper guidance and upbringing. They must install in their children the fear of God, which goes along with Love as the greatest commandment God gave to us. It is of note today that most children from broken homes become an obstacle to the society at large since there is no environment of love in their growing up. Let us be grateful of our homes and families and values this union that are given to us by God not man.

"I believe that children are the future. Teach them well and let them lead the way. Show them all the beauty they posses inside. Give them a sense of pride. Let the children's laughter remind us of how we used to be." **(Whitney Houston)**

"It is easy to love the people far away. It is not always easy to love those close to us. It is easier to give a cup of rice to relieve hunger than to relieve the loneliness and pain of someone unloved in our own home. Bring love into your home for this is where our love for each other must start." **(Mother Teresa)**

"Train up a child in the way he should go, and when he is old he will not turn from it." **(Proverbs 22:6)**

"The most influential of all educational factors is the conversation in a child's home." **(William Temple)**

"Feeling grateful or appreciative of someone or something in your life actually attracts more of the things that you appreciate and value into your life." **(Christiane Northrup, M.D)**

"The love of family and the admiration of friends are much more important than wealth and privilege." **(Charles Kuralt)**

"It is not what you do you're your children, but what you taught them to do for themselves, that makes them successful human beings." **(Anna Landers)**

"The great danger for family life, in the midst of any society whose idols are pleasure, comfort and independence, lies in the fact that people close their hearts and become selfish." **(Pope John Paul II)**

"Our job is not to toughen children up to face a cruel and heartless world. Our job is to raise children who will make the world little less cruel and heartless." **(L.R Knost)**

"A man should never neglect his family for business." **(Walt Disney)**

"A child educated only at school is an uneducated child." **(George Santayana)**

The Media

The mass media and the social media such as television, radio programs, newspapers, face book, twitter, my space, youtube etc should assist in preaching the message of love, tolerance, and forgiveness to their listening audience as against the dissemination of negative messages such as violence, nudity, sexuality, arrogance to list a few. This medium imparts a lot of us and we want to begin to act like our idols and mentors we watch on TV. Programmes with selective guardiance should be aired more progating love amongus us.

"The media is the most powerful entity on earth. They have the power to make the innocent guilty and make the guilty innocent, and that's power, because they control the minds of the masses." **(Malcolm X)**

"The most powerful tool of deformation and propaganda is the media. Never believe everything you read on the net or paper." **(Prince Ndu Ibeto)**

"If you are not careful the newspapers will have you hating the people who are being oppressed, and loving the people who are doing the oppressing." **(Malcolm X)**

Trials and tragedy

My family has experienced some tragedies here and there but to God be the glory we are still hanging on there. The Love we exhibited and shared still abides in our hearts and spirits. In quiet succession unimaginable things have happened. In 1994 I lost an Uncle Mr. Lazarus Ogbuagu in a very mysterious way. In 1997 my father also disappeared in mysterious circumstance till date nobody has been able to say exactly what happened. Instead people took advantage of our situation to defraud us, accusations and counter accusations were made, and unnecessary fingers were pointed. Enemies' emerged from nowhere. People who were supposed to stand by us deserted us. This was indeed a terrible period for us. God gave my mother strength to stand dispute all odds as she was in the centre of it all, I wonder how many people will go through all this setbacks and still show love to people, I had all sort of stories, personally I don't think I could pass through such and still remain the same. God does not fail He is the same today, tomorrow and forever. I thank God for giving me such a strong willed woman as a Mother and pray that God should continue to strengthen her and give her the grace to continue with her call and destiny with Him God Almighty.

"Life happens don't try to understand the mysteries of life. God has not forsaken you. God has not forgotten you. Trial come to strengthen you, not break you. Get a blessing from the lesson. After your toughest trails will be your greatest triumphs." **(Tony A Gaskin Jr)**

"There is no education like adversity." **(Benjamin Disraeli)**

"It is not what you have experienced that makes you greater, but what you have faced, what you have transcended, what you have unlearned." **(Ben Okri)**

"When you get through whatever it is you are going through, you are going to be much better off. In the midst of a challenge, our eyes are opened, our minds blown to new levels of awareness. When you get through this, you are going to be something else...a better, stronger you!" **(Iyanla Vanzant)**

"The greater your capacity to love, the greater your capacity to feel the pain." **(Jennifer Aniston)**

In 1999 my mother's immediate younger brother Mr. Samuel Akpua (Ejee Abba) was gunned down in front of his house leaving behind a young widow and five beautiful children. In 2000 I lost a mentor chief J. C. Onwubuya (Ichie Okutalukwu Abagana) who died three days to his 70th birthday and instead of friends, family members supporting the bereaved family, they were fighting with them. At the age of 34, In 2008 my first cousin engineer Ferdinand Chukwuemeka Akpua (Ferdinando) was gunned down coming out from the bank as a result of business deal gone bad, out of greed and selfishness leaving behind a newly wedded wife with a five or six months pregnancy, thus denying an unborn child the provision, protection, guidance, caring and loves of a father.

To the glory of God a bouncing baby boy was born into the Akpua family though cannot replace the big gap that has been felt as a result of Ferdinand death. For me losing four prominent persons in my life that were my mentors in a space of seven years was a heavy blow that I cannot measure till this day. In 2012 while in South Africa I lost yet another father figure in the person of Mr. Simon Obidigbo (Ossai), at the age of 63 a down to earth man that stood into the gap of my missing father, he was always there at our disposal at any time, whenever he was been called upon for advise or solving an internal family dispute ,his said death or illness that led to his death once again a mysterious one ,with him one tenth of my being died, they say the good ones die so early in life what a great lose Mr. Obidigbo was to mankind and humanity. Another blow yet again to me, at the age of 39 my first cousin from my paternal side Mrs. Chinenye Emelife left this hazard world in March 2014, the good ones seem to be departing so soon, people that have the fear and love of mankind, that have touched the dying world with their deeds and kindness, so painful I won't see her again. A true sister has departed and left me once more to cry, the eye of the Family has been snatched forcefully by the cold hand of death. Chinenye seem to be my type of person always interested in the unity fo the family and likes to carry everyone around making sure theat love flows in the family, supporting in any way she can to see the advancement of humanity. The issue here is not death, but when young men and women are forcedly taken away from us without them getting to reach their destiny with God. We are all going to died at one point or the other in our lives, if you take a look at all this wonderful people I have lost to Mother Nature, they still have a lot to offer and have not yet reached their prime that is where I have a problem. In the end judgement is of the Lord alone not of man.

"The saddest thing about betrayal is that it never comes from your enemies, it comes from your friends and loved ones." **(Unknown)**

"There's a world in which reasons are made up because reality is too painful." **(Barry Diller)**

"We will never understand certain kind of pain until it happens to us." **(Paulo Coelho)**

The lingering thought of my father a second lieutenant in the Biafra army, disappearing at the age of 52 or so, without a single trace is the most mysterious thing I have come to live with till date and will remain so till I die. After waiting for twelve years without any clue of what might have happened to Chief Clement Ogbuagu, the family decided to put everything to rest by conducting his funeral without a body done traditionally and leaving everything to fate and God. Not to not to mention the gunning down of my uncle Samuel Akpua (Ejee) at an untimely age of Forty Three, in front of his house, the mentor that bought me my first travelling box and took me to my first holidays. The brave Ejee that never believed any living person could intimidate him not to talk of killing him throw the spine off my nerves, wherever he might be today he will be crying loud and saying me of all persons as he believed too much in himself, I so much believe in the confidence I had whenever Ejee was around me, to me he was my god on earth, or the agonizing death of my uncle Lazarus Ogbuagu at the age of 37, if such like this could happen to this brave warriors of mine then nobody is safe. I felt a huge gap since all what I was suppose to learn from these young men while growing to be a man was taken forcefully away from me. Chief J. C. Onwubuya (Ichie Okutalukwu) was the last stray that break the camels back when I was beginning to get close to him death strike again at the age of seventy depriving me once again knowledge one could not buy.

I won't forget my mother Achala ugo strong and industurous women, the backstabbing from people she loved and catered for, people she bought cloths for, paid their school fee, gave money for their children upkeep all become overnight enemies claiming all those things she was doing was that she was collecting their luck, A women that brought light into the ogbuagu family with her hard work and the spirit of togetherness, What an irony? Life can be very cruel, if you have never felt such type of betrayal before you will not understand what she went through even to be accused that she knew what happened to her husband she laboured with was the greatest understatement I have ever heard.

To God be the glory she survived all setbacks in life, and in business. All this incidents have given me a scar in my heart on how wicked the world is. I always have this in mind and it keeping coming to me in my vision that no matter how bad it was there is still light in the other side of the tunnel. God will cause even the worst things to come together for good. Hold on to the promises of God, no matter what you see on the outside. God is good. If He allows something bad to happen, you may not understand it, but you can hold on to His goodness.

"If memories are used to rekindle old hatreds, it will lead us back to continuing hatred and conflict. But if memory is used to rebuild, or to begin new relationships that is where hope lies." **(Pumla Gobodo Madikizela)**

"You cannot hate others & be filled with the love of God! Don't let anyone or anything make you bitter & rob you of blessing. Let it go!" **(Paula White)**

"Love will find a way through paths where wolves fear to prey." **(Lord Bryon)**

The best way to judge people is to love them. You are not called as a spiritual detective. Stop finding faults and flaws of people as if there is a reward for it. You are commanded by God to love people and not judge them because it was the side of Jesus that was pierced and not yours. Grow up and see people the way God sees them and you will deal with them kindly! Jesus Is Lord" I had to ponder and ask myself what the world was turning into. Why the fighting, witch-hunting and the killing? If love does really exist in the right sense, things like these should not be heard at all. People who kill people forget that one day they will have to die as well. They have to be accountable to God for the things they did on earth.

I appeal to this generation to turn around and practice true love; to show forgiveness to people who may have offended them just as our Father in heaven will forgive us. Let us stop taking away people God has made. Let us allow everyone to exploit the full potential God has given to each and every one of us before we go to our grave. However no matter what your situation or circumstances, you always have a choice of responding in either negative way or a positive way the decision is yours to show love to all and believe in God that all is well.

"Always remember that there is no fear in love. But perfect love drives out fear **(1st John 4:18)** but what is perfect love? You have probably heard the answer before God is perfect love."

"Forgiveness and love cannot be earned, deserved, bought, sold, won, or forced. They are gift and should never be taken for granted or expected only accepted." **(Anna La Torres)**

"I would rather have one Rose and a kind word from friends while I am here than a whole truckload when I am gone." **(Thumi Tshanyela)**

"Some family tree has beautiful leaves and some have just a bunch of nuts. Remember it is the nuts that make the tree worth shaking." **(Unknown)**

"Life never ran out of mysteries. The more you want to understand it, the more it becomes complicated so why worry life will go on and on." **(Prescilla Corpus)**

"Tragedy, sadness, loneliness, betrayal, frustration, bitterness, envy, ungrateful and despair taught me that life is really a beautiful thing, if it wasn't I wouldn't be able to recognize that anything was wrong." **(Anna La Torre)**

The fact that the world has been turned into a place of regret, bitterness, disappointment to many doesn't mean love, and God fearing people do not exist. During our trials and tribulations some friends and families stood firmly behind my family. They were there from the onset till date. They have been of assistance to us morally, financially, spiritually and in so many other ways. It is for this reason I wish to mention few of them. My sincere thanks goes to the Onwubuya Family, Amobi family, Obidigbo family, Anaekwe Family, Etusi family, Ejinidu family, Agummadu family, Ogbonna family, Ezeibe family, Ogidi family, Anigbogu Family, Nwazojie Family, Oraka Family and others I may not be able to mention. And more importantly to the family of Late Chief and Mrs. Gabriel Onuorah (Ichie Akubueziokwu, Dike Udum Abagana) that has been of the uttermost assistance to me in my life. I can never forget what they did for me! They took me as one of them, housed me, clothed me; fed me, and provided for all my needs.

"There can be no greater gift than that of giving one's time and energy to help others without expecting anything in return." **(Nelson Rolihlahla Mandela "Madiba)**

"Kindness and love open the doors to one's soul." **(Anthony Douglas Williams)**

"Kindness is the language which the deaf can hear and the blind can see." **(Mark Twain)**

"Kind words do not cost much. Yet they accomplish much." **(Blaise Pascal)**

"Hatred and anger are powerless when met with kindness." **(Malcolm X)**

"Too often we underestimate the power of a touch, a smile, a kind word, a listening ear, an honest compliment, or the smallest act of caring, all of which have the potential to turn a life around." **(Leo Buscaglia)**

"Wherever there is a human being, there is an opportunity for a kindness." **(Seneca)**

They are a family with a very loving heart though we were not related by blood, but we were from the same town Abagana. Emeka Basil Onuorah the first son to late Chief/Sir Gabriel and Chief Mrs. Justina Onuorah (Gabbson) was my class and house mate at Christ the Kings College Onitsha. He brought me into this beautiful family. The Ogbuagu's and Onuorah's families were bonded as both families exchanged visits to their various homes in Lagos and Onitsha. This is what friendship and love should be. Anthony Onuorah (Akuwanta) did everything in his capacity to assist me whenever I ran to him for help. The Onuorah Family members such as: Uchenna, Ejike, Nonso, Chiamaka and Ngozi took me as one of them. My heart is still with them so is my prayers. They will always be part of me and I won't forget the remarkable role they have all played in my life.

"The best and most beautiful things in the world cannot be seen or even touched – they must be felt with the heart." **(Helen Keller)**

"It is necessary to help others, not only in our prayers, but in our daily lives. If we find we cannot help others, the least we can do is to desist from harming them" **(Dalai Lama)**

"All the beautiful sentiments in the world weigh less than a single lovely action." **(James Russell Lowell)**

"Happy are those who dare courageously to defending what they love." **(Ovid)**

Let's endeavour to show love to all of God's creation. Let's live and dream love in every aspect of our lives, in our relationships is it in church, at home, our work place, or our business dealings. We should always show mercy and have the spirit of forgiveness to all that have wronged us. As you read this chapter kindly sit and ponder have you really shown love to people around you? If you have not it is not too late to start doing so.

"Always do right. This will gratify some people and astonish the rest." **(Mark Twain)**

"Leave life passionately, love unconditionally, and hope for the best, laugh your heart out, cry when needed. Learn from the past. But most of all remember whatever is meant to be will eventually find its way to you." **(Evelyn Bumpers)**

"Everyone says love hurts, but that is not true. Loneliness hurts, rejection hurts, losing someone hurts, and envy hurts. Everyone gets these things confused with love. But in reality love is the only thing in this world that covers up all pains and makes someone feel wonderful again. Love is the only thing in this world that does not hurt." **(Sumit Kumar)**

"Life can't be measured by the achievement and awards given to us; but the caring and kindness we've shown to a lot of people we meet especially the less fortunate ones." **(Unknown)**

"I asked for strength and God gave me difficulties to make me strong. I asked for wisdom and God gave me problems to solve. I asked for prosperity and God gave me brawn and brains to work. I asked for courage and God gave me danger to overcome. I asked for patience and God placed me in situation where I was forced to wait. I asked for love and God gave me troubled people to help. I asked for favours and God gave me opportunities. I asked for everything so I could enjoy everything. I received nothing I wanted, I received everything I needed" **(Facebook friend)**

"God grant me the serenity to accept things I cannot change, the courage to change the things I can and the wisdom to know the difference." **(Unknown)**

"O Lord even in my most stressful moment may I find rest in you. May the work that I do and the way that I do them bring love, hope, peace, joy, faith, strength and life to all I come in contact with this day today and forever." (Unknown)

"My little children let us not love in word, neither in tongue; but indeed and truth." **(1st John 1:8)**

"If you are a child of God learn to: feed the hungry; give water to the thirsty; clothe the naked; shelter the homeless; stretch a hand to the fallen; visit the captive; rebuke the sinner; educate the ignorant; be patience with the doubtful; comfort the sorrowful; tolerate the blunderer; forgive the offender; pray for your enemy; soothe the sick; bury the dead. Man, observe daily the foregoing works of compassion and the inner recesses of God shall be yours." **(Rev Chidozie Ejimadu)**

Let us preach and practice love to all we meet along the road for our creator in heaven wants from us to be our brother's keeper in truth and in spirit. Our parents didn't tell us the truth when we came into this world, all they did was welcome us with a smile despite the fact that we came in crying. As we grew older; we found out life is not as it seems, our parents' smiles couldn't hide the fact any longer. It is now factual that not every smile, gift, disappointment, blessing, or favour seems to be what it is. We all came into this **"Battle Field"** named 'The World' not knowing where life was going to take us. **CHANGE** recognizes no comfort. It's always less painful to accept it now rather than to admit it later, so as we sail through life; it also unfolds. Let us **SEEK FOR GOD'S GRACE** to rightfully identify and embrace change intensely and most importantly, **GRACEFULLY. SHALOM** to everyone as we get to learn the hard lessons of life. Accept life as it unwraps its mystery.

The power to heal lies within you and your acceptance that there are things beyond the power of our will. Nobody can heal on your behalf it is your choice to make. The journey to self healing comes after the journey of self-discovery. Learn to let old things go before you take a step forward, otherwise you'll keep on shrinking. Nothing in life is permanent, except the illusions we choose to hold on to. We choose our own traps. When we string our traps we have to leave behind the **Trapping.** Pretending to be what others expect you to be diminishes you. When we try to control others we experience a world of frustration and disappointment. When we control our own minds, we become aware of the beauty around us. Take back your life from whoever you left it with.

Every day, we create our world anew through our choices; what we choose to see, what we choose to hear, what we choose to feel are the daily gift we give ourselves. Another person's actions mean nothing until we choose the interpretation. How you choose to interpret another person's behaviour is more about what you think you need than about them. What you think you need is limited by your fears and expectations. What you could be is infinitely greater. People do things for their own reasons not yours, your worth can never be determined by others.

"You hand over your God-given power, when you allow "WHAT" other people think about you, to control "HOW" you think about yourself. They live in your head "RENT FREE." **(Hasheem Francis, CEO Built to Prosper)**

"As long as we don't forgive people who have hurt us, they occupy a rent-free space in our mind!" **(Khetho Nemudzivhadi)**

In conclusion, Freedom is a lonely space. There's a wonderful opening for you to heal, when you understand fear you can do anything, this includes the fear of the unknown. If you don't choose your path, you'll land up being boiled by those wanting to exploit you. The price of freedom is taking responsibility for one's own choices this includes your "**Happiness**". Being needy is a baggage that weighs you down, leave behind your need for others to be there for you. Leave behind your need to be loved and accepted.

Leave behind your desire to control and possess, with this you will embark on the most wonderful adventure of your life- a pilgrimage into your heart where you can find true happiness." **Happiness**" comes through experience. What matters is not what you do for others but what you are to yourself. Choose to be happy. The greatest sense of all is insight which is your "**Happiness.**" Allow the eagle within you to soar. Follow your heart to find your soul, when it just feels right it is. Focus your full attention on what is unfolding now. At the end there is love. Happiness comes through experience. **Choose to be happy;** it starts with self love and self acceptance I am not advocating for self absorbing, conceited way. This form of self love is self less. You give more than you take.

You offer without being asked. You share when you don't have much. You find happiness by making others smile. You love yourself because you are not all about yourself. You are happy with who you are because you make others happy around you. Loving yourself is not about being selfish, self –satisfied, or self centred. It's about accepting your life as a gift to be nurtured and shared as a blessing to others. Instead of dwelling on your disappointments, betrayals, imperfections, failing, or your mistakes, focus on your blessings and contributions you can make, whether it's a talent, knowledge, wisdom, creativity, hard work, or a nurturing soul. You don't have to live up to anybody else's expectations. You can define your own version of perfection. Self acceptance and self love are important but often misunderstood concept these days. You should love yourself as a reflection of God's love and someone put on this earth to make a unique contribution. Bear this in mind as I rest my case no one on this earth can succeed without benefitting from the wisdom, the kindness, or the helping hands of others reach out to the world and be blessed with its resources. I have come to the realisation that to be a blessing to other people you need to be a blessing to yourself, because there is no way you can give what you don't have . Start this wonderful Joy by cherishing your life, and all what you have and the rest will take it due place in your life.

"The ultimate lesson all of us have to learn is unconditional love, which includes not only others but ourselves as well." **(Elisabeth Kubler-Ross)**

"Beauty is whatever gives joy." **(Edna St. Vincent Millay)**

You will change the world by loving yourself, by enjoying life, by making your personal world a dream of heaven, The message that you deliver to yourself, your husband/wife, children and friends will all change when within yourself love abides. Once you change the message you deliver to yourself which centres around happiness, you are happier, and just being happier, the people who live around you will also benefit. Your effort is really for everyone, because your joy, your happiness, your heaven are contagious. When you are happy the people around you are happy too, and it inspires them to change their own world. We represent a whole legacy and our legacy is love; it is joy, its happiness. Let's enjoy this world. Let's enjoy one another. We are meant to love one another, not to hate one another.

Let's stop believing that our difference makes us superior or inferior to one another. Let's not believe that lie. Let's not be afraid that our different colour makes us different people. We have a message to deliver, and that message is our legacy which is imbedded in love. When we were children, we received the legacy of our parents and ancestors. We received a wonderful world, and it's our turn to offer our children and grand children a planet where they live a wonderful and as well as we do now. Let love, compassion, joy, peace and harmony be our watch word and the world will be a better place.

"Love yourself first and everything else falls into line. You really have to love yourself to get anything done in this world." **(Lucille Ball)**

"Self-love is the source of all our other loves." **(Pierre Corneille)**

"Within YOU right now is the power to do things you never dreamed possible. This power becomes available to you, as soon as you change your mindset from the ideas of "I'm not good enough" "I'm not worthy" "I don't deserve it." **(Hasheem Francis, CEO Built to Prosper)**

"Realize that true happiness lies within you. Waste no time and effort searching for peace and contentment and joy in the world outside. Remember that there is no happiness in having or in getting, but only in giving. Reach out. Share. Smile. Hug. Happiness is perfume you cannot pour on others without getting a few drops on yourself." **(Og Mandino)**

"You have to love yourself before you can love someone else. Giving all of yourself and not receiving the same in return will leave you empty and depressed in the end." **(Tony Gaskin)**

"Don't wait around for other people to be happy for you. Any happiness you get you've got to make yourself." **(Alice Walker)**

"Let us be grateful to the people who make us happy; they are the charming gardeners who make our souls blossom." **(Marcel Proust)**

"There are two basic motivating forces: fear and love. When we are afraid, we pull back from life. When we are in love, we open to all that life has to offer with passion, excitement, and acceptance. We need to learn to love ourselves first, in all our glory and our imperfections. If we cannot love ourselves, we cannot fully open to our ability to love others or our potential to create. Evolution and all hopes for a better world rest in the fearlessness and open-hearted vision of people who embrace life." **(John Lennon)**

"Happiness comes more from loving than being loved; and often when our affection seems wounded it is only our vanity bleeding. To love, and to be hurt often, and to love again, this is the brave and happy life." **(J. E. Buckrose)**

"Not everyone you love is going to love you back. That is why it's important for you to love yourself." **(Unknown)**

"There will always be something that's not right about you to a person who's not right for you." **(Trent Shelton)**

"When it comes to love, compassion, and other feelings of the heart, I am rich." **(Muhammad Ali)**

God is love; his children are love. Currently, we have forgotten that our true self is love hence we hate ourselves and hate other people (for as the individual does to his self he does to other selves; hate yourself and you hate other people, love yourself and you love other people). Our world is a place of lovelessness hence a world at war with itself, a world of conflict. Africans sold their people into slavery and learned not to love their people. They need to be taught to love themselves and each other. God's purposes for each of us is that one should love one's self and love other persons (and since all of us are part of God, loves God).

Our covenant (contract) with God and all his sons is that we must love us and all people. Since at the moment we disobey that contract and allow our ego, the means of separation, to lead us to hate folks we must find a way to transform our ego to ego of love. If possible set your ego aside and see the Christ in you and in all people. Christ is love so love him (you and all people). But if you insist on being ego then do what the nineteenth century Indian saint, Ramakrishna, said: use your ego to love other egos and in so doing bring our world to the gate of heaven, and attain what Bahaullah (a nineteenth century Iranian messenger of God) called the lesser peace (Bahaullah taught that all people are one, that men and women are equal; he asked folks to love one another to attain what he called the lesser peace while we are still in forms; the greater peace is attained in formless heaven). When you love, you get hurt. When you get hurt, you hate. When you hate, you try to forget. When you try to forget, you start missing. And when you start missing, you'll eventually fall in Love and start all over again. When we choose to love, or to allow our minds to be one with God, then life is wonderful. When we turn away from love, the pain sets in. Love is the answer to it all Love again.

The goal of this book is to help replace our mutual attacks with mutual love. When we overlook our attacks (work to correct them) and love each other we transform our world into a loving world; a loving world is a peaceful and happy place. A world where we love each other is a world that finally obeys the will of God, for God wills that His children love Him and love each other. When we love God and each other, that is, obey the will of God, we transform the world from the kingdom of the ego (hate) to the Kingdom of God (love). The world then becomes a place of light forms and from that purified world it re-enters the formless world of God, heaven (in the world of light forms, photons, each of us still has a body but that body is made of pure light, not the congealed light called atoms, elements, molecules).

"Our highest power is love, and it is one thing each of us has an unlimited amount of. How much love do you give to others in one day? Each day we have an opportunity to set out with this great, unlimited power in our possession, and pour it over every person and circumstance. Love is appreciating, complimenting, feeling gratitude, and speaking good words to others. We have so much love to give and the more that we give, the more we receive. May the joy be with you" **(Rhonda Byrne)**

"Don't seek love. Let love seek you. But love yourself enough to receive love with an open mind when it visits you!! Don't be a slave to your past experience. Collections of experience are called wisdom. Life is not about the past, we cannot do anything about. It's about the present that we can do something about." **(Sibongile Radebe-Nwazulu)**

"Sometimes, you may feel like NOTHING you do is good enough & a certain person in your life will NEVER change. Remember this: You plant, GOD grows. So, keep planting & loving. Stay focused." **(Heather Lindsey)**

"Whatever is not an expression of love is an expression of fear. Withholding love for any reason is a sign that we are crying out in fear. Fear of being hurt. Fear that our love will not be reciprocated. When you feel afraid, acknowledge it. Then love yourself through it." **(Iyanla Vanzant)**

Nothing changes but everything changes. Nothing stays the same yet everything stays the same. Live fully in the moment that you find yourself in. Every day brings awareness into your routine. Happiness is contained in the detail. Change your focus to change your experience. Zoom out for understanding. Zoom in for happiness. Live in vigorous pursuit of all the wonders that God has given us on this earth. Every now and then, cut loose and do something just for fun, something unpredictable and see the Joy it will bring to your heart.

Living is giving. Living is giving your best self away. Living is helping someone every day. Living is giving more than you can get, it's treating an animal like a person, instead of a pet, it's helping the handicapped across the street, and it's smiling at the new person at work that you meet. It is respect for all Nations, Colour and Creed. It is sharing and caring for your neighbour's needs one of God greatest laws you can live and believe that Moses gave us, the more give the more you will receive. Personally irrespective of my ordeal I still believe that love heals all wound, Love supersedes everything on earth and love bears all things, I look upon the lord for strength in my weakness from whence cometh help, in Psalm 121 he said behold he that keepth Israel shall neither slumber nor sleep. The Lord is the keeper; the Lord is the shade upon thy right, that the sun shall not smite thee by day or the moon by night. The Lord shall preserve thee from all evil; He shall preserve the going out and thy coming in from this time forth and for ever more Amen.

"When we love, we always strive to become better than we are. When we strive to become better than we are, everything around us becomes better too." **(Paulo Cohelo)**

"Go out into the world today and love the people you meet. Let your presence light new light in the hearts of others." **(Mother Teresa)**

"Let us always meet each other with smile, for the smile is the beginning of love." **(Mother Teresa)**

"Every action of our lives touches on some chord that will vibrate in eternality." **(Edwin Hubbell Chapin)**

"My wealth is in my knowledge of self, love, and spirituality." **(Muhammad Ali)**

"Spread love everywhere you go: first of all in your own house. Give love to your children, to your wife or husband, to a next door neighbour. Let no one ever come to you without leaving better and happier. Be the living expression of God's kindness; kindness in your face, kindness in your eyes, kindness in your smile, kindness in your warm greeting." **(Mother Theresa)**

"Love the post! It is heart-warming, endearing and quite engaging! I am who I am, peculiar as I may seem to you; I'm the absolute most awesome being to another! Most importantly though, I do not seek your approval nor do I feel the need for it because I was not created by you. I am Blessed to be who I am, so be happy that I am happy with me being me instead of judging what you have not taken the most minute and fragmented of time to understand! Let's just love one another with our entire idiosyncrasy! Jehovah created us differently for the love of diversity, if there was no darkness the light would not know that it is the light and therefore would not be able to glow!!!" **(Iyanla Vanzant)**

A woman came out of her house and saw 3 old men with long white beards sitting in her front yard. She did not recognize them. She said "I don't think I know you, but you must be hungry. Please come in and have something to eat.""Is the man of the house home?" they asked."No", she replied. "He's out." "Then we cannot come in", they replied.

In the evening when her husband came home, she told him what had happened. "Go tell them I am home and invite them in!" The woman went out and invited the men in" "We do not go into a House together," they replied. "Why is that?" she asked. One of the old men explained: "His name is Wealth," he said pointing to one of his friends, and said pointing to another one, "He is Success, and I am Love." Then he added, "Now go in and discuss with your husband which one of us you want in your home."The woman went in and told her husband what was said. Her husband was overjoyed. "How nice!!" he said. "Since that is the case, let us invite Wealth. Let him come and fill our home with wealth!" His wife disagreed. "My dear, why don't we invite Success?" Their daughter-in-law was listening from the other corner of the house.

She jumped in with her own suggestion: "Would it not be better to invite Love? Our home will then be filled with love!" "Let us heed our daughter-in-law's advice," said the husband to his wife. "Go out and invite Love to be our guest." The woman went out and asked the 3 old men, "Which one of you is Love? Please come in and be our guest."Love got up and started walking toward the house. The other 2 also got up and followed him. Surprised, the lady asked Wealth and Success: "I only invited Love, Why are you coming in?" The old men replied together: "If you had invited Wealth or Success, the other two of us would've stayed out, but since you invited Love, wherever He goes, we go with him. Wherever there is Love, there is also Wealth and Success!!!!!!"

A story as narrated by Ugochukwu Ikedife. In life no matter what you are passing through, what you do, how rich you are; who you know, what you have achieved, if there is no love around you there is no true happiness. I have come to know that from my true life experiences. Love is power, Love is wealth, Love understands, Love is health, Love is spiritual, and Love is God.

Date with a woman. Read on you will be touched too.
After 21 years of marriage, my wife wanted me to take another woman out to dinner and a movie. She said I love you but I know this other woman loves you too and would love to spend some time with you. The other woman that my wife wanted me to take out was my mother who has been a widow for 19 years, but the demands of my work and my three children had made it possible to visit her only occasionally. That night I called to invite her to go out for dinner and a movie. 'What's wrong, are you well, she asked? My mother is the type of women who suspect that a late night call or a surprise invitation is a sign of bad news.' I thought that it would be pleasant to be with you,' I responded "Just the two of us."

She thought about it for a moment, and said,' I would like that very much. The Friday after work, as I Dr.ove over to pick her up I was a bit nervous. When I arrived at her house, I noticed that she too seemed to be nervous about our date. She waited in the door with shawl on. She had set her hair and was wearing the dress that she worn to celebrate her wedding anniversary. She smiled from a face that was as radiant as an Angel's.' I told my friends that I was going out with my son, and they were impressed.' She said, as she got into the car, 'They can't wait to hear about our date. We went to a restaurant that although not elegant, was very nice and cozy.

My mother took my arm as if she were the first lady. After we sat down,' I had to read the menu, large print. Half way through the entries, I lifted my eyes and saw mom sitting there staring at me. A nostalgic smile was on her lips, it was I who used to have to read the menu when you were young, she said.' Then it's time that you relax and let me return the favours, I responded. During the dinner, we had an agreeable conversation, nothing extra ordinary, but catching up on recent events of each other's life. We talk so much that we missed the movies. As we arrived at her house later, she said,' I'll go out with you again, but only if you let me invite you.' I agreed. How was your dinner date? Asked my wife when I got home.' very nice. Much more so than I could have imagined.' I answered.

A few days later, my mother died of massive heart attack. It happened so suddenly that I didn't have time to do anything for her. Sometime later, I received an envelope with a copy of a restaurant receipt from the same place mother and I had dined. An attached note said. 'I paid this bill in advance. I wasn't sure that I could be there, but nevertheless, I paid for two plates one for you the other for your wife. You will never know what that night meant to me. I love you, my son.' At that moment, I understood the importance of saying in time; I love you and give our loved ones the time that they deserve.

Nothing in life is more important than God, your family and friends. Is it our mansions? Is it our cars? Is it our bank accounts? We will leave them and go one day. It is time to give our loved ones the time they deserve, shower our love to them, tomorrow might be too late; these things cannot be put off till some other time. Let this message go around pass to a child, to an adult, to your parent, to your friends, to your mates or someone you care for. Let love be the reason for your existence. Love is good, love is sweet, and love is God. **(Contributed by Kingsley Madu)**

"In competition of love we'll all share in the victory, no matter who comes first." **(Muhammad Ali)**

CHAPTER 6
WINNING THE HEART OF YOUR LOVED ONES VOLUME ONE

This Chapter will help in various marriages, relationships, intended marriages, and relationships. If you are planning to win over a woman or a man's heart, it is words like these that bring back the flames, the spark, fire, desire if used the right way. After reading this chapter you will find every reason to exploit the various avenues in winning the heart of your loved ones. By sending those sms, mails, letters you will be putting smiles in their faces and hearts. Love should govern us in all we do on earth." Wives submit yourselves unto your own husbands, as unto the lord. For the husband is the head of the wife, even as Christ is the head of the church: and he is the saviour of our body. Husband love wives even as Christ also loved the church and gave himself for it. He that loveth his wife loveth himself" **(Ephesians 5 verse 22 to 26/28)**

Marriages are crumbling in our present generation because of lack of true Love and the spirit of forgiveness amongst partners. People go into marriages for the wrong reasons. Marriages and relationships are now meal tickets for many as a means of survival and the real meaning of love have been given a back seat, if there is love there is happiness and prosperity. Love brings out the inner joy in a person and extends one's life span. After marriage the showing of affection should not stop, sharing messages like this are important for the renewal of Love. Men wept your women of their feet's. Women put smiles on the faces of your men. Let us stop going into marriages and relationships for the wrong reason. Love should govern all we do in our daily lives .Love is great, love is good, love is sweet.

They say a happy heart is a happy person. Welcome to the dream land of possibilities.

"Once in his life, every man is entitled to fall madly in love with a gorgeous redhead." (Lucille Ball)

Ten commandment of Love

1. Love me and accept I am your best choice.

2. Learn my weak and strong points, likes, and dislikes.

3. Respect me, I will respect you, never neglect me.

4. Problems are part of life, never yell at me.

5. Advice me rather than criticize me.

6. Forgive and forget my past mistakes, never look for fault.

7. We both contributed to make a quarrel don't blame me alone. Better one side wins the argument.

8. Let us settle our difference before we go to bed, evaluate your friends and their advices.

9. Accept your mistakes and ask for forgiveness.

10. Remember to pray to God he will solve all our problems.

Love is when you have strong communication with that person; you and she can speak on any subject, no matter how painful. Good or bad you won't abandon each other, its mutual respect. You believe in that person and want to share your life with the person as long as the man in heaven keeps life in you. If the person leaves your life it's like a piece of you is missing or has died. Professor Chinua Achebe "Author and writer Things Fall apart".

1. Love is patient, love is kind, and love is not jealous or boastful. It is not arrogant or rude. Love does not insist on its own way, it

is not irritable or resentful. It does not rejoice at wrong but rejoice in the right. Love bears all things, believes all things, hopes for all things, and endures all things.

2. You make me think too much about love. You make me lose sleep thinking of you. Sometimes I think I am going crazy thinking of you; not to worry I like the feelings I get thinking of you.

3. I can't sms you my heart. I can't fax you my smile, but I can tell you that you are in my heart and when I think of you I smile.

4. Some people are separated by time, some by differences, some by distance, some by pride, but no matter how far you are and how busy we may be you will always be special to me. My wish is to be with you right now. I miss you.

5. If I should live without you by my side, what kind of empty life would that be?

6. When I look at you something tells me that you are the kind of girl that I can be down for.

7. Take my heart and let it be consecrated unto your heart, take my moments and my day make it yours, to comfort and cherish, because it is the place to abide.

8. Don't believe in stories but actions, don't believe in dreams but realities, and don't give up your faith in love because it is a certainty of everlasting happiness.

9. Hours passed, minutes and seconds without hearing your voice makes me feel insecure and not loved.

10. Someone close to my heart always gets my first message for the day.

11. My dear, do you know there's a sexy beautiful angel in heaven? Hey don't worry I won't tell them where you are. I miss you.

12. No Garden is fully complete without rose to make it sweet. No life is ever full of fair without someone to share it. Thanks for being a rose in my life. I love you.

13. A Great Relationship Happens, When Two People Who Truly Understand Each Other, and Love Each Other for Who They Are, Come Together and Create Something Stronger, That Neither of Them Could Ever Be on Their Own. I love you.

14. When I met you I had no reason. When I fell in love with you I had no reason for it and I don't think I will find a reason to leave you.

15. I want you to know from the bottom of my heart that I do love you. You are special and I won't let you go.

16. In pretence that I am glad you went away, the wall of loneliness is closing on me every day, wander if I am dying in silence and nobody knows it but me, when will I see you again.

17. You made me understand the true meaning of love that dictionary cannot give me.

18. The sun went down in my life when you walked out of my life. The rain cease falling and the moon died that same day you stopped being my lover. Please come back to me.

19. This is just a reminder of my undying love for you, whatever it takes, no matter what it means, I will love you forever.

20. Someday someone might come into your life and love you the way you've always wanted. If your someday was yesterday, learn. If your someday is tomorrow, hope and if your someday is today... Cherish...♥

21. Believe me ever since you came into my life I have been drunk loving you. Please whatever is the magic don't stop it.

22. Don't place me in your eyes I might fall as tears, but keep me in your heart so that every beat remind you that I am there for you.

23. When you care about someone engrave his/her name in a circle. Not a heart because the heart can be broken, but circle continues forever. Your name is my circle.

24. I need the strength of a woman from you, in difficulty you are there, in painful moment you bear, in rough times you stand by me, when it is tough you encourage me. That is the strength of a woman.

25. I know you have always doubted my love perhaps because I am a ladies' man but then you occupy a prime place in my heart and life.

26. Do people really know what love is? I don't think they know but I know love means you.

27. You may be out of my reach but not out of my mind. You may be out of my sight but not out of my heart. I may not tell you that I miss you, but I always do.

28. Missing you is my habit, thinking of you is my addiction, to see you is always my wish, not to hurt you is my prayer. Lots of love.

29. When you are alone I will be your shadow. When you need to laugh I will be your smile. If you want a hug I will be your pillow. And any time you need a friend I will be there, and be the best I can.

30. I don't have the measles, I am not confined to bed ,aspirin won't help because It isn't my true love, true love doesn't have a happy ending, that is because it doesn't have an ending. A heart truly in love never loses hope but always believes in the promise of Love.

31. Headache I don't have, back ache or flu is not for me, what I am going through is more serious than those. I am missing you.

32. I almost thought God doesn't exist until He led me to your path. You are God sent praise the Lord.

33. Love is the greatest thing that can happen to anybody which should be shared and reciprocated.

34. Love and time are the only two things in the entire world and all of life that cannot be bought but only spent.

35. I asked God for a flower He gave me a garden, I asked for a river He gave me an ocean, I asked for an angel He gave me you.

36. Love is gentle, love is kind, love is when two hearts combine, love is hopeful, love is strong, and giving, love is the sources of Joy in living.

37. When I don' call it is not cause I am not thinking about you I am just giving you time to miss me.

38. You made me believe that no matter how many times love been hurt, how many times I have been broken hearted I should still believe in love.

39. When the night comes, look at the sky, if you see falling stars don't wonder. Why? Just make a wish, trust me, it will come true because I did and I found you.

40. Press down if you miss me.... I am impressed, you are so sweet, and ok you can stop, still pressing down???? You really miss me neh?? I miss you too ooohhh, I have never being better. Thanks this will make me smile the whole day.

41. I am sorry you felt abandon. I missed you and thought of you every second. Now I am back never to leave your presence again.

42. Let ocean run dry or the sky turn blood red, for as long as I breathe the air of life, I will always be there for you, unless you tell me otherwise.

43. Our record shows your sex account is in arrears please, have sex to avoid being sexually blacklisted. I miss you.

44. I made a cup of coffee especially for you, I found out there is no sugar but don't worry the sender is sweet.

45. Have you ever loved someone or something so much that no matter what, you cannot let go of that, which I find in you.

46. You are the dance, I am the drummer, and together we are in harmony.

47. I am sitting at dinning, trying to read the paper as silence take over my room, I made my favourite Coffee but it doesn't taste the same, nothing seems to matter because all I want and think of is you.

48. When I look at you, I see something that I love very much, I see me.

49. The first day I saw you I said to myself you are a queen you belong to me.

50. Stop running away from my love, my love will not hurt you but will only bring much happiness than your happy heart can hold.

51. You don't know how much I admire you. Let's therefore put on love which binds us together in perfect harmony that is what the bible says.

52. If tomorrow comes I will still be waiting for you. If today expires I will still be here waiting for you. They may take the world from me but not my love.

53. They were doing a head count of all angels in heaven, there was trouble the sweetest and most beautiful angel was missing. Please let them know you are okay.

54. Even without seeing you even without saying a word even without sending messages I never fail to think of you.

55. The very first time I saw you I know you were specially sent to me by nature to comfort me.

56. Without you there is no reason to live.

57. My life has never been so sweet, never been so interesting, never been so wonderful, never been so exciting, and never had a reason of living until I found you.

58. Because you are the best thing that has ever happened to me, if we are meant to be together we will be, and if not God knows the best. But know this I do love you from the bottom of my heart.

59. Despite the fact that love is an emotion that comes and goes my love for you is a fact it will always remain constant through thick and thin.

60. It is good to have money and things it can buy, but it is even better to check once in a while and make sure we haven't lost the things money can't buy; people like you.

61. Our meeting has been destined from above. Since that sweet day, hardly does a day pass without me thinking about you and wishing you are always by my side.

62. Every life in this world is written by God's own hands that is why I am thankful because as He wrote my life, He included you as a beautiful part of it. I love you.

63. When I found you, love returned to my life .glow surfaced in my heart, radiance brightened my face and I discovered how sweet love could be. I will always love you.

64. I like your walking strides it takes me to heights where angels elide. I like your beckoning eyes they give me confidence where hope seems lost. I like you aquiline nose it is so beauteous like the Lord's Prayer. I like your spellbinding accent even angels borrow it to sing heavens eulogies. I like your natural hue it is allergic and resistant to peroxide cosmetic gimmicky. I like your charisma; I like everything about you that is why I love you.

65. I want you to know that you are very special in my life especially at this period when love is mostly shared by two hearts that care for each other. I love you.

66. If you spend too long holding to the one who treats you like a potion you will miss finding the one who treats you like a priority. You are my priority stay with me I love you.

67. If I had a flower for every time you made me laugh and smile. I would have the most beautiful garden to walk in forever. Thanks for your love.

68. Sometimes we are only given few minutes to be with the one we love, and thousand hours to spend thinking of them. I am thinking of you right now.

69. I will never get tired of loving you. You are one of blessings that I value the most. Thank you for making me feels special every day.

70. "If you live to be a hundred, I want to live to be a hundred minus one day so I never have to live without you. I Love you so much" **(A. A. Milne)**

71. In life you will meet someone who captures your heart, mind & soul. You will have feelings you never felt before. Your love for them will outweigh any obstacles. Your heart will never lie to you so do not try to fight what its feeling.

72. Let every day be a dream you can touch, let every day be love you can feel, let everyday be a reason to live because life indeed is beautiful.

73. Relationships are nurtured and maintained and for it to linger sometimes one party sacrifices a lot to maintain it.

74. I never believed I could love, I never believe I could care; I never believed there was a place for love in my heart. I never believe I could stay with my heart to one heart until you came into my life; then my unrelieved turned to believe. Please remain in my life I want to keep on believing.

75. If I was a star I would shine for you, if I was a bird I would fly for you, if I was an angel I would look after you but since I am only human I can only think of you.

76. I never thought I could love or care until I met you, for heaven began the day we first met and dreams of love were filled. You became my other half, the half that filled me with sweet thoughts. Please remain with me, for someone like me is hard to come by.

77. Please listen to my heart beat, altogether it does not always take words to say what is in our heart. The force is sometimes too strong to resist.

78. You are more precious to me than anyone else in the world, if I searched for horizons distant oceans or undiscovered stars I would never find anyone to love the way I love you, you are my sunrise, my sunset, my eternity and that is forever.

79. If I could list the wonderful things I love you are my dear, I would still be adding to the list day in day out. The understanding ways you have your gentleness, your smile, the loving care you take of me that makes life so worthwhile, you are kind and thoughtful too that is why darling I couldn't help but fall in love with you.

80. I know I have said before that I love you and tried to tell you how much you really mean to me but I wonder if you really know how strong and sincerely my emotions are and how deeply touched I am by your feeling.

81. Love is the only flower that grows without any aid of season.

82. Our love means more to me than anything else in the world. From the very first moment I felt happy to be by your side. There is no where better to be than in your arms. And I know that in closeness, beyond words, you alone will be the love of my life forever.

83. On the pile of bricks I would write I miss you and I hope one falls on your head so you know how it hurt to miss someone special.

84. I phoned 10111 to report a missing person and they told me that the fact that I miss you doesn't make it a police matter.

85. To be disturbed by the beep of your phone means that somebody somewhere remembers, loves and cares for you.

86. East and west, north and south when I was weak you were my voice. When I could not speak you took pains away from me with your kiss. You are the light on the dark side of my life.

87. I wonder what the world will be like if anything happens to our dream. Baby, you mean so much to me that I will always keep praying that our heavenly father keeps our candle light burning.

88. This morning I searched my purse I found nothing. Then I searched my pocket they too were empty. When I searched my heart I found you and I realized how rich I am.

89. Love is when you take away that feeling, that passion and that romance in a relationship and find out that you still care about that person.

90. A strong bond doesn't need daily chats, visits, or gift. As long as love lives in our heart and we can count on each other, true love never departs.

91. Sometimes I forget to ask if you are ok, sometimes I even miss to say hi, but it doesn't mean that you are forgotten I am just lazy like you.

92. I want to live in your eyes, die in your arms, and buried in your heart.

93. True love hardly takes centre stage, rather it is found in the quiet of everyday.

94. Love is always bestowed as a gift, freely, willing and without expectation, we don't love to be loved we love to love.

95. Love is not blind it sees more not less, but because it sees more it is willing to see less.

96. Knowing you was not a mistake, loving you I don't regret, giving you care is what I am willing to do, missing you is my sickness, hoping that the cure will be found. I miss and love you.

97. Always draw a circle around the ones you love, never draw a heart because heart can be broken but circles are never ending. Thanks for being in my circle.

98. You never lose by loving; you always lose by holding back. Love is an act of endless forgiveness, a tender look which becomes a habit. I love you.

99. Never waste an opportunity to say I love you to someone you really love. It's not every day you meet a person with the magic of falling in love.

100. When time comes for you to give your heart to someone, make sure you select someone who will never break your heart, because broken hearts does not have a spare part, I am the one I will cherish your heart like a gold mine.

101. My Love, nothing else matter to me in life but you. You are the light that makes my life so bright. You are the Joy that gladdens my lonely heart. Being in love with you my happiness is guaranteed; because I feel we are made for each other. Time and tide won't change my love for you. Together we shall always be come rain or shine. I love you.

102. Yesterday I walked into the church I knelt down before the alter I said Lord I love you , I also love her Amen, out of the church my heart as light as an angels kiss back home I thought princess you are all I have.

103. One and one is two we all know, but I can prove different because when two hearts that truly love and care for each other ,then one and one is one because our love has made us one, let's keep it that way and let's make us a mystery to all. I love you.

104. Have you ever loved somebody so much it made you cry, that is how my love for you is.

105. I promise to live each day with you as if it were my last; to be honest with you , even though it may sometimes hurt, to tell you everything all my feelings as well as my thought. I promise you all the little happiness I am capable of giving to let nothing keep us apart as long as we both want to be together, to lend you my advice, but not demand that you take it. I promise to share your sorrow as well as your joy, and as for as long as you will accept it, I promise you all my love.

106. Infatuation is when you find someone absolutely perfect. Love is when you realize they arent' perfect and it doesn't matter. I want to tell you I love you.

107. No matter how strong of a person you are. There is always someone who can make you weak. You are that person to me. I love you with all my heart.

108. "I love that feeling of being in love, the effect of having butterflies when you wake up in the morning. That is special." (Jennifer Aniston). This is the feeling I get knowing I have you in my life. I love you

109. Immature love says: 'I love you because I need you.' Mature love says 'I need you because I love you. Mature love is what I feel for you

110. True Love means

Find a guy who call you beautiful instead of hot, who calls you back when you hang on him, who will stay awake just to watch you sleep...wait for the guy who kisses your forehead who wants to show you off to the world when you are in your sweats...who holds your hand in front of his friends...wait for the one who is constantly reminding you of how much he cares about you and how lucky he is to have you.

Just think about it, there was a blind girl who hated herself because she was blind. She hated everyone except her loving boyfriend. He was always there for her. She told her boyfriend, if I could only see the world, I will marry you. One day someone donated a pair of eyes to her, when the bandages came off; she was able to see everything including her boyfriend. He asked her, now that you can see the world, will you marry me? The girl looked at her boyfriend and saw that he was blind. The sight of his closed eyelids shocked her. She hadn't expected that. The thought of looking at them the rest of her life led her to refuse to marry him.

Her boyfriend left in tears and a day later wrote a note to her saying, "**Take good care of your eyes, my dear; for before they were yours, they were mine.**" This is how the human brain often work when status changes. Only very few can recall the difficult times they had in the past and those who stood by them in those painful moments. Life is a gift.

Today before you say an unkind word, think of someone who can't speak. Before you complain about the taste of your food, think of someone who has nothing to eat. Before you complain about your husband or wife, think of someone who is crying out to God for a companion. Today before you complain about life, think of someone who died too early on earth. Before you complain about children, think of someone who desires to have children but is barren. Before you yell at your house help for not cleaning your dirty house to shine like snow, think of people who live in the street.

Before whining about the distance you have to drive, think of someone who walks the same distance (with their feet). And when you are tired and complain about your job, think of the unemployed, the disabled, and those who wish they had your job. Before you think of pointing a finger or condemning another, remember that not one of us is without sin and when depressing thought seems to get you down put a smile on your face and think you are alive and still around. I pray these ideas moves around the entire universe. **(Anonymous)**

CONCLUSION

Having read through the six chapters of this book, I am of the firm belief that your attitude and perception of the way you view life will be changed for the better. The insight of knowledge that will be acquired from this book will renew your way of reasoning and will help to improve your standard of living, uplift your soul and wellbeing, make you a good leader if you are in the business of leading people, help you to locate your calling, assignments and destiny with God and choosing career that gives you joy. I believe that we as individuals can gain much more if we become the CEOs of our lives and take control our thinking and actions in order to achieve our goals and aspirations.

I want you to know that in order for the world to believe in you, you first need to believe in yourself. This is because you are God's chosen vessel, not the worlds. Share all you have gained and learned from this book with family, friends, associates, you're your colleagues. Make it a point of duty to carry the motivational and inspirational words at the back of your mind every day of your life. God bless you! And thank you for investing in your growth and development.

Comrade Raphael Ikechukwu Ogbuagu "Ik Poly" (Odiraa Chukwu Mma)

BIBLIOGRAPHY

1. Bishop Macedo, Edir Are We All God's Children? :2007 **(Publisher Unipro Rio De Janeiro)**

2. Bishop Oyedepo, David.O .Pillars of Destiny: August 2008 **(Published Dominion Publishing House Lagos Nigeria)**

3. Covey, Stephen. Principle of Centered leadership: 1992 **(Published Simon & Schuster UK Ltd)**

4. Collin, Jim, Good to great: Oct 16 2001 **(Publisher: Harper Business)**

5. Collin, Jim, How the mighty fall and why some company never give in: May 19, 2009 **(Publisher: Harper Business)**

6. Napoleon Hill, Think and grow Rich 2004 **(Publisher Cornwell, Ross)**

7. Jafolla Richard, Soul Surgery: Jun 1, 1982 **(Publisher: DeVorss & Company)**

8. Kegan's scientific research

9. Motseoa Lugemwa, Take Control of your destiny Strategy and Personal Success 2010 **(Publisher Lugemwa Motseoa)**

10. Mandino Og, Return of the Ragpicker: Jan. 1, 1993 **(Publisher: Bantam)**

11. Maxwell, John, Leadership Gold: Lesson I've learned from a lifetime of leading" Apr. 1, 2008 **(Publisher: Thomas Nelson)**

12. Maxwell, John, The 21 irrefutable law of leadership. Sept.18, 2007 **(Publisher Thomas Nelson)**

13. Maxwell, John Maxwell daily planner: Jan 2010 **(Publisher Struik Christian Gifts South Africa)**

14. McGinnis, Alan Loy .Power of optimism: Aug 19, 1994 **(Publisher: Harper Paperbacks)**

15. Osuji, Ozodi Rehumaizing and civilizing African People and the Society

16. Pastor Adeoye, David Olatunde: The way to the top in life 2000-2007 **(Publisher King's   Publisher Lagos Nigeria)**

17. Pastor Adeoye, David Olatunde. Don't Mind them, you are destined for Greatness: 1999-2007 **(Publisher King's Publisher Lagos Nigeria)**

18. Pastor Ndeda, Elias .Seed of his word: 2000 **(Publisher Elias Ndeda Ministries SouthAfrica)**

19. Peter Laurence Johnston Peter principle: 1969 **(Publisher Bantam)**

20. Ponder .D.Randall. Entrepreneur made easy series: 2005 **(Publisher Ep Entrepreneur Press)**

21. Professor Achebe, Chinua. Anthills of Savannah: 1987 **(Publisher Heinemann published)**

22. Professor Achebe Chinua, Things Fall Apart: 1958 **(Publisher Heinemann published)**

23. Randolph John, The wings as Eagle: Jan 1, **2002 (Publisher: Whitaker House)**

24. The Top 10 Leadership Qualities **(David Hakala)** on March 19, 2008

25. Williamson Marianne. A return of love, Reflections on the Principles of A Course in Miracles, 1992 **(Publisher: HarperCollins)**

26. Zelinski, Ernie J. Retirement wisdom you won't get from your financial Advisor Sept. 1, 2009 **(Publisher: Visions International Publishing)**

ABOUT THE WRITER

Comrade Raphael Ikechukwu Ogbuagu (Odiraa Chukwu Mma, Abagana) popularly known as Ik Poly was born in Ajegunle; in the city of Lagos, Nigeria. He hails from Abagana in the Njikoka Local Government of Anambra State. He did his primary school at St Mary Primary School and later joined Awodi Ora Primary School both in Ajegunle in Lagos. He did his secondary school at Christ the King's College, Onitsha in Anambra State and obtained a Higher National Diploma in Business Administration and Management from Federal Polytechnic Oko in Anambra State. He also holds qualifications in Human Resources and Customer Care Management from University of South Africa (UNISA). He is a motivator and an inspiration to all that have close contact with him. He is a leader dedicated to service. He has held various positions that include: Class Labour Prefect, House Captain of Okagbue House, Senior Store Keeper, Director of Socials of Association for Business Administration and Management, Vice Chairperson and Chairperson Apapa Development Association (ADAS) of which he is a founding member and Head Neo Black Movement of Africa Worldwide South Africa Chapter.

He is currently Financial Secretary Abagana Welfare Union South African Branch, Chairperson Nigerian Union Roodepoort Ward, Public Relations Officer Anambra State Association South African Chapter, and the pioneer Chairperson of the Westrand Brothers Association whose vision is to re-brand Nigeria in South Africa and spread its tents to the poor; orphanages and schools in the society. He is a member of the Welfare Committee of Gauteng Branch of Nigerian Union South Africa, Abagana Welfare Union South African Branch, and Anambra State Association South Africa. He serves in the education, labour and training and the art, culture and heritage working groups as a representative of (JMAP). He has a heart for charity and is a volunteer in various associations such as the Faith Foundation, Dora Ark Orphanage home, Khayelitsh a home for abandoned boys, Naladi People Centre, an association for abused women and children, to mention but a few. He seats on the board of

Christian for Peace in Africa. Raphael is a believer of African culture and tradition and is a co-founder of Westrand Palace, an organization that sustains and promotes the Igbo culture in South Africa.He is also a co founder Anamanbra State Association westrand Chapter.

He played soccer for Awordi Ora Primary School, junior and senior football teams of Christ the King's College Onitsha; he captained the Wilmer Crescent/Abukuru Football Team in Lagos. He also played for Black Stars Lagos, Junior Leopard, and Dende/Nnanna Bombers both in Onitsha. Raphael is a great lover of football hence as the chairperson of Westrand brothers association he formed Westrand football club for leisure and to keep fit. His experience and active participation in sports has distinguished him as an astute sports analyst/commentator. For his participation, he has won many awards and accolades. These include: Mr. Federal Polytechnic and Mr. Ultimate in Oko Polytechnic etc. Both awards were male dominated competitions. Participants were judged based on their physical appearance, intelligence quotient (IQ), singing/dancing skills, bravery, and ability to adapt and survive in difficult situations etc. He has a flair for acting and has appeared as a guest actor in one of South Africa's popular soapies; Isidingo

He is a human rights activist and a social crusader who fights against social ills such as xenophobia, human trafficking, forced labour, child abuse, and other injustices which violates and diminishes the dignity of human beings. He has dedicated much of his time to pursue social justice and the equality of all people regardless of creed, sex, or colour. His passion lies with working with young people. He is the author and publisher of the book hard lessons of life, our goals can contradict our values and Unlocking the soul of humankind through words of wisdom and laughter. He has taken into writing as a passion and has written articles for Roodepoort Records and North side Chronicles. He is the host of a programme titled Empowering and Uplifting your Soul with Westside FM live radio station in Kagiso west of Johannesburg.

Here are what others people had to say about Hard Lessons of Life and Self-healing

I have read the Book "Hard Lessons of Life and Self-Healing"; it social and spiritual worth as a product of inspiration to many who shall avail themselves of the book, cannot be quantified. I so much believe that the level of readability will increase, as Mr. Raphael has not only demonstrated eloquent inspirational prowess, but was able to unlock ancient mysteries, that which has been known by seekers of truth and divinity to inspires and motivate the ordinary minds into performing extraordinary feats. Only the deep can call on the deep. Raphael in his book kept calling and is still calling through his self-explanatory inspirational monograph the ordinary mind's brightest realm of self-realization; a book compiled as an outstanding intellectual piece. This work is masterfully scripted and I recommend it to emerging generation of young thinkers on their path to economic, political and psychosocial revolutionary revival. *(HRH Dr. Carl Nosakhare Oshodi-Isibor Paramount Ruler; Okodonutese Kingdom, Executive Director; Safety 2000 Limited. Writer, Poet, Civil Right Activist, Public Affairs Analyst)*

In this book Raphael guides us on a spiritual journey of life using Christ as a perfect example to follow. He touches different issues like pain and poverty, but also hope and joy. This book offers us a unique experience to understand ourselves through Christ at our deepest level. It also gives us courage and hope of becoming the masters of our destiny in a righteous way. This is one of the most influential books for the mind and spirit that I have read. A great master piece indeed!!! *(Zanele Ndlovu Author of the book Umakhweyana)*

I have read "The book hard lessons of life and self-healing" time and time again; and have distilled from its pith and marrow the enduring canons of discipline, humility, simplicity, integrity, courage, hope, faith and perseverance. You need the unbreakable empathy of this book you who are in the throes of desolation. If you are experiencing crushing challenges – if you are at the mercy of disappointments – you need the friendship of this book. You, who desire to construct for others ceaseless clean rivers of compassion, first read this book. You need this book you who are blessed with the wings of the eagle, but crave to fly higher. If you are already seated on the mountaintop, but desire not to lose your seat, please read "Hard lessons of life and self-healing." *Rev. Chidozie Ejimadu (LL.B Hons, Clergyman, Writer, Poet, Community Facilitator, Activist, Secretary General, Ohaneze Ndigbo South Africa)*

In this remarkable book, Raphael shares powerful mirror image strides to assist one overcome past hurt, shame, self-critics, hatred, unforgiveness and become more compassionate , loving and accepting themselves through self-actualization ,discovery and creating a more positive self-image .This book guides one into the importance of self-healing even before seeking professional help. Self-healing is a comprehensive approach to increase your personal power, challenging your inner critics as well as celebrating your personal strength which will ultimately define your core value in life. I strongly recommend the book to anyone who may have gone through any form of challenges at any point in life. *(Mrs. Amaka Nnodu, BSc. UNN, MSc Wits, Energy Engineer, University of Johannesburg)*

I knew Raphael way back struggling with everyday life which transforms him to become a today motivational speaker. His works dwell on building personal character, achieving private victory and expand it to public victory. The collection of past scholar quotes in his works present a strong aspiration that can awake once inner spirit towards recognition of self. It is a MUST read for everyone. *(Dr. Duaka Ifeanyi, PhD)*

My true calling is something I hide behind reason. It's the thing I will do on the side, a well-loved hobby. Why on earth would I do that when I know what I want to do? Fear that I won't make it? "Hard Lessons of Life & Self-healing "challenges that; Your calling. In the book pages, my calling has found a way to slip into my mind and dig out the things that are truly meaningful to me. I think one needs to read this book because you owe it to yourself.

It's knowledge that actually teaches you how to discover your calling through hard lessons of life and through spirituality. This is not another book of practical advice, or just some fluffy quotes. This is "Hard Lessons of Life and Self-Healing" and I wholeheartedly recommend it. *(Sibongile Radebe-Nwazulu Columnist Nigeria Voice Newspaper)*

There are valuable lessons to be learned from reading this book, and they can be applied, to one's life as well as one's business. If you don't take time to read this book, you will truly be missing the opportunity to get "Net Ready" on how to live your life successfully and achieve optimum growth in your business. This is a revolutionary text, it is uplifting and inspiring, it shows us what we can be as well as how we can achieve this organizationally and structurally. It is a book for those who are striving for the best in themselves and others. It has the capacity to change lives, because it shows us a way to develop who we are. *Chief (Hon) Stanley F. Nwokocha (MNES), Oratory Skill Developer, Policy Maker, and a Creative Thinker.*

Raphael Ogbuagu in this remarkable book, managed to craft 'a map in words' for all persons that journey through the tumultuous quest that is life. In his avant-garde style, he interestingly presents the reader with the enthusiasm, caution, drive, ambition, initiative, determination, enterprise, hope and inspiration for every step in the journey. I recommend this book as an essential for all who journey through the chaos that is life. It is a guiding rudder when in turbulent seas, a warning sign when at crossroads, a compass pointing to the northern star, a soothing balm when bruised, succor when marooned, and fair wind when ready to sail. This map in words has valuable rules and cannons encoded in it, which at every twist and turn is a source of invaluable directives useful for the reader in business, politics, faith, religion, relationships and in all life endeavors. It is a must read. *(Sunny-Unachukwu John Esq. Writer, Poet, Magazine Publisher & Community Organizer)*

This is a great book to share with all who are in leadership positions and those who are aspiring to be in that position. This book will motivate and inspire you when that position began to feel like a heavy rock that you cannot come from under. Jesus gave us the gift of the Holy Spirit to lead us and guide us through the labyrinth of life, with this gift God will enable us to do great things for the betterment of humankind no matter how large or how small the endeavour. Learn how to be a good leader by following the Leadership Style of Jesus Christ. *(Dr Ludella Lewis PhD, President of Ludella Lewis & Company, Accounting, Taxes & Payroll)*

It is with full humility and honour that I should write about this humble leader. A short description of you and your work goes thus' A work of direction towards the full realization of your full potential in the writing world" your involvement and numerous achievement has really set you apart from your peers. A book of, if you can think it you can do you. This book is recommended for all. *(Hon Chima.C. Onyeagba Umealo Bsc, Pgd Absu, CEO Fassy IT company, President, Melose and Angel Nigerian Ltd. Deputy President Ohaneze Ndi Igbo South Africa)*

www.ingramcontent.com/pod-product-compliance
Lightning Source LLC
Chambersburg PA
CBHW060004100426
42740CB00010B/1388